NEW AMERICANISTS A Series Edited by Donald E. Pease

IN THE NAME
OF NATIONAL SECURITY

Hitchcock, Homophobia, and

the Political Construction of Gender

in Postwar America

ROBERT J. CORBER

DUKE UNIVERSITY PRESS ■ Durham and London ■ 1993

Second printing, 1996

© 1993 Duke University Press

All rights reserved

Printed in the United States of America

on acid-free paper ∞

Designed by Cherie Holma Westmoreland

Typeset in Eras Bold display and Palatino

text by Keystone Typesetting, Inc.

Library of Congress Cataloging-in-Publication

Data appear on the last printed page of

this book.

Frontispiece art based on a still from

Strangers on a Train © 1951 Warner Bros.

Pictures Inc. Renewed 1979 Warner Bros.

Inc. All Rights Reserved.

IN MEMORY OF

JOAN IRENE TENNAL CORBER

CONTENTS

ACKNOWLEDGMENTS

In the course of writing this book, I have incurred more debts than I can possibly acknowledge here. I would like to express my appreciation to Lynne Curtis and Erika King for providing emotional and intellectual support during a particularly difficult period in my academic career. I am also indebted to Elizabeth Helsinger for encouraging me to pursue my interests in gender studies at a crucial stage in my intellectual development. Although this book bears little resemblance to the dissertation I wrote under her supervision at the University of Chicago, it was in Beth's workshop on feminist criticism and theory that I first began to think about the political construction of gender and sexual identity.

Many friends and colleagues have commented on parts or all of the manuscript. I would like to thank in particular Lauren Berlant, Teresa de Lauretis, Jane Gallop, and Loren Kruger; they will recognize how much I have benefited from their comments and criticisms. I would also like to thank Jonathan Arac who generously agreed to read the entire manuscript. Jonathan's combination of scholarly rigor and critical finesse has greatly influenced my reconstruction of Cold War liberal discourse, although obviously he is not responsible for the book's shortcomings. I owe a special debt to Donald Pease whose incisive comments on an earlier version of the manuscript led me to rethink my argument in crucial ways. The subtlety and complexity of Don's thinking about the Cold War and its impact on American culture has been my model throughout. My greatest debt is to Kent Sargent who encouraged me to pursue this project when it was still only an article. Without his support and encouragement I could not have written this book. Finally, I would like to dedicate this book to my mother's memory. In many respects, this project began as an attempt to understand the political and sexual taboos of my childhood, which included not being allowed to watch *Strangers on a Train* when it was

x   shown on television because, according to my mother, it was a film about "homos."

A version of chapter 2 appeared in *Discourse* 13, no. 2 (Spring–Summer 1991): 58–82. A version of chapter 3 appeared in *boundary 2* 19, no. 1 (Spring 1992): 121–48. I would like to thank the publishers of both journals for kindly allowing me to reprint this material.

INTRODUCTION

In *The Vital Center*, his highly influential revisionist history of the liberal tradition published in 1949, Arthur Schlesinger heralded the emergence of a new generation of liberal intellectuals whose faith in human nature had been shattered by the extermination of millions of Jews and the dropping of the atomic bomb. Unlike older liberals, whose cultural politics had been influenced by the Communist-dominated Popular Front, Schlesinger's generation had supposedly learned to question the efficacy of human agency. The rise of totalitarianism had revealed to it a "new dimension of experience—the dimension of anxiety, guilt, and corruption," which taught it to view conflict as an inevitable part of the human condition.[1] Schlesinger explained that "the Soviet experience, on top of the rise of fascism, reminded my generation rather forcibly that man [sic] was, indeed, imperfect, and that the corruptions of power could unleash great evil in the world."[2]

Although his claim that his generation was united in the belief that human nature was inherently corrupt may have been wishful thinking, Schlesinger was not alone in wanting to reclaim liberalism from the influence of the Popular Front. Lionel Trilling, for example, similarly thought that the liberal tradition had been seriously compromised by the fellow traveling of the 1930s. In the preface to *The Liberal Imagination* (1950), he argued that the postwar critic's primary responsibility was "to recall liberalism to its first essential imagination of variousness and possibility, which implies the awareness of complexity and difficulty."[3] Leslie Fiedler made a similar argument in "Hiss, Chambers, and the Age of Innocence," an essay published in *Commentary* in 1950 in which he claimed that "we who would still like to think of ourselves as liberals must be willing to declare that mere liberal principle is not in itself a guarantee against evil."[4]

In claiming that the liberal tradition had been seriously compromised in the 1930s, anti-Stalinist intellectuals such as Schlesinger, Trilling, and Fiedler participated in the production and consolidation of the political and cultural settlement historians of postwar American society often call *the Cold War consensus*.[5] Under the terms of this settlement, the only way in which women, African Americans, and other historically disenfranchised groups could gain recognition for their contributions to the war effort was by limiting their demands for such recognition. Underlying Trilling's and Fiedler's argument that postwar critics had a responsibility to return liberalism to its first principles was a desire to distance themselves from the more controversial aspects of the New Deal (recognition of the right of workers to strike, the implementation of social programs that benefited women, African Americans, and other disenfranchised groups). According to Trilling and Fiedler's argument, the institution of policies that sought to democratize social relations owed more to the influence of the Popular Front than to liberalism's "first essential imagination," and because such policies had allegedly been inspired by the Communist party, they were considered un-American. Thus the political and cultural settlement underwritten by cultural critics who were committed to reclaiming liberalism (hereafter the postwar settlement) was primarily an attempt to manage and contain the political claims of organized labor, women, and minorities. By exaggerating the influence of the Popular Front on the New Deal, anti-Stalinist intellectuals were able to neutralize the potential antagonism of these disenfranchised groups, and in exchange for their submission, they were allowed to participate more fully in the postwar culture of consumption.

The primary purpose of this book is to clarify the attempts of liberals to manage and contain the demands of women and minorities for greater recognition by situating a group of films Hitchcock made in the 1950s in relation to the postwar settlement. I use the films to demonstrate how these liberals achieved and retained hegemony over American society in the 1950s by producing a united cultural front that not only incorporated the interests of women and other historically disenfranchised groups (gays, lesbians, African Americans) but also organized them into a popular and seemingly unified collective will dedicated to containing communism. At the same time, I use the films to expose the contradictions in this dominant construction of social reality, contradictions that eventually led to the collapse of the Cold War consensus amid the crisis of cultural legitimation in the 1960s. Situating the films in relation to the postwar settlement shows that

Cold War liberals (by which I mean liberals who wanted to preserve the legacies of the New Deal while reclaiming liberalism from the cultural politics of the Popular Front) used hysteria over the possibility that the federal government had been infiltrated by Communists, homosexuals, and lesbians to prevent competing constructions of social reality from mobilizing popular support. I argue that by exploiting the wave of anti-Communism unleashed by the McCarthy hearings, Cold War liberals virtually guaranteed that the postwar settlement operated unconsciously, that it determined, without appearing to do so, a definition of reality to which Americans consented freely and spontaneously because it seemed to correspond to their lived experience.[6] That is to say, Cold War liberals were able to determine the way in which Americans thought and lived their relations to the world by limiting the fund of interpretive possibilities available to them for understanding their lived experience. I try to show that in so doing, they gained control over the production of the postwar subject.

The most common approach to the films I examine in this book has been psychoanalytic.[7] Indeed, several of the films I discuss have been central to the formulation of Lacanian theories of the cinematic apparatus. For example, in "Visual Pleasure and Narrative Cinema," an essay that continues to shape discussions of the organization of the look in classical Hollywood cinema, Laura Mulvey uses *Rear Window* (1954) and *Vertigo* (1958) to substantiate her claims about the voyeuristic economy of the filmic text.[8] Mulvey tries to show that both films thematize the voyeuristic structure of filmic pleasure, which they locate in the scopic regime of the male spectator's psychical economy.[9] Elaborating Hitchcock's own critique of the representational strategies of filmic discourse, she argues that because women in classical Hollywood cinema invariably signify sexual difference, they threaten the male spectator with castration. For this reason, the camera resorts to framing them as icons, or objects to be looked at, that interrupt the film's narrative flow. Rather than subjects who solicit the male spectator's identification, women in classical Hollywood cinema function as objects of visual pleasure, thereby allowing the male spectator to elude the threat of castration signified by their image. In a famous shot-by-shot analysis of *North by Northwest* (1959), Raymond Bellour makes a similar argument about the narrativizing of sexual difference in classical Hollywood cinema.[10] He claims that Hitchcock's films are con-

4   structed along an Oedipal trajectory that ultimately disavows sexual difference. He suggests that the male spectator derives sadistic pleasure from the fragmentation of the woman's body by the framing of the camera because it reassures him of the totality and coherence of his own body, and thus he can return her look without fear of castration.

In adopting a historical rather than a strictly psychoanalytic approach to these and other films Hitchcock made in the 1950s, I aim not to reject Lacanian theories of the cinematic apparatus so much as to expose their limited ability to elucidate the complex operations whereby the filmic system inserts a subject originally constructed across a multiplicity of conflicting discourses into a relatively fixed subject position. I want to show that the use of Lacanian psychoanalysis in film theory has tended to repress the historicity of the cinematic apparatus. The claim that Hitchcock's Oedipalized narratives restage the subject's entry into the symbolic order by reenacting the mirror phase as defined by Lacanian psychoanalysis reduces the cinematic apparatus to a totalizing system that automatically inserts the spectator into a fixed, stable subject position. In contrast, I stress the historicity of the subject, its construction in relation to a plurality of competing discourses that include, but are not limited to, those that regulate the production of sex, gender, race, and class at a particular historical moment. Following Teresa de Lauretis, I conceive of subjectivity as an ongoing, continuous construction that is renewed daily through the individual's always provisional encounter with the institutions, discourses, and practices that structure her/his relation to the world.[11] That is to say, I assume that subjectivity does not constitute a stable identity but a constantly shifting series of ideological positions that the individual reworks into a personal, subjective construction that necessarily reflects the specificity of her/his personal history. Thus I treat the cinematic apparatus as a machinery for ideological investment in which the subject is constructed but not exhausted. Because the individual's often conflicting investments in the discourses that address her/him as a subject always reflect the specificity of her/his personal history, the cinematic apparatus can never wholly determine the construction of her/his subjectivity.

At the same time, however, I also try to show that the textual strategies developed by the film industry for absorbing the spectator in the diegesis enabled the classical text to partially suture the spectator's subjectivity.[12] One of my basic assumptions is that hegemonic practices necessarily emerge in a heterogeneous social field crisscrossed by competing ideological positions; the purpose of such practices is to contain the excess meaning of the social, or the part of the social that remains outside its system of representation and therefore threatens to destabilize or rupture it. I follow Ernesto Laclau and Chantal Mouffe in conceiving of the social as both the infinite play of differences and the attempt to fix or halt that play in a structured network of meaning.[13] Although the social is always structured around a constitutive impossibility that necessarily thwarts any attempt to suture it as a totality, all social formations develop articulatory practices, or *nodal points,* that partially fix the excess meaning of the social in an organized and relatively closed system of differences.[14] For this reason, at the same time that the individual occupies a multiplicity of contradictory subject positions, s/he also feels constrained to construct from those positions a relatively stable, or hegemonized, identity.[15] Indeed, the very instability of the individual's subjectivity, its construction across variable axes of difference, is one of the necessary conditions for the hegemonic articulation of a partially fixed identity.

In claiming that the films discussed in this book helped to underwrite and legitimate the postwar settlement, I take for granted that filmic discourse in the 1950s constituted a nodal point that partially fixed the individual's identity in a relatively coherent and unified ensemble of differences. As noted earlier, my principle objection to Lacanian theories of the cinematic apparatus is that they tend to ignore the historical specificity of fantasy and desire, their relation to historically specific social technologies such as the filmic system. Lacanian film theory tends to treat the cinematic apparatus as fulfilling rather than as constituting the fantasies that organize and define the dominant forms of male and female subjectivity at a particular historical moment. According to this theory, the male spectator derives pleasure from the fragmentation of the woman by the framing of the camera because it enables him to elude a threat of castration that not only preexists his position as a spectator but also is constitutive of his subjectivity.[16] In contrast, my use of psychoanalytic theory stresses the way in which the cinematic apparatus implants desire in the spectator by positioning her/him as a subject of historically specific fantasies. I assume that fantasy works to limit the potentially endless dispersal

6   and displacement of the individual's desire; that is to say, it provides the coordinates of the individual's desire by organizing and regulating it.[17] Fantasy is not the object of the individual's desire but its setting, or mise-en-scène, and it functions as the frame that enables her/him to desire. In the fantasy scenario, the individual's desire is not fulfilled so much as it is constituted. Through fantasy, the individual learns how to desire.[18] Fantasy orients or grounds the individual's desire by determining which objects s/he will invest with desire and try to obtain. Thus its role in the construction of the individual's subjectivity is originary.

I use this aspect of fantasy to explain how the films Hitchcock made in the 1950s were able to insert a spectator whose subjectivity was originally constructed across a multiplicity of competing discourses into a relatively stable subject position. I try to show that Hitchcock's films provided the spectator with the coordinates of her/his desire. Using the psychoanalytic theory of fantasy described above, I suggest that Hitchcock's films did not fulfill the spectator's desire so much as constitute it. They limited the potentially endless dispersal and displacement of the spectator's desire by bringing it into alignment with the nation's security interests. That is to say, they determined the objects the spectator invested with desire and tried to obtain. The spectator of Hitchcock's films not only accepted the emergence of the national security state as politically necessary but actively contributed to its reproduction by conforming to the dominant constructions of gendered identity. In other words, Hitchcock's films functioned as fantasy scenarios that rendered the spectator's insertion within the discourses of national security not only desirable but pleasurable. They helped to organize the spectator's sexuality according to a series of identifications and object attachments that corresponded to the nation's security interests. By invoking the homophobic categories of Cold War political discourse, in particular the construction of "the homosexual" and "the lesbian" as security risks, Hitchcock's films virtually guaranteed that gender and nationality functioned as mutually reinforcing categories of identity. The spectator of his films no longer participated in a plurality of contending social formations but became a subject of historically specific fantasies that contributed to the establishment and consolidation of the postwar settlement.

My emphasis on the construction of subjectivity across a multi-

plicity of conflicting discourses as one of the necessary conditions for
the hegemonic articulation, or partial suturing, of identities seems
particularly relevant to a study of postwar American culture. America
in the 1950s experienced the emergence of an increasingly heterogeneous and antagonistic social field in which the proliferation of
differences threatened to lead to a generalized crisis of identities. For it
was in the 1950s that homosexuals and lesbians, as well as other historically disenfranchised groups (middle-class heterosexual women,
African Americans), began again to organize politically. Homophile
organizations such as the Mattachine Society and the Daughters of
Bilitis, founded in 1950 and 1955, respectively, openly challenged the
medicalization of same-sex eroticism and pioneered a minoritarian, or
subcultural, model of gay and lesbian identities.[19] Appropriating the
rhetoric of the civil rights movement, such organizations claimed that
gay men and women were members of an oppressed minority whose
civil rights had been systematically violated by the American government. In so doing, they contested the dominant construction of social
reality, which represented the Oedipal structure of the middle-class
nuclear family as natural, and made possible the emergence of new
subjectivities. In constructing an alternative representation of social
reality that stressed the history of oppression gay men and women
shared, they helped to organize gay and lesbian identities into a
relatively coherent and unified ensemble of differences. However, in
trying to establish a set of experiences that all gay men and women
supposedly had in common, they also tended to hypostatize gay and
lesbian identities. The construction of gay and lesbian identities from a
minoritarian perspective was an exclusionary process that marginalized and suppressed forms of gay and lesbian subjectivity that were
considered potentially damaging to the homophile movement. Those
who were excluded from this process included gay men such as the
founders of the Mattachine Society, who were former members of the
Communist party and who were committed to theorizing gay and
lesbian oppression from a Marxist perspective that related it to other
forms of oppression (race, class, and gender), and lesbians who fre-
quented gay bars and engaged in butch-femme role playing.[20]

As stated earlier, I use Hitchcock's films to show that one of the
ways that Cold War liberals tried to contain the increasing heterogeneity of American society was by linking questions of gender and

sexual identity directly to questions of national security. I focus in particular on the attempts of Cold War liberals to counteract the emergence of an alternative construction of social reality that called into question the pathologizing of gay and lesbian subjectivity by politicizing same-sex eroticism. On the one hand, the dominant discourse of same-sex eroticism claimed that homosexuality and lesbianism represented developmental disorders and therefore could not be considered categories of identity similar to other categories of identity, such as race and gender. According to the federal government, if gay men and women felt alienated from mainstream American society, that was because they were maladjusted; their problems were not political but personal and were best remedied in a doctor's office. On the other hand, the dominant discourse of same-sex eroticism tried to show that homosexuality and lesbianism promoted communism and fellow traveling and therefore politicized gay and lesbian identities. During its highly publicized hearings in the 1940s and early 1950s, the House Un-American Activities Committee did not limit its investigation to the Communists and fellow travelers who had supposedly infiltrated the federal government, but extended it to include homosexuals and lesbians who "passed" as heterosexual. On the basis of testimony from psychiatrists and other medical "experts" who testified that they were susceptible to blackmail by Soviet agents because they were emotionally unstable, homosexuals and lesbians were officially identified as national-security risks. As a result, more homosexuals and lesbians were expelled from the federal government in the 1950s than were suspected Communists and fellow travelers.[21]

The publication of the Kinsey reports on male and female sexual behavior, in 1948 and 1953, respectively, only reinforced the politicization of homosexuality and lesbianism. In revealing the diversity of sexual practices Americans of both sexes engaged in, the Kinsey reports seemed to confirm the increasing heterogeneity of American society. Indeed, the reports contributed to the emergence of alternative constructions of social reality by demonstrating through the use of scientific data that homosexuals and lesbians were not "maladjusted" individuals who were emotionally unstable but productive members of society who did not differ significantly from heterosexuals. At the same time, however, the reports contributed to the crisis precipitated by the discovery that homosexuals and lesbians could "pass" as heterosexual by calling attention to the differences not only among Americans but within them as well. The reports provided scientific evidence suggesting that sexual identities were fluid and unstable rather than exclusively and permanently heterosexual or homosexual. Many of the individuals interviewed by Kinsey and his colleagues had engaged in same-sex practices regularly as adolescents but had become exclusively heterosexual as adults; others continued to engage in same-sex practices, despite being married and having children. In demonstrating that sexual identities were fluid and unstable, the reports hindered the attempts of gays and lesbians to define themselves as members of an oppressed minority and contributed to the growing crisis over national security. Following publication of the Kinsey reports, homosexuals and lesbians were thought to threaten national security not only because they were emotionally unstable and susceptible to blackmail but also because they might convert heterosexuals to their "perverted" practices by seducing them.

Focusing on the films Hitchcock made in the 1950s enables me to stress the centrality of the politicization of same-sex eroticism to postwar American culture and to show that it was one of the necessary conditions for the establishment of the postwar settlement. I argue that the crisis over the government employment of an indeterminate group of gay men and women who "passed" as straight not only reflected anxiety over the increasing heterogeneity of American society but also provided Cold War liberals with a mechanism for containing the emergence and consolidation of alternative social formations. The juridical construction of "the homosexual" and "the lesbian" as security risks all but guaranteed that homosexuality and heterosexuality became relatively fixed positions in an antagonistic relation. Because of the politicization of same-sex eroticism, Americans felt constrained to structure their sexual identities into relatively coherent ensembles of differences and to define themselves almost wholly in terms of those ensembles. One of the consequences of the definition of homosexuality and lesbianism as threats to national security was that in the 1950s sexual orientation became as crucial a determinate of social identity as race and gender. Moreover, the politicization of homosexuality and lesbianism was used to contain resistance to the terms of the postwar settlement. The discourses of national security positioned those Americans who refused to consent to the terms of the postwar

10   settlement as homosexuals or lesbians who threatened to undermine national security. The emergence of the national security state virtually insured that Americans scrutinized themselves for any indication of sexual and/or political deviance that might call into question their loyalty to the nation. The "enemy within" was not limited to the Communists, homosexuals, and lesbians who had supposedly infiltrated the federal government, but included the individual's own psyche. Generally considered the site of unconscious, potentially transgressive desires that s/he could not control, the individual's psyche constantly threatened to betray her/him into committing deviant sexual and/or political acts that conflicted with the nation's security interests.

This explains more fully why I have chosen to adopt a historical rather than a strictly psychoanalytic approach to the films Hitchcock made in the postwar period. It is my contention that in the context of the politicization of homosexuality and lesbianism, Hitchcock's ratification of a psychoanalytic understanding of male and female subjectivity was ideological. I try to show that his films contributed indirectly to the pathologizing of same-sex eroticism by suggesting that in order for the individual to achieve a relatively stable heterosexual identity, s/he had to successfully negotiate the Oedipus complex. Thus the application of psychoanalytic categories to his films by Lacanian film critics seems circular. It ignores the extent to which psychoanalysis was itself one of the major ideological tropes of the postwar period. I argue that in narrativizing the male and female Oedipal trajectories, Hitchcock tried to suture the spectator's subjectivity. Inserting the spectator into an Oedipalized subject position enabled him to contain the crisis of representation to which the proliferation of differences had led. The emergence in the 1950s of alternative constructions of social reality such as those that challenged the juridical construction of "the homosexual" and "the lesbian" as security risks threatened to disrupt the representational system of classical Hollywood cinema. The spectator's participation in a multiplicity of contending social formations meant that s/he might resist the attempts of the filmic system to interpellate her/him into an ideological position. One of the ways in which Hitchcock tried to forestall this potential crisis was by constructing his films along the male and female Oedipal trajectories. Narrativizing sexual difference enabled him to organize the spectator's sexuality according to a set of identifications and object attachments that were compatible with the terms of the postwar settlement. In refusing to occupy the Oedipalized subject position Hitchcock's films made available to her/him, the spectator risked positioning her/himself as the lesbian or homosexual of contemporary juridical discourse. Thus Hitchcock's Oedipalized narratives worked to contain the spectator's political and sexual indeterminacy, the construction of her/his subjectivity across variable axes of difference. By occupying the subject position Hitchcock's films made available to her/him, the spectator became complicit with her/his own Oedipalization, which in the 1950s was tantamount to accepting the terms of the postwar settlement.

But this does not explain why I have chosen to limit the focus of this book to Hitchcock. For if, as I have been claiming, filmic discourse was one of the principal nodal points that in the 1950s partially fixed the excess meaning of the social in a relatively closed system of differences by suturing individual identities, then the work of other directors would have served my purposes equally well. Yet locating Hitchcock's films in their historical context has struck me as a particularly urgent task. As I noted above, many of the films I discuss have been used to formulate Lacanian theories of the cinematic apparatus. These theories tend to ignore the historicity of filmic pleasure, its discursive construction in a specific historical context and in relation to hegemonic social and political structures. Lacanian film theorists seem to assume that voyeurism and other forms of desire preexist the cinematic apparatus and are not constituted by it.[22] By examining Hitchcock's films in the context of the postwar settlement, I want to call attention to the problems with this refusal to historicize filmic pleasure. I try to show that Hitchcock's films participated in a regime of pleasure that was specific to the postwar period and that helped to consolidate the emergence of the national security state. But I have also chosen to limit my focus to Hitchcock because his films provide particularly obvious examples of the political construction of gender in postwar America. Film theorists have long noted that Hitchcock's films engage issues of gender and sexual identity. In adopting a historical rather than a strictly psychoanalytic approach to his films, I want to show that his engagement of these issues was to a large extent determined by the politicization of homosexuality and lesbianism in the 1950s. The use of Lacanian psychoanalysis in film theory has tended to suppress this aspect of his work.

12   My goal in examining the political construction of gender in Hitchcock's films is to show that Hitchcock's representational practices were
complicit with the dominant construction of social reality under the
postwar settlement. Hitchcock's ratification of a psychoanalytic understanding of male and female subjectivity worked to limit the fund
of interpretive possibilities available to Americans. The spectator of
Hitchcock's films tended to subjectivize her/his experience of social
reality, to understand it psychologically rather than historically or
materially. In constructing his films along an Oedipal trajectory, Hitchcock virtually guaranteed that the spectator experienced as subjective
relations that were in reality political and social. That is to say, the
spectator of his films tended to experience her/his lived relations to the
world as originating in her/himself rather than in concrete historical
circumstances. I try to show that Hitchcock's tendency to subjectivize
the individual's experience constitutes one of the principal links between his films and the anti-Stalinist project of Cold War liberals. In
chapter 1, I argue that Cold War liberals wanted to reclaim "reality"
from Popular Front writers, and so they tried to shift attention from
the material world to the individual's subjective experience of it by
defining reality in such a way that it did not lend itself readily to a
Marxist analysis. Cold War liberals argued that reality did not exist
independently of the individual but was experienced subjectively.
Privileging modes of representation that stressed the highly mediated
relation between the individual and the material world, they claimed
that the Popular Front critique of American society was crudely positivistic because it focused on the capitalist relations of production at
the expense of the construction of subjectivity. For example, Robert
Warshow, whose film criticism appeared regularly in *Partisan Review*
and *Commentary,* attacked William Wyler's film, *The Best Years of Our
Lives* (1946), because it meticulously recreated the everyday life of
small-town America and emphasized the historicity of the postwar
subject, its construction in relation to historically specific institutions,
discourses, and practices.[23]

In chapter 1, I discuss Warshow's film criticism in relation to Lionel
Trilling's essay on the first Kinsey report, originally published in *Partisan Review* in 1948 and reprinted in *The Liberal Imagination* (1950), to
show that this attempt to establish an alternative system of representation, a system more appropriate to the anti-Stalinist agenda of liberal

intellectuals because it denied the importance of material conditions, relied heavily on the politicization of homosexuality and lesbianism. I argue that Trilling tried to link the Kinsey report to the Popular Front critique of American society. Trilling claimed that the report promoted the Stalinization of American culture because it tried to show that homosexuals and lesbians were as "normal" as heterosexuals. In using scientific data to support its claims, the report supposedly contributed to the crisis over national security. It suggested that reality existed independently of the individual and could be measured quantitatively. In chapter 3, I show, in relation to *Rear Window,* that this attempt to discredit the representational practices of the Popular Front by linking them to the crisis over national security was part of a larger project undertaken by Cold War liberals to develop a critical practice that was materialist but discarded the category of class. Cold War liberals wanted to show that America's economic recovery rendered the Marxist analysis of the capitalist relations of production irrelevant. The conditions of the postwar period supposedly required a set of categories different from the ones Popular Front intellectuals had developed in the 1930s for analyzing America's social and political structures. Cold War liberals tried to avoid the economic determinism of Popular Front intellectuals by stressing the importance of status rather than of class in determining the structure of American society. But in discarding the category of class, they merely succumbed to another kind of reductionism. They resorted to arguing that psychological rather than historical categories of analysis explained McCarthyism, and thus they psychologized the social relations of the period.

But my aims are not limited to demonstrating how Cold War liberals were able to produce a relatively united cultural front that combined a multiplicity of dispersed wills with heterogeneous and contradictory aims into a single collective will based on a shared interpretation of reality. I am also interested in using Hitchcock's films to expose the inconsistencies in the liberal interpretation of reality, inconsistencies that eventually led to the collapse of the postwar settlement in the 1960s. At the same time that the films I discuss participated in the dominant system of representation, they also inadvertently called attention to a surplus of meaning that remained uncontained by the liberal interpretation of reality and thus threatened to destabilize or rupture it. In chapter 2, for example, I show that the proliferation of

14   competing constructions of same-sex eroticism in the 1950s led to a
crisis in Hitchcock's system of representation because it problematized
his use of identification as his primary mode of address. Using Freudian theory, I argue that the process of identification involves the
repression of a potentially destabilizing homosexual object cathexis
between the male heterosexual spectator and the hero: the male heterosexual spectator must first desire the hero before he can identify
with him. Turning to *Strangers on a Train* (1951), I then suggest that the
politicization of same-sex eroticism in the postwar period made this
aspect of identification highly problematic. By encouraging the male
heterosexual spectator to identify with the hero of his film, Hitchcock
threatened to reinforce rather than to counteract the instability of his
sexual identity and in so doing to position him as "the homosexual"
who supposedly threatened national security. Hitchcock resorted to
ratifying the homophobic categories of Cold War political discourse in
order to suture the male heterosexual spectator's subjectivity.

In other words, I try to show that even those films of Hitchcock's
that were most governed by the organizing principles of the Cold War
consensus inadvertently called attention to a surplus of meaning that
remained uncontained by the dominant construction of social reality
and therefore made possible the emergence of alternative constructions. Although *Strangers on a Train* ratified the politicization of same-
sex eroticism by showing that male homosexuals constituted a security
risk, it unintentionally acknowledged the homoerotics of male spectatorial pleasure. In chapter 3, I suggest that *Rear Window* similarly
exposed the inconsistencies in the liberal interpretation of reality. On
the one hand, Hitchcock's attempts to depoliticize voyeuristic desire
by recontaining it within the private sphere corresponded to the liberal
critique of McCarthyism. Hitchcock implicated the cinematic apparatus in the rise of McCarthyism by suggesting that the voyeuristic
economy of spectatorial pleasure had been corrupted by the scopic
regime of the national security state. On the other hand, Hitchcock's
attempts to reprivatize spectatorial pleasure called attention to the
limits of the postwar settlement. Hitchcock inadvertently acknowledged that the Cold War consensus was experienced differently by
individuals who were positioned differently within the social formation (by race, class, and gender) by trying to show that what Lisa
Fremont (Grace Kelly) lost in the public sphere (a highly successful

career as a model) she gained in the private (a sexually satisfying marriage). Obviously, Hitchcock would hardly have made such a claim if
Lisa had been a man. Thus the film was unwilling to accommodate
Lisa's interests except within the confines of the middle-class nuclear
family.

In chapter 4, I continue to situate Hitchcock's films in relation to
the postwar settlement by examining the way in which they simultaneously reinforced and undermined the liberal interpretation of reality, but with the aim of problematizing Hitchcock's status as an auteur.
It is my contention that the auteur theory, as it was elaborated in the
1950s by American critics and directors, was complicit with the emergence of the national security state. I argue that in promoting his
reputation as a director who had overcome the constraints of industrial production and "authored" his films, Hitchcock tried to position
himself as a unified and coherent subject who occupied the Oedipalized subject position inscribed in his films. Although, in the wake of
poststructuralist theory, auteurist criticism has become highly problematic, critics continue to treat Hitchcock as the originating agency of
his films. They attribute to his corpus a monolithic, homogeneous
system of representation that installs him as the stable point of authorial origin. In contrast, I conceive of Hitchcock as a subject in history,
constituted in and through discourse. I try to show that Hitchcock
spoke from a position within a network of discourses that placed
considerable constraints on his textual practices. This network was not
limited to the textual system of classical Hollywood cinema but included the discourses that governed the construction of male subjectivity at the particular historical moment in which he worked as a
director. Moreover, this network was a site of intense ideological
struggle (especially in the 1950s, when gender and nationality functioned as mutually reinforcing categories of identity) and thus was
not fixed but constantly shifting. Focusing on the differences between
the two versions of *The Man Who Knew Too Much* (1934, 1956), I assert
that Hitchcock's textual practices were necessarily conditioned by the
emergence of the national security state and reflected the construction
of his subjectivity in relation to the discourses of national security.

In the remaining two chapters, I argue that in calling attention to a
surplus of meaning uncontained by the dominant system of representation, Hitchcock's films inadvertently suggested that the discourses

16   of national security could not exhaust all social experience and that
their ability to regulate and define the social field was necessarily
limited because it was based on exclusions and repressions. I contend
in chapter 5 that *Vertigo* exposed the discrepancy between the actual
experiences of real historical Hispanic men and women and the representation of those experiences by official histories of the United States.
In reconstructing the story of Carlotta Valdez, a Hispanic woman who
was seduced and abandoned by her Anglo lover in the nineteenth
century, *Vertigo* challenged the official representation of the nation's
past as a continuous, linear narrative and indicated the possibility of
constructing a counterhistory that more accurately represented the
nation's past because it included stories like hers. The film's emphasis
on the inaccuracies of official history unintentionally showed that
social reality was not only an effect of representation but also its
excess, or what remained uncontained by representation and therefore threatened to destabilize or rupture it.

In chapter 6, I claim that in exposing the exclusions and repressions on which the dominant construction of social reality was based,
Hitchcock inadvertently showed that power relations in the 1950s
were reversible. I argue that *Psycho* (1960) constituted a mirror image
of *North by Northwest* in that it inverted the earlier film's representation
of the operations of power in postwar America. *Psycho* represented a
kind of paranoid fantasy in which the discourses of national security
not only failed to gain the individual's free and spontaneous consent
to the postwar settlement but actually encouraged her/his resistance
to it. Whereas in *North by Northwest* Hitchcock demonstrated how the
discourses of national security produced fantasies that brought the individual's desire into alignment with the nation's security interests, in
Psycho he demonstrated how the discourses of national security produced counterfantasies, or fantasies that organized the individual's
sexuality according to a set of identifications and object attachments
that conflicted with the nation's security interests. Still, in stressing the
limited ability of the discourses of national security to organize and
define the social field, *Psycho* indicated the possibility of constructing
an alternative representation of social reality that was more inclusive
than the one constructed by Cold War liberals. *Psycho* inadvertently
showed that the social field was made up of a multiplicity of competing discourses that were historically produced and reproduced

through the practices of everyday life and that implicated the individual in contradictory ways.

In the Name of National Security, then, places as much emphasis on the contradictions and inconsistencies as on the unity and coherence of the dominant construction of social reality in the postwar period. Although I try to show that in defining reality in such a way that it did not lend itself readily to a Marxist analysis, Cold War liberals were able to produce a single, collective will from a multiplicity of wills with heterogeneous and contradictory aims, I also try to show that their definition of reality was not a given, but faced constant competition from alternative definitions, and that they had to renew its hegemony continuously. This explains more fully why the films I examine simultaneously reinforced and undermined the postwar settlement. They were part of a constantly shifting discursive horizon in which the dominant construction of social reality underwent continuous revision and thus made possible the emergence of alternative constructions. To emphasize this constantly shifting horizon, I address a different aspect of the political construction of gender and sexual identity in postwar America in each of the chapters on the films. I divided these chapters into three parts. They begin with a theoretical account of a set of problems specific to postwar American culture, proceed to a reconstruction of the set of discourses that functioned as the political preconscious of the film under discussion, and conclude with a demonstration of how that film was at once complicit with and critical of the dominant construction of social reality in the 1950s.[24] Chapters 4 and 6 deviate slightly from this organization in that their reconstruction of the political pre-conscious of the film that is their primary focus is limited to other films Hitchcock made.

I chose to organize the chapters in this way for two reasons. First, I wanted to clarify the complex relation between the films and the dominant construction of social reality by locating them in the specific network of discourses in which they participated. Second, I wanted to emphasize the extent to which the construction of gender and sexual identity was governed by the discourses of national security. Each of the films I examine calls attention to a different aspect of the organization of gender relations in the postwar period. Consequently, reconstructing their political pre-conscious helps to show that the politicization of gender and sexual identity in the 1950s was crucial to the

18   production and reproduction of the Cold War consensus. Examining
Hitchcock's films in the context of the emergence and consolidation of
the national security state suggests that the juridical construction of
"the homosexual" and "the lesbian" as security risks provided the
American government with a mechanism for containing resistance to
the postwar settlement. Thus I have tried to organize this book in a
way that allows me not only to situate Hitchcock's films in relation
to the Cold War consensus but also to establish crucial connections
between gender, national identity, and national security in postwar
American society.

DRAPED IN THE AMERICAN FLAG
Cold War Liberals and the Resistance

to Theory

In those years, I was told, when I became terrified, vehement, or lachrymose:
It takes time, Jimmy. It takes time. I agree: I still agree: though it certainly didn't
take much time for some of the people I knew then—in the Fifties—to turn
tail, to decide to make it, and drape themselves in the American flag. A
wretched and despicable band of cowards, whom I once trusted with my life—
friends like these!
—James Baldwin, Preface to the 1984 edition of *Notes of a Native Son*

War is hell, even when it's a cold one.—The Professor, *North by Northwest*

In *The Vital Center* (1949), one of the most influential books of the
postwar period, when Arthur Schlesinger, Jr., wanted to emphasize
the conspiratorial nature of the American Communist party, he compared it to the gay male subculture. Engaging in the kind of political
tactics perfected by McCarthy and his followers, Schlesinger alleged
that the American Communist party had an "underground arm, oper-
ating apart from the formal organization of the [party] and working as
the American section of the Soviet secret intelligence corps."[1] According to Schlesinger, this arm was composed of "secret members" (127)
who were committed to infiltrating and subverting the American government through covert strategies. Unknown to one another, these
members reported directly to a representative of the party's National
Committee and interacted with one another in ways that allegedly
resembled homosexual "cruising." Although they supposedly had no
local affiliations, were exempt from party discipline, and were "unknown to most of their Party brethren" (127), Schlesinger claimed that
these members could recognize one another almost instinctively. He
suggested that they could "identify each other (and be identified by
their enemies) on casual meeting by the use of certain phrases, the

names of certain friends, by certain enthusiasms and certain silences" (127). Contributing to the anti-Communist hysteria then sweeping the nation, Schlesinger compared the way in which these members identified one another to the way in which he alleged homosexuals made contact when looking for sex. He charged that their methods of making contact were "reminiscent of nothing so much as the famous scene in Proust where the Baron de Charlus and the tailor Jupien suddenly recognize their common corruption . . ." (127).

Comparing the way in which the "secret" members of the Communist party supposedly interacted to the way in which homosexuals identified one another when looking for sex enabled Schlesinger to accomplish two things crucial to the project undertaken by Cold War liberals in the 1950s to reclaim liberalism from its history of Communist fellow traveling. First, it helped to consolidate the Cold War consensus by making membership in the Communist party and other forms of political dissent seem "unnatural." Second, it helped to insure that gender and nationality functioned as mutually reinforcing categories of identity by suggesting that engaging in homosexuality and other "perverted" sexual practices was un-American. Like other anti-Stalinist intellectuals, Schlesinger refused to believe that Americans joined the Communist party because they were genuinely committed to communism. He thought that Marxist categories of analysis were simply not applicable to postwar American society. He pointed out that America had witnessed the longest period of liberal government in its history and that the labor movement had won major concessions from American industries. For this reason, he tried to explain membership in the Communist party psychologically. He suggested that despite the economic prosperity of the postwar period, America still had "its quota of lonely and frustrated people, craving social, intellectual and even sexual fulfillment they cannot obtain in existing society" (104). For such people, the discipline of the Communist party, its demand for unceasing loyalty, was supposedly not an obstacle but an attraction. Membership in the party offered such people the possibility of belonging to a group. Schlesinger speculated that "communism fills empty lives. Surrender to the Party gives a sense of comradeship in a cause guaranteed by history to succor the helpless and to triumph over the wealthy and satisfied" (105). In other words, membership in the party did not reflect a commitment to Marxist

ideology but a longing for comradeship fostered by the atomization of
postwar American society.

According to the implications of this argument, Americans who
thought of themselves as part of the gay and lesbian subcultures that
began to emerge in the postwar period in large urban areas, or who
joined the Mattachine Society, an organization founded in Los Angeles in 1950 that defined gay men and women as members of an
oppressed minority with its own distinct culture, could be seen as
disloyal citizens engaged in a conspiracy to overthrow the American
government. In suggesting that Americans joined the Communist
party for psychological rather than ideological reasons, Schlesinger
identified the party as a kind of subculture, or alternative social formation, in which members defined themselves wholly in terms of their
membership in the party. He claimed that party members willingly
subjected themselves to the sort of "intensive personal supervision,
only to be duplicated in a religious order or a police state" (105). A
clause in the party constitution allegedly forbade members from enter-
ing into relations with "enemies of the working class," but Schlesinger
claimed that it was rarely invoked because most members "voluntarily
renounce non-Party friendships and activities" (106). Indeed, most
members supposedly became so dependent on the party psychologically that "the threat of expulsion strikes them as excommunication
would a devout Catholic" (106). In this way, Schlesinger obliquely
suggested that gay men who considered themselves members of an
oppressed minority or who participated in the gay subculture were as
un-American as communists who threatened national security as well.
Their identities as homosexuals were supposedly in tension with their
identities as patriotic Americans and threatened to displace them.
Arguing that Americans joined the Communist party because they
wanted a "sense of comradeship" and not because they were committed to Marxist ideology enabled Schlesinger to reduce membership
in the Communist party to a form of identity politics. Schlesinger tried
to show that communism was no longer a system of political beliefs
but had become a category of identity that competed with other categories of identity such as race, class, and nationality. In so doing, he
implied that membership in the Communist party was "unnatural."[2]
Americans who were members of the Communist party resembled
homosexuals in that the bonds uniting them in a common struggle

against the capitalist state were supposedly stronger and more enduring than the bonds uniting them as Americans.

In indirectly suggesting that membership in the Communist party constituted a form of homosexuality, Schlesinger sought to reclaim liberalism from the "taint" of its history of Communist fellow traveling. In the 1930s, many liberal intellectuals had embraced the Popular Front and its materialist critique of American society; in so doing, they seriously compromised the liberal tradition, which became associated with the Stalinization of American culture.[3] Schlesinger tried to reclaim liberalism from its allegedly tainted past by declaring the emergence of a "new and distinct political generation" (vii) that had supposedly rejected the cultural politics of the Popular Front and remained faithful to liberal principles. Using his own political development as an example, he explained that his generation of liberal intellectuals had come of age at a time when liberalism had dominated American politics. This new generation of liberal intellectuals supposedly had no reason to embrace the Marxist critique of the capitalist relations of production because Keynesian economics and the emergence of the welfare state had rendered Marxist categories of analysis obsolete. Schlesinger argued that the New Deal had shown that "democracy was capable of taking care of its own" (viii). Moreover, unlike the generation of liberal intellectuals who had come of age during the Progressive Era, he and his contemporaries did not believe in the perfectibility of human nature. With the collapse of the Soviet "experiment" and the rise of fascism, he and his contemporaries had discovered "a new dimension of experience—the dimension of anxiety, guilt and corruption" (ix). Thus they could no longer believe in the possibility of progress. Schlesinger explained that events like the Holocaust and the constant threat of nuclear war "reminded my generation rather forcibly that man [sic] was, indeed, imperfect, and that the corruptions of power could unleash great evil in the world" (ix).

To show that a "new and distinct" generation of liberal intellectuals had truly emerged in the postwar period, Schlesinger undertook a critique of American society that was materialist but that discarded the category of class and thus could not be confused with the cultural politics of the Popular Front. Although he acknowledged the role material conditions played in determining contemporary social relations, he minimized the importance of the capitalist relations of pro-

duction and limited his critique of postwar American culture to industrialization. He claimed that science and technology, rather than the
capitalist mode of production, were responsible for the emergence in
America of an atomized, impersonal society dominated by mass culture. Thus he urged critics of contemporary American society to direct
their criticisms "not against any particular system of ownership, but
against industrial organization and the post-industrial state, whatever
the system of ownership" (3). In this way, Schlesinger formulated a
critique of postwar American culture that, despite its focus on material
conditions, remained grounded in the liberal tradition and was clearly
not Marxist. His emphasis on the role of science and technology in
determining contemporary social relations divested Marxism of its
explanatory power. If industrialization rather than the capitalist mode
of production was responsible for the atomization of postwar American society, then Marxist categories of analysis were no longer applicable to contemporary social relations. Schlesinger thought that the only
way in which Americans could contain Soviet expansionism and win
the Cold War was by creating social and political structures "within
which the individual can achieve some measure of self-fulfillment" (3).
Such structures must "succeed where the ancient jurisdictions of the
family, the clan, the guild and the nation-state have failed. [They]
must solve the problems created by the speed-up of time, the reduction of space and the increase in tension. [They] must develop new
equivalents for the sanctions once imposed by custom and by reli-
gion" (4).

Arguing that the problems facing postwar American society were
social and political rather than economic was a strategy anti-Stalinist
intellectuals frequently adopted in order to invalidate the Marxist
critique of the capitalist relations of production. Schlesinger's discussion of mass culture and the problems it posed for contemporary
society in many respects anticipated Hannah Arendt's *Origins of Totalitarianism* (1951), which in the 1950s became the standard interpretation
of the emergence of the totalitarian state.[4] In *The Origins of Totalitarianism*, Arendt claimed that totalitarianism constituted an entirely new
form of power and could not be adequately explained by the category
of class. She argued that the totalitarian state could not be considered a
traditional dictatorship because it operated "according to a system of
values so radically different from all others, that none of our traditional

legal, moral, or common sense utilitarian categories could any longer help us to come to terms with, or judge, or predict [its] course of action."[5] Making this claim enabled her to discard the category of class as irrelevant to the analysis of the rise of the totalitarian state. She located the emergence of totalitarianism in mass psychology and defined totalitarian movements as "mass organizations of atomized, isolated individuals" (323) who had no class affiliations and were disaffected from traditional political parties. Recalling Schlesinger's argument that the Communist party appealed primarily to "lonely, frustrated" Americans, she speculated that totalitarianism attracted the "completely isolated human being who, without any other social ties to family, friends, comrades, or even mere acquaintances, derives his [sic] sense of having a place in the world only from his belonging to a movement, his membership in the party" (323–24). In other words, Marxist categories could not adequately explain the emergence of the totalitarian state.[6] If totalitarian movements were made up of "atomized" individuals who had no class or party affiliations, then the most useful categories for analyzing the emergence of totalitarianism were psychological.

In stressing the psychological rather than the economic factors that had led to the emergence of totalitarianism, Arendt adopted Schlesinger's strategy for invalidating the Marxist critique of the capitalist relations of production. Anticipating Arendt's argument, Schlesinger claimed that totalitarian movements appealed primarily to "atomized" individuals who had difficulty adjusting to the complexities of capitalist societies. According to him, the individuals who joined totalitarian movements reveled "in the release from individual responsibility, in the affirmation of comradeship in organized mass solidarity" (54). They were easily swayed by totalitarian propaganda because it provided them with an answer to "the incoherence and apparent uncontrollability of industrial society" (53–54). Arendt similarly emphasized the psychological appeal of totalizing theories that tried to account for every aspect of an individual's experience. Like Schlesinger, she claimed that the "masses" longed for a "completely consistent, comprehensible, and predictable world" (352) in which the merest coincidence was invested with meaning. Totalitarian propaganda supposedly appealed to the "masses" because it transformed "chaotic and accidental conditions into a man-made pattern of relative consistency" (352). In this way, both Schlesinger and Arendt implied that Marxist theory was totalitarian because it was totalizing. In suggesting that social relations were necessarily determined by the dominant mode of production, Marxist theory allegedly treated mere coincidences as if they were part of a "man-made" pattern or design; in so doing, like totalitarian propaganda, it misled the "masses" into believing that experience was predictable rather than random and indeterminate. Both Schlesinger and Arendt thought that no theory could adequately explain the complex structure of capitalist societies. Arendt objected to totalitarian propaganda because it tried to spare the masses "the never-ending shocks which real life and real experiences deal to human beings and their expectations" (353).

Both Schlesinger and Arendt, then, tried to divest Marxist theory of its explanatory power by claiming that totalitarianism and other complex social phenomena reflected the atomization of contemporary social relations and were not reducible to the category of class. According to them, experience consisted of "never-ending shocks" that defied analysis because they could not be predicted or determined in advance; consequently, Marxist theory could not adequately explain the complexity of capitalist social formations. In what follows, I want to examine this attempt to invalidate Marxist categories by shifting attention from the material world to the individual's subjective experience of it. I will argue that Cold War liberals tried to divest Marxist theory of its explanatory power because they wanted to reclaim "reality" from Popular Front intellectuals whose materialist critique of American society had become hegemonic. In stressing those aspects of postwar American society that Marxist theory could not adequately explain or that did not readily lend themselves to a Marxist critique because it lacked a fully developed theory of subjectivity, Cold War liberals sought to limit the fund of interpretive possibilities available to postwar Americans for making sense of their lived experience. If Cold War liberals were right in claiming that experience was composed of "never-ending shocks" that did not correspond to existing theoretical paradigms, then the most useful categories for analyzing the complex structure of American society were psychological. Invalidating the category of class enabled Cold War liberals to produce a relatively united cultural front that combined a multiplicity of dispersed wills with heterogeneous and contradictory aims into a single collective will based on a shared interpretation of reality. By focusing on those aspects of the individual's experience that resisted theoretical elaboration, Cold War liberals established an interpretation of reality to which Americans consented because it seemed to correspond to their lived experience.

Redefining Reality:
Cold War Liberals and the Subjectivization of Experience

Perhaps the most explicit attempt by a Cold War liberal to reclaim "reality" from Popular Front intellectuals was Lionel Trilling's highly influential essay "Reality in America," included in *The Liberal Imagination* (1950) but originally published in *Partisan Review* and the *Nation* in two separate parts. In "Reality in America," Trilling attacked the Popular Front critique of American culture as crudely positivistic. Like Schlesinger, he thought that liberalism had been seriously compromised by its history of fellow traveling, and he wanted to reclaim it by repudiating the Marxist interpretation of reality. He adopted Schlesinger's strategy and tried to discredit historical materialism by arguing that it simply ignored or suppressed those aspects of an individual's experience that resisted theoretical elaboration or that did not correspond to its theoretical paradigm. In the preface to *The Liberal Imagination*, he resorted to the language of psychoanalysis, comparing liberalism to a "human entity" and claiming that its "conscious and unconscious life . . . are not always in accord."[7] He argued that liberalism continued to dominate American politics because it "unconsciously limits its view of the world to what it can deal with, and it unconsciously tends to develop theories and principles, particularly in relation to the nature of the human, that justify its limitation" (xiii). In this way, he not only discredited the Popular Front critique of capitalism by suggesting that it overlooked the "reality" of capitalist social formations, but he also legitimated the use of psychological categories by treating liberalism as a "human entity" that could be psychoanalyzed. If liberalism resembled a "human entity," if it had a "conscious" and an "unconscious" life, then the most useful categories for analyzing its history were psychological.

Trilling's example in "Reality in America" of liberalism's "unconscious" tendency to suppress those aspects of American society that did not lend themselves readily to a materialist critique was V. L. Parrington's history of American letters, *Main Currents in American Thought* (1927). Trilling objected to Parrington's reconstruction of American literary history because of its positivistic assumptions about the nature of reality. He alleged that Parrington naïvely assumed that there was "a thing called *reality*. It is one and immutable, it is wholly external, it is reducible. Men's minds may waver, but reality is always reliable, always the same, always easily to be known" (4). Consequently, Parrington tended to judge the classics of American literature according to how faithfully they represented reality rather than according to their literary merits. Parrington was supposedly incapable of appreciating writers who did not work within the realist tradition or who did not share his positivistic assumptions. Trilling thought that Parrington politicized American literary history unnecessarily and suggested that "whenever he was confronted with a work of art that was complex, personal and not literal, that was not, as it were, a public document, Parrington was at a loss" (4). Trilling tried to show that Parrington's obviously partisan reconstruction of American literary history exemplified the way in which Popular Front critics politicized American culture and allowed politics to distort their interpretations of American literature. Because he did not realize that "there is any other relation possible between the artist and reality than this passage of reality through the transparent artist" (5), Parrington dismissed an entire tradition of American writers whose politics did not correspond to his own. Indeed, he seemed to consider writers who did not share his simplistic understanding of the relation between literature and society unworthy of inclusion in the canon because they were undemocratic. According to Trilling, Parrington met "evidence of imagination and creativeness with a settled hostility the expression of which suggests that he regards them as the natural enemies of democracy" (5).

Trilling singled out Parrington's history of American letters because he considered it representative of the dominant attitudes of the American middle class. Greatly exaggerating his influence as a literary historian, Trilling claimed that Parrington had "had an influence on our conception of American culture which is not equaled by that of any other writer in the last two decades" (3). For Trilling, this meant that Parrington's simplistic understanding of the relation between literature and society enjoyed considerable currency and influenced the way in which Americans conceived their relation to the world. Trilling argued that Parrington's partisan readings of the classics of American literature rarely encountered resistance from other literary historians because they expressed "in a classic way the suppositions about our culture which are held by the American middle class so far as that class is at all liberal in its social thought and so far as it begins to understand that literature has anything to do with reality" (3). In other words, Trilling interpreted the continuing popularity of Parrington's study to mean that a consensus had emerged with respect to the structure of American society. The American middle class was receptive to Parrington's reconstruction of American literary history because it shared his assumptions about the nature of reality. Like Parrington, it tended to reduce the complex relation between literature and society to the simplistic formula, "Most writers incline to stick to their own class" (4). Trilling stressed Parrington's reductive approach to issues of literary production because he considered it an indication that the cultural politics of the Popular Front continued to influence the self-understanding of the American middle class. Despite their inadequate theorization of the relation between base and superstructure, Popular Front intellectuals had been able to win Americans over to their interpretation of reality because it seemed based on common sense.

In using Parrington's history of American letters as an example of liberalism's "unconscious" tendency to simplify the "reality" of America's social and political structures, Trilling seriously misrepresented Parrington's cultural politics. To begin with, the Communist party did not embrace the Popular Front as a strategy for uniting the American Left in a common struggle against fascism until 1935, and Parrington's reconstruction of American literary history owed more to the cultural politics of the Progressive Era than to a serious engagement with Marxist theory. Indeed, what distinguished him as a literary historian were not his positivistic assumptions about the nature of reality so much as his emphasis on the role of social conflict in determining the course of American history.[8] Moreover, F. O. Matthiessen's *American Renaissance* (1941) had replaced Parrington's book as the most influential reconstruction of American literary history by the time Trilling revised his essay for inclusion in *The Liberal Imagination*. Trilling indirectly acknowledged this when he added a paragraph to the revised version of the essay in which he stated that "Parrington lies twenty years behind us, and in the intervening time there has developed a body of opinion which is aware of his inadequacies and of the inadequacies of his coadjutors and disciples" (10). But, as Jonathan Arac has shown, Trilling deliberately did not mention Matthiessen's book because it undermined his argument about liberalism's "unconscious" tendency to suppress those aspects of American culture that did not correspond to its theoretical paradigm (a tendency that, in this particular instance, Trilling clearly shared).[9] Although Matthiessen's history of American letters was deeply indebted to the cultural politics of the Popular Front and thus was as partisan as Parrington's, it could not be accused of reducing the classics of American literature to a superstructural expression of the capitalist mode of production. Still, singling out Parrington's book rather than Matthiessen's enabled Trilling to exaggerate the threat the continuing influence of the Popular Front posed to American society. If Trilling was right, if the American middle class as a whole did indeed share Parrington's simplistic understanding of the relation between base and superstructure, then the nation's security was threatened internally as well as externally. In greatly exaggerating the continuing popularity of Parrington's study, Trilling created the impression that the American middle class was thoroughly Stalinized.

Using Parrington rather than Matthiessen as an example of liberalism's unconscious tendency to simplify reality enabled Trilling to define reality in such a way that it did not lend itself readily to a Marxist critique. In opposition to Parrington, Trilling argued that reality did not exist independently of the individual, but was experienced subjectively. Thus the individual's relation to reality was not transparent, but highly mediated. The individual could not perceive reality objectively because her/his relation to it was subjective. Stressing the highly mediated relation between the individual and reality allowed Trilling to retrieve an entire tradition of American writers who had been relegated to the ash heap of American literary history by Popular Front critics who considered them elitist and inaccessible to the "people." Trilling wanted in particular to reclaim Hawthorne for the liberal tradition. Whereas Parrington dismissed Hawthorne as a romantic who psychologized the relation between the individual and reality, Trilling praised him for focusing on the individual's subjective experience of reality: "The man who could raise those brilliant and serious doubts about the nature and possibility of moral perfection, the man who could keep himself aloof from the 'Yankee reality' and who could dissent from the orthodoxies of dissent and tell us so much about the nature of moral zeal, is of course dealing exactly with reality" (9). In this way, Trilling suggested indirectly that the Marxist conceptual apparatus, which lacked a fully developed theory of subjectivity, could not adequately explain American literary history.[10] His insistence that American literature could not be reduced to a superstructural expression of the capitalist mode of production invalidated Marxist categories of analysis by shifting attention from the material world to the individual's subjective experience of it. Because reality did not exist independently of the individual, but was experienced subjectively, the most useful approach to American literature was psychoanalytic.

Trilling was not alone among Cold War liberals in trying to reclaim Hawthorne for the liberal tradition. Schlesinger also praised Hawthorne for his willingness to dissent from the orthodoxies of dissent.[11] Like Trilling, Schlesinger greatly admired Hawthorne's novel *The Blithedale Romance*, because of its fictionalized account of the utopian experiment at Brook Farm. According to Schlesinger, Hawthorne's criticisms of the utopian reformers who settled at Brook Farm foretold the emergence of the totalitarian state and accurately described the authoritarian personality and its totalitarian will to power. Schlesinger speculated that Hawthorne's refusal to embrace the liberal pieties of his age enabled him to extrapolate "unerringly from the pretty charades of Brook Farm to the essence of totalitarian man [sic]" (162). Thus Schlesinger seems to have shared Trilling's assumptions about the complex relation between the individual and reality. Schlesinger admired Hawthorne's novel because its criticisms of the utopian movement were supposedly not specific to Jacksonian America but foretold the rise of totalitarianism; that is to say, they did not try to generalize a historically specific set of experiences but conveyed abstract, universal truths about human nature and its potential for evil. The implications of this reading of Hawthorne's fictionalized account of Brook Farm should be obvious. In praising Hawthorne as a realist who accurately represented the "reality" of utopian movements in general, Schlesinger and Trilling invalidated the Marxist conceptual apparatus as a tool for analyzing American culture. Schlesinger apparently agreed with Trilling that reality did not exist independently of the individual but was subjectively experienced. Thus writers who focused on the material world rather than on the individual's subjective experience of it lacked insight into the complex nature of American society and did not deserve inclusion in the canon. For if reality was subjectively experienced, the role of material conditions in determining the individual's relation to it was trivial and not worth examining.

To help explain Trilling's focus on the individual's subjective experience of reality, I want to compare "Reality in America" to two essays by James Baldwin that originally appeared in *Partisan Review* but were included in *Notes of a Native Son* (1955). In elaborating a theory of subjectivity that was very different from Trilling's, these essays suggest that Trilling's rejection of Marxist categories reflected not only his belief that American literature could not be reduced to a superstructural expression of the capitalist mode of production, as contemporary Marxist theory suggested, but also his desire to suppress issues of ethnicity that threatened to lead to a backlash against Jewish intellectuals and undermine his authority as one of America's leading cultural critics. At first glance, Baldwin appeared to reiterate Trilling's criticisms of liberalism's "unconscious" tendency to suppress those aspects of American society that did not correspond to its theoretical paradigm (which, no doubt, accounts for their publication in *Partisan Review*).[12] For example, in "Everybody's Protest Novel," which first appeared in *Partisan Review* in 1949, he seemed to echo Trilling when he accused liberal critics of reducing the highly mediated relation between literature and society to a simplistic formula that emphasized the category of class at the expense of the other categories of identity that influenced the individual's subjective experience of reality. Reminding liberal critics that literature was not a branch of sociology, he warned that "our passion for categorization, life neatly fitted into pegs, has led to an unforeseen, paradoxical distress; confusion, a breakdown of meaning."[13] Moreover, in "Many Thousands Gone," which was originally published in *Partisan Review* in 1951, he suggested that the social protest novel did not accurately represent reality in America because it ignored the individual's subjective experience of the material world. Again seeming to echo Trilling's criticisms of liberalism, he asserted that "the reality of man [sic] as a social being is not his only reality and that artist is strangled who is forced to deal with human beings solely in social terms" (33). Baldwin, then, seems to have shared Trilling's assumptions about the nature of reality. The individual's experience of reality was subjective and could not be reduced to her/his identity as a social being. Liberal critics who stressed the relation between the individual's experience of the material world and her/his identity as a social being ignored the complexity of reality and tried to make it fit neatly into pegs.

This emphasis on the complex relation between the individual and reality, an emphasis he shared with Trilling, did not mean, however, that Baldwin thought that the individual's identity as a social being did not influence her/his subjective experience of the material world or that writers should ignore the historicity of the individual's subjectivity, its construction in relation to historically specific discourses, practices, and institutions. On the contrary, as a gay African-American intellectual, Baldwin was particularly interested in establishing a connection between the individual's identity as a social being and her/his subjective experience of the material world, and he called into question Richard Wright's status as a representative African-American writer whose best-selling novel, *Native Son*, accurately represented African-American experience. For example, he criticized Wright, not because he treated Bigger, the protagonist of *Native Son*, purely as a social being, but because he did not seem to realize the extent to which Bigger was a social being. Wright supposedly did not understand that as an African American, Bigger had internalized the racist stereotype of "the nigger" and could not avoid coming to terms with it. Baldwin claimed that he knew of no African American who had not been forced "to make his [sic] own precarious adjustment to the 'nigger' who surrounds him and to the 'nigger' in himself" (38). It was this aspect of Bigger's identity as a social being that Wright supposedly overlooked when he focused on the material conditions of African-American life rather than on Bigger's subjective experience of them. Wright apparently did not realize that African-American identity was a subjective construction and that all African Americans had to negotiate the stereotype of "the nigger." Baldwin claimed that *Native Son* "lacked any revelatory apprehension of Bigger as one of the Negro's realities or as one of the Negro's roles" (39). In other words, Wright's novel simplified the complexity of African-American oppression. Racist ideol-

ogy had concrete, material effects and conditioned the construction of
African-American subjectivity. Wright did not fully understand the
nature of Bigger's tragedy. It was not that Bigger had been denied the
opportunity to achieve the American dream but that he had "accepted
a theology that denies him life, that he admits the possibility of being
sub-human and feels constrained, therefore, to battle for his humanity
according to those brutal criteria bequeathed to him at his birth" (23).

Because he did not seem to understand that Bigger's identity as a
social being and his subjective experience of the material world were
mutually reinforcing, Baldwin questioned whether Wright was genuinely interested in working to eliminate the structural inequalities
between Blacks and whites or whether he resented the fact that African Americans were excluded from the American dream. Baldwin was
critical of social protest novels because he thought they led to compla-
cency. Rather than challenging the reader's assumptions about American society, they only reinforced them. Social protest novels had become "an accepted and comforting aspect of the American scene,
ramifying that framework we believe to be so necessary" (19). Although Baldwin acknowledged that *Native Son* was not like other
social protest novels in that it was the "most powerful and celebrated
statement we have yet had of what it means to be a Negro in America"
(30), he nevertheless thought that by ignoring the concrete, material
effects racist ideology had on the construction of African-American
subjectivity, Wright helped to perpetuate the stereotype of "the nigger." To begin with, in refusing to acknowledge that Bigger's crimes
were not creative acts but capitulations to the racist stereotypes that he
had inherited as a social being, Wright simply reinforced the com-
monly held assumption that all African-American men were potential
rapists and murderers. Moreover, Wright's focus on the material conditions of African-American life seemed to suggest that Blacks were
inferior to whites. In claiming that the only way in which Bigger could
redeem his manhood was through rape and murder, Wright reassured
white readers that "black is a terrible color with which to be born" (30).
In other words, Wright ignored the complexity of African-American
culture, its richness and diversity. His focus on the injustice of Bigger's exclusion from the American dream inadvertently denigrated the
"complex techniques [Blacks] have evolved for their survival" (35) and
seemed to suggest that they were culturally, as well as economically,

impoverished. Baldwin complained that Wright's novel seriously misrepresented "the relationship that Negroes bear to one another, that depth of involvement and unspoken recognition of shared experience which creates a way of life" (35). This did not mean that Baldwin thought Wright should have blindly celebrated the "techniques" African Americans had developed for resisting their oppression, or that he should have ignored the economic forces that conditioned African-American experience. Rather, Baldwin was critical of Wright because he thought Wright's understanding of historical materialism was too narrow and did not extend to the construction of African-American subjectivity in relation to the stereotype of "the nigger."

Baldwin, then, in claiming that Wright did not adequately address the individual's complex relation to reality, was not interested in shifting attention from the material world to the individual's subjective experience of it. He was critical of Wright because Wright ignored the materiality of ideology, its concrete effects on the construction of African-American subjectivity. Wright did not seem to understand that Bigger's crimes indicated that he had internalized racist constructions of Black male identity. In becoming a rapist and a murderer, Bigger merely fulfilled white America's expectations. In this respect, Baldwin's criticisms of Wright differed significantly from Trilling's criticisms of Parrington. Although Baldwin seemed to share Trilling's assumptions about the nature of reality in that he criticized Wright for ignoring the construction of Bigger's subjectivity in relation to racist constructions of African-American male identity, he was not interested in shifting attention away from the historical specificity of the individual's identity as a social being. Rather, he wanted to show that the individual's subjective experience of the material world was complexly related to her/his identity as a social being. Baldwin suggested that the most disturbing aspect of the stereotype of "the nigger" was that it provided American society with "the force and the weapons to translate its dictum into fact, so that the allegedly inferior are actually made so, insofar as the societal realities are concerned" (20). Thus Baldwin thought that *Native Son* failed as a social protest novel because it did not adequately address the complexity of America's racist structures and limited its materialist critique of African-American oppression to Bigger's economic disenfranchisement.

In marked contrast to Baldwin, Trilling *did* want to shift attention away from the individual's identity as a social being. Indeed, as a Jewish intellectual, he had a vested interest in suppressing the relation between the individual's identity as a social being and her/his subjective experience of the material world. After all, many of the Communists and fellow travelers exposed by the McCarthy hearings were Jewish, and Trilling seemed to fear that the anti-Communist hysteria unleashed by the hearings would lead to a backlash against Jewish intellectuals who, like him, had been active in the Popular Front. He tried to deny that the individual's subjective experience of the material world was complexly related to her/his identity as a social being or that ideology had concrete, material effects on the construction of the individual's subjectivity. Indeed, in claiming that reality did not exist independently of the individual, he tried to deny that the individual had an identity as a social being. For if reality was purely a subjective construction, the individual's identity as a social being could not influence her/his experience of it. Trilling also tried to deny that the individual's subjective experience of the material world was partially determined by her/his identity as a social being, because he thought that stressing the historical specificity of the individual's relation to reality would revalidate the use of the Marxist conceptual apparatus, despite its lack of a fully developed theory of subjectivity. For if the individual's relation to reality was indeed partly a reflection of her/his identity as a social being, critics could no longer justify claiming that Marxist categories were irrelevant to postwar American culture. With its emphasis on the importance of the individual's social identity, the Marxist conceptual apparatus could help to explain the historical specificity of the individual's relation to the material world.

Trilling's desire to suppress issues of ethnicity by shifting attention away from the individual's identity as a social being is perhaps most apparent in his essay, "The Kinsey Report," which first appeared in *Partisan Review* in 1948. Trilling's criticisms of the Kinsey report on male sexual behavior, which was published in 1948, were remarkably similar to his criticisms of Parrington's partisan reconstruction of American literary history. He suggested obliquely that Kinsey's use of scientific data to analyze male sexuality threatened to consolidate the Stalinization of American society. He claimed that the report focused on the historical specificity of the individual's identity as a social being to the exclusion of her/his subjective experience of reality. He dis-

36   missed the report as a crude Marxist document that simplified the
individual's complex relation to reality and implied that it demonstrated the continuing influence of the cultural politics of the Popular
Front on American society.[14] He accused Kinsey and his colleagues of
defining sexual behavior too narrowly, using the term "sexual behavior" to designate "only that behavior which is physical" (230).
Restricting their definition of sexual behavior to that which is physical
was supposedly part of a covert strategy to extend Marxist categories
to the area of human sexuality. Defining sexual behavior purely in
physical terms enabled them to exclude psychoanalytic categories
from their analysis. Indeed, they sought to demonstrate that psychoanalytic categories were irrelevant to the study of human sexuality.
Trilling argued that in treating sexuality as a purely physical phenomenon that could be measured quantitatively, Kinsey and his colleagues
tried to suppress the "connection between the sexual life and the
psychic structure" (232). They wanted to legitimate the use of Marxist
categories, and so they treated the emotions "very much as if they
were a 'superstructure'" (232). In other words, Trilling tried to suggest
that Kinsey and his colleagues wanted to replace the Freudian conceptual apparatus with the Marxist conceptual apparatus as the most
useful tool for analyzing the construction of the individual's subjectivity. Inappropriately applying the Marxist conception of the relation
between base and superstructure to human sexuality, the report reduced the individual's subjectivity to an unmediated reflection of
her/his sexuality.

Trilling objected to the report's use of the Marxist conceptual
apparatus not only because it reduced the individual's subjectivity to a
"superstructure" that was an unmediated reflection of her/his sexuality, but because it shifted attention from the individual's subjective
experience of reality to her/his identity as a social being.[15] He complained that in replacing Freudian with Marxist categories, the report
"explicitly and stubbornly resists the idea that sexual behavior is involved with the whole of the individual's character" (238). He did not
find the report's approach to sexuality convincing because it contradicted the "findings" of psychoanalysis, which supposedly showed
that sexuality was "an important clue to, even the crux of character"
(238). Moreover, in denying that the individual's sexuality was the
"crux" of her/his character, Kinsey and his colleagues ignored the

relation between subjectivity and sexual identity. Trilling was disturbed by the report because it challenged the medicalization of homosexuality and other allegedly perverted sexual practices. Trilling charged that the report's definition of sexuality as a purely physical phenomenon that had no connection to the individual's emotional life encouraged the conclusion that the difficulty many homosexuals had adjusting to society was "the result of no flaw in the psyche itself that is connected with the aberrancy but is the result only of the fear of social disapproval of [their] sexual conduct" (238). Trilling, then, objected to the report because its attempt to reverse the medicalization of homosexuality implied that the individual's experience of her/his sexuality was directly related to her/his identity as a social being. According to Trilling, if homosexuals had difficulty adjusting to society, it was because they were emotionally disturbed, not because society treated them as though they were sexually aberrant.

But Trilling's complaint that the report did not adequately address the relation between the individual's subjectivity and her/his sexual identity did not mean that he thought Kinsey and his colleagues should have ignored the individual's identity as a social being or that the individual's identity as a social being bore no relation to her/his subjectivity. Trilling's criticisms were riddled with contradictions. On the one hand, he claimed that the report exaggerated the importance of the individual's identity as a social being by suggesting that it governed the construction of her/his subjectivity. On the other hand, he argued that the report underestimated the importance of the individual's identity as a social being because it denied that the individual's sexuality constituted the "crux" of her/his character. He asserted that in treating sexuality as a purely physical phenomenon that could be measured quantitatively, Kinsey and his colleagues implied that "a fact is a physical fact, to be considered only in its physical aspect, and apart from any idea or ideal that might make it a social fact, as having no ascertainable personal or cultural meaning and no possible consequences—as being, indeed, not available to social interpretation at all" (242). In other words, Trilling considered the report's approach to sexuality seriously flawed because it did not adequately address the construction of the individual's subjectivity in relation to her/his identity as a social being. While the report tried to show that the individual's subjective experience of her/his sexuality reflected her/his identity as a social being, it also tried to show that the individual's sexual practices did not constitute the "crux" of her/his character because they supposedly bore no relation to her/his identity as a social being. Kinsey and his colleagues wanted to discourage society from judging the individual on the basis of her/his sexual practices, and so it treated sexuality as a physical rather than a social or a cultural "fact."

In claiming that the report did not adequately address the relation between the individual's identity as a social being and the construction of her/his subjectivity, Trilling contradicted his own argument about the nature of sexuality. On the one hand, he suggested that sexuality was subjectively experienced and thus did not reflect the individual's identity as a social being. Homosexuals had difficulty adjusting to society because they suffered from an arrested sexual development, not because they were persecuted. On the other hand, he claimed that the individual's sexual practices could be used to judge her/his identity as a social being because they constituted the "crux" of her/his character. His use of the Freudian conceptual apparatus was as reductive as the report's use of the Marxist conceptual apparatus.[16] Invoking psychoanalytic theory, he challenged the report's attempt to reverse the medicalization of homosexuality. Although he conceded that many psychoanalysts no longer thought of homosexuality as a developmental disorder that required treatment, he suggested that "their opinion of the etiology of homosexuality as lying in some warp . . . of the psychic structure has not, I believe, changed. And I think they would say that the condition that produced the homosexuality has produce [sic] other character traits on which judgement could also be passed" (240–41). In other words, rather than discarding the report's reductive categories, Trilling merely reversed them. At the same time that he accused Kinsey and his colleagues of reducing the individual's subjectivity to an unmediated reflection of her/his identity as a social being, he reduced the individual's identity as a social being to an unmediated reflection of her/his subjectivity. He continued to define homosexuality as a developmental disorder that originated in a "warp" of the individual's subjectivity. The individual's identity as a social being functioned as a "superstructure" that reflected her/his subjectivity. Thus, whereas it was inappropriate to judge the individual on the basis of ethnic identity because it supposedly bore no relation to her/his subjectivity, it was appropriate to judge the individ-

ual on the basis of sexual practices because they supposedly determined her/his identity as a social being. In this way, Trilling diverted
attention from Jewish intellectuals who, like him, had been active in
the Popular Front and directed it toward the homosexuals and lesbians
whom he had already associated with threats to national security.

Trilling tried to show that the report's definition of sexuality as a
purely physical phenomenon that had no connection to the individual's subjectivity was part of a covert strategy to revalidate the use of
the Marxist conceptual apparatus because he wanted to exaggerate the
Stalinization of American culture. Claiming that the report did not
adequately address the relation between the individual's subjectivity
and sexual practices because it wanted to reverse the medicalization of
homosexuality enabled him to link the report to the forces that supposedly threatened to subvert the nation from within. He considered
the report a representative American document that, in denying that
homosexuality constituted a developmental disorder that reflected a
"warp" in the individual's subjectivity, tried to establish a "democratic
pluralism of sexuality" (241). In this respect, Trilling's criticisms of
the report were remarkably similar to his criticisms of Parrington's
Main Currents in American Thought. Like Parrington, who supposedly
insisted on judging the classics of American literature according to
their politics rather than according to their literary merits, the report
showed "a nearly conscious aversion from making intellectual distinc-
tions, almost as if out of the belief that an intellectual distinction must
inevitably lead to a social discrimination" (241–42). Indeed, the report's refusal to treat the individual's sexual practices as the crux of
her/his character reflected political considerations rather than the "realities" of human sexuality. The report supposedly shared Parrington's
assumption that "all social facts—with the exception of exclusion and
economic hardship—must be accepted, not merely in the scientific
sense but also in the social sense, in the sense, that is, that no judg-
ment must be passed on them, that any conclusion drawn from them
which perceives values and consequences will turn out to be 'undemocratic' " (242). In this way, Trilling tried to link the report to the
cultural politics of the Popular Front. Although it was a scientific study
that examined male sexual behavior, Trilling believed that it belonged
to the same tradition of cultural criticism as Parrington's *Main Currents
in American Thought*.

Trilling's desire to link the report to the Popular Front critique of American society helps to explain his focus on the report's most controversial aspect, namely, its attempts to reverse the medicalization of homosexuality by demonstrating through the use of scientific data that homosexuals are as "normal" and as "well-adjusted" as heterosexuals.[17] Stressing the report's controversial position on homosexuality allowed Trilling to suggest that the report belonged to the same tradition of cultural criticism as Parrington's history of American letters. He tried to identify the report with the cultural politics of the Popular Front by claiming that its emphasis on the relation between the individual's identity as a social being and the construction of her/his subjectivity was politically, rather than scientifically, motivated. According to him, the report tried to establish a "democratic pluralism" of sexuality in which homosexuals would no longer be judged on the basis of their sexual practices. In this way, Trilling used the report's position on homosexuality to suggest that its findings conflicted with the nation's security interests. After all, the report's attempt to reverse the medicalization of homosexuality contradicted the position of the American government, which had recently begun to expel gay men and women on the grounds that they constituted a security risk.[18] The report, Trilling asserted, not only tried to legitimate the use of Marxist categories by demonstrating their applicability to sexuality, but also tried to promote greater tolerance of homosexuality.

Trilling, then, used the report's controversial attempt to reverse the medicalization of homosexuality to discredit its representation of reality in America. In suggesting that the individual's sexuality was a purely physical phenomenon that had no connection to her/his subjectivity, the report embraced a definition of reality that was diametrically opposed to Trilling's and that seemed to reflect the continuing influence of the Popular Front on American culture. Whereas Trilling tried to show that reality did not exist independently of the individual but was subjectively experienced, the report tried to show that reality did exist independently of the individual and could be measured quantitatively through the use of scientific data. For this reason, the report's status as a best seller threatened to undermine Trilling's efforts to shift attention from the material world to the individual's subjective experience of it. The report's attempts to establish a "democratic pluralism" of sexuality in which homosexuals and other sexual minorities were no longer persecuted focused attention on the relation between the individual's identity as a social being and the construction of her/his subjectivity. Thus, in locating the report in the same tradition of cultural criticism as Parrington's *Main Currents in American Thought,* Trilling tried to contain the threat it posed to the project undertaken by Cold War liberals to reclaim "reality" from Popular Front intellectuals. Trilling implied that the report's use of scientific data conflicted with the nation's security interests because it suggested that reality existed independently of the individual and could be measured quantitatively. According to him, the report's attempt to show that the individual's subjectivity reflected her/his identity as a social being amounted to a materialist critique and thus was complicit with the infiltration of the American government by Communists, homosexuals, and lesbians.

Simply Expressing a Point of View:
Robert Warshow and the Refusal to Theorize

Not all Cold War liberals were interested in suppressing the relation between the individual's identity as a social being and the construction of her/his subjectivity, and in the remainder of this chapter I want to examine Robert Warshow's essays on film and other aspects of American popular culture in order to clarify the place of identity politics in the critical discourse of Cold War liberals. Warshow's essays, which constitute a sustained critique of the American culture industry in the postwar period, suggest that Cold War liberals tended to emphasize the importance of the individual's identity as a social being only when it was politically expedient and promised to advance their ideological project. An editor of *Commentary* who contributed regularly to *Partisan Review,* Warshow resembled other Cold War liberals in that he tried to reclaim reality from Popular Front intellectuals by claiming that American popular culture was wholly Stalinized. He shared Trilling's assumption that reality did not exist independently of the individual, and, like Trilling, he tried to shift attention from the material world to the individual's subjective experience of it. He refused, for example, to theorize his relation to American popular culture and claimed that, as a cultural critic, he merely expressed a point of view. In the preface to

The Immediate Experience, a collection of his essays published post-humously in 1962, he claimed that his film criticism was not like other film criticism because it was highly personal. He supposedly did not approach film as a critic but as a "man looking at a movie."[19] Thus, unlike other film critics, he did not slight "the actual, immediate experience of seeing and responding to the movies as most of us see them and respond to them" (xxv) but tried to capture it as it really was.[20] That is to say, he did not approach film from a rigid theoretical perspective but tried to convey his own subjective experience of viewing films. He claimed that his only ambition as a critic was "to produce a body of criticism dealing with specific films and types of films, with certain actors, certain themes, and with two or three of the general problems which may point toward a theory" (xxviii).

Because they corresponded to their own emphasis on the individual's subjective experience of reality, Warshow's highly personal essays on American popular culture earned him the admiration and respect of other Cold War liberals. For example, in his introduction to *The Immediate Experience*, Trilling praised Warshow for refusing to theorize his relation to American popular culture and suggested that Warshow's insistence on expressing his own highly personal point of view accounted for "the tone of honesty that we hear in [his] work, . . . the rejection of attitude in favor of understanding" (xxi). Although Trilling conceded that "the categories of history and politics were essential to [Warshow's] thought" (xxi), he did not question Warshow's claim that he was not interested in producing a theory of film, only a body of criticism that pointed in the direction of a theory. Tacitly comparing him to cultural critics like Parrington, he asserted that Warshow "never, in his idea of himself as an intellectual, conceived of himself as being 'on the stage of history,' as having a 'role' assigned to him by the *Zeitgeist*" (xxi). Thus Warshow's claim that American popular culture was wholly Stalinized was not partisan but factual. Unlike Parrington and other critics influenced by the cultural politics of the Popular Front, Warshow did not consider himself a world historical individual destined to change the course of American history, and his cultural criticism could not be seen as promoting the political agenda of Cold War liberals. Yet Warshow's refusal to theorize his relation to American popular culture did not mean that his cultural criticism was not motivated by political considerations, nor that he did not approach

American popular culture from a rigid theoretical perspective. For in focusing on his own subjective experience of viewing film, he rigidly adhered to the theoretical stance of Trilling and other Cold War liberals who wanted to suppress the role of material conditions in determining the individual's relation to reality.

That Warshow's approach to American popular culture was indeed rigidly theoretical is perhaps most obvious in "The Legacy of the 30's," which first appeared in *Commentary* in 1947. Few Cold War liberals were as convinced as Warshow that the Popular Front continued to influence the cultural politics of the American middle class, and in "The Legacy of the 30's" he stressed the difficulty of establishing an approach to film that had not been influenced in some way by the Popular Front critique of American society. Although he conceded that support for the American Communist party had eroded considerably since the 1930s, he claimed that "the terms of discussion are still fixed by the tradition of middle class 'popular front' culture which [the party] did so much to create, and we are still without a vocabulary to break through the constriction it imposes on us" (5). Indeed, he thought that the cultural politics of the Popular Front continued to influence the self-understanding of the American middle class, despite the anti-Communist hysteria sweeping the nation. He argued that Stalinism no longer represented a point of view, but had become "a psychological and sociological phenomenon" (7). It had supposedly destroyed "the emotional and moral content of experience, putting in its place a system of conventionalized 'responses'" (7). Thus the individual's subjective experience of reality was no longer spontaneous but corresponded to the Popular Front critique of American society. He alleged that the individual responded to reality as though it existed independently of her/him and could be measured quantitatively through the use of scientific data. Moreover, the individual tended to see a connection between her/his subjective experience of the material world and her/his identity as a social being. S/he continued to think in terms of the social and economic forces that conditioned the construction of her/his subjectivity.

Warshow stressed the extent to which the Popular Front continued to influence the cultural politics of the middle class because he thought that most cultural criticism represented a "conventionalized response" that did not adequately address the function of popular culture in American society. Warshow defined popular culture as "the screen through which we see reality and the mirror in which we see ourselves" (8). In many respects, the primary function of popular culture was to conventionalize the individual's response to reality.[21] Warshow explained that popular culture was supposed to "relieve one of the necessity of experiencing one's life directly" (7). Popular culture enabled the individual to negotiate the complexities of capitalist societies by simplifying her/his relation to them. Popular culture provided her/him with a "fixed system of moral and political attitudes" (7) that protected her/him from the "shock," or unpredictability, of experience. Thus popular culture gave American society "its form and its meaning" (8). Defining popular culture in these terms allowed Warshow to exaggerate the continuing influence of the Popular Front. Ironically, his response to popular culture was itself conventionalized. Although his cultural criticism had obviously not been influenced by the Popular Front critique of American society, he allowed a "fixed system" of political beliefs to determine his response to film and other aspects of popular culture. In defining popular culture as the "screen" through which Americans saw reality, he adopted the tactics of Trilling and other Cold War liberals for discouraging resistance to the postwar settlement. For if popular culture did indeed constitute the "screen" through which Americans saw reality, its Stalinization constituted a threat to national security. Warshow tended to totalize the influence of the culture industry on postwar American society. He assumed that Americans consumed popular culture passively rather than critically and were therefore incapable of resisting Communist propaganda.

Warshow's claims that critics of American popular culture continued to be influenced by the cultural politics of the Popular Front and thus were partisan rather than "objective" also represented a conventionalized response that contributed to the consolidation of the postwar settlement. Echoing Trilling's criticisms of Parrington, Warshow argued that because cultural critics saw reality through the "screen" of popular culture, they were incapable of representing reality accurately and tended to write from the point of view of their identities as social beings. Indeed, their responses to reality were wholly unreliable. They constantly measured their experiences against a "fixed system" of politically correct attitudes and had no interest in experiencing reality directly without the "screen" of popular culture. Warshow claimed that the contemporary critic could not write "objectively" about film and other aspects of popular culture because "he [sic] lives within the mass culture, he meets experience through the mass culture, the words and ideas that come to him most easily, most 'naturally,' are the words and ideas of mass culture" (9). Thus, in order for cultural critics to represent reality accurately, they had to distance themselves from popular culture. For distancing themselves from popular culture would enable them to develop "some method of understanding and communicating experience directly as it really is, as it really feels" (9). But clearly, cultural critics who distanced themselves from popular culture would not have been in a better position to communicate experience as it really was; rather, they would have been in a better position to communicate experience according to how Cold War liberals thought it should be. That is to say, they would have been able to communicate experience in a way that no longer reflected their identities as social beings but was highly personal. Thus they would still have been measuring their experiences against a "fixed system" of politically correct attitudes; the only difference would have been that their approach to popular culture would have been more in keeping with Warshow's.

Somewhat ironically, Warshow's example of a cultural critic who saw reality through the "screen" of popular culture was Lionel Trilling. He criticized Trilling's novel *The Middle of the Journey* (1947), which recounted Trilling's political experiences in the 1930s in fictionalized form. In the character of John Laskell, Trilling tried to recreate the experience of an entire generation of liberal intellectuals who were active in the Popular Front but eventually became disillusioned with its populist rhetoric. Warshow claimed that Trilling was less interested in faithfully recreating the experience of being a Communist fellow traveler in the 1930s than in repudiating liberalism's "tainted" past. Trilling's reconstruction of his political experiences implied that Americans joined the Communist party or became fellow travelers for intellectual rather than psychological reasons. He tried to suppress the fact that "the middle class which experienced Stalinism was in large part a Jewish middle class, driven by the special insecurities of Jews in addition to the insecurities of the middle class in general" (13). Warshow interpreted Trilling's inability to communicate his political experiences as they really were as an indication that he was overly inserted into the discourses of the American culture industry. Trilling's responses to reality were as conventionalized as those of the Stalinists whom he attacked in the novel. His refusal to examine the subjective dimension of his involvement in radical causes reduced him "to the level of his subject; like the Stalinists themselves, he can respond to the complexity of experience only with a revision of a doctrine" (15). This did not mean, however, that Warshow considered the individual's identity as a social being more important than her/his subjective experience of the material world. He sought to establish a connection between the construction of the individual's subjectivity and her/his ethnic identity in this particular instance because he wanted to explain why so many Jewish intellectuals had been active in the Popular Front. If Jewish intellectuals had been quick to embrace the Marxist critique of the capitalist relations of production, that was because they were subject to "special insecurities" that were directly related to their status as Jews. That is to say, their involvement in the Popular Front reflected their exclusion from mainstream American society rather than a genuine commitment to Marxist ideology.

Warshow, then, used his critique of Trilling's novel as the occasion to explain, and hence discount the importance of, the involvement of Jewish intellectuals in radical causes in the 1930s. He tried to persuade readers that Jewish intellectuals did not actually believe the Marxist critique of the capitalist relations of production but that the "special insecurities" to which they were subject as social beings made them susceptible to Communist propaganda. Warshow reinforced his criticisms of Trilling by tacitly comparing him to Leo McCarey. He criticized McCarey's rabidly anti-Communist film *My Son John* (1951) for the same reasons that he criticized *The Middle of the Journey*.[22] In a review of *My Son John*, originally published in *American Mercury* in 1952, he argued that the film "might legitimately alarm any thoughtful American, whether liberal or conservative" (113). Like Trilling's novel, the film supposedly represented a conventionalized response to reality that failed to communicate experience as it really was. McCarey lacked insight into the complex psychology of Communists and fellow travelers, and his fanaticism led him to misrepresent, if not underestimate, the danger the continuing influence of the Popular Front on the American middle class posed to the nation. McCarey was so rabidly anti-Communist that he could not "imagine why anyone might become a Communist, what inner needs of the personality might be served" (119). Moreover, the film suggested that Communists and fellow travelers were easier to identify and expose than they actually were. His characterization of John (Robert Walker), a rising young government official who is an agent of the Soviet Union, relied too heavily on stereotypes and misled the audience. According to War-show, the typical member of the Communist party was not "pompous, supercilious, as sleek and unfeeling as a cat, coldly contemptuous of his [sic] father, patronizing to his mother" (114). Nor was the typical member of the Communist party overtly homosexual or lesbian. Rather, s/he was usually the epitome of "stodgy respectability" (119) with Ivy League credentials. In other words, McCarey's use of a "fixed system" of representing Communists and fellow travelers led him to underestimate the nation's vulnerability to Communist infiltration. Because the typical member of the Communist party could "pass" as a respectable American, s/he could avoid exposure and subvert the nation from within.

McCarey's use of a "fixed system" of representation was also problematic because it supposedly prevented him from examining the psychology of his characters. His focus on the conflict between John and his father captured a typical American drama and had the potential to communicate experience as it really was for middle-class Americans. Warshow claimed that there was no drama more typical of the American middle class than that in which "children so often become alienated from their parents, going beyond them in education and social status until the parents, who may have made great sacrifices to accomplish precisely this result, find themselves excluded from the triumph they have prepared" (114). But McCarey supposedly allowed his desire to expose the Communists, homosexuals, and lesbians who had infiltrated the American government and threatened to subvert it from within to displace his interest in this typical American drama. Rather than exploring the structure of the American family, McCarey reduced the complex relationships between parents and children to a political allegory. He lacked the "compassionate detachment" (115) necessary to represent the American family realistically, and the conflict between John and his father became "so naked and intense that it [took] on the quality of a nightmare" (115). Just as in the character of John he unintentionally misrepresented the threat that Communists and fellow travelers posed to national security, in the character of the father he unintentionally exposed the dangers of rabid anti-Communism. He expected the audience to regard the father's ignorant and bigoted statements "not as an excusable want of intelligence, but as a higher form of wisdom" (116). Indeed, McCarey's rabid anti-Communism constantly threatened to deteriorate into a hysterical diatribe against intellectuals and their influence on American society. His emphasis on John's sophistication as an intellectual, a sophistication that pitted him against the father, seemed to suggest that "he had picked up his Communism as another man might pick up a love of chamber music, simply as part of his cultural furniture (there are such Communists, of course, but they do not become spies)" (119).

In criticizing Trilling and McCarey for failing to assume an attitude of "compassionate detachment" with respect to the Stalinization of American society, Warshow did not mean to suggest that writers should always avoid approaching reality from the perspective of their identities as social beings. For example, in "Clifford Odets: Poet of the Jewish Middle Class," an essay that first appeared in *Commentary* in 1946, he praised Odets for faithfully recreating the reality of Jewish experience in America. But in praising Odets as a "poet" who communicated the experience of the Jewish middle class as it really was, Warshow avoided discussing his involvement in the Group Theater, as well as the explicit political content of his plays, which were often dismissed as propaganda for the labor movement. Although Warshow acknowledged that Odets had been heavily influenced by the cultural politics of the Popular Front and that he used his plays to convey "something like the direct apprehension of sociological truth" (26), he limited that truth to Odets's ability to represent Jewish immigrant life as it really was. Indeed, he claimed that despite their explicit political content, Odets's plays offered the Jews in the audience "a continuous series of familiar signposts, each suggesting with the immediate communication of poetry the whole complex of the life of the characters: what they are, what they want, how they stand with the world" (24). This purportedly truthful description of the experience of the Jewish middle class compensated for the "intellectual shallowness" (24) of Odets's cultural politics, and accounted for "the spectacular achievement which makes him a dramatist of importance" (24). In other words, although Odets approached experience from the perspective of his identity as a social being, what distinguished him from Trilling and McCarey was that he did not allow his cultural politics to interfere with his "compassionate detachment" from reality. Odets supposedly wrote more as a Jew than as an intellectual committed to Marxist ideology. He did not measure his experiences against a "fixed system" of politically correct attitudes. In this way, Warshow tried to protect Odets from the anti-Communist hysteria of the period. Odets had been subpoenaed by the House Un-American Activities Committee in 1941 to answer questions concerning Communist infiltration of the film industry, and he was subpoenaed to appear before it again in 1951.[23] In canonizing Odets as a "poet" of the Jewish middle class rather than as a propagandist for the Popular Front, Warshow tried to divert attention away from his membership in the Communist party and to reclaim his plays for the postwar settlement.

As a critic of the American culture industry of the postwar period, then, Warshow tended to privilege modes of representation that psychologized reality. Like Trilling and other Cold War liberals, he wanted to reclaim reality from Popular Front intellectuals, and so he celebrated writers who focused on the individual's subjective experience of the material world. He praised Odets as a poet of the Jewish middle class not because he wrote from the perspective of his identity as a social being, but because he was able to communicate experience as it really was, despite the fact that he wrote from the perspective of his identity as a social being. Warshow's tendency to privilege modes of representation that psychologized reality was perhaps most obvious in "The Anatomy of Falsehood," a review of the film *The Best Years of Our Lives* (1946), which was originally published in *Partisan Review* in 1947. Directed by William Wyler, *The Best Years of Our Lives* was one of the most popular films of the postwar period and received several Academy Awards, including one for best picture.[24] Although it was praised by critics such as André Bazin because of its realistic representation of small-town America, it was attacked by anti-Stalinist intellectuals because they considered it a populist melodrama in the same tradition as Frank Capra's films.[25] For example, in "Everybody's Protest Novel," Baldwin suggested that the film suffered from the same problems as the social protest novel. Despite its meticulous reconstruction of small-town life, the film was a fantasy, "connecting nowhere with reality, sentimental . . ." (19). Warshow similarly criticized the film for being overly sentimental. He complained that the film treated politics as "a problem of personal morality" (110) that could be solved in the private sphere. Like Capra's *It's a Wonderful Life* (1946), it reduced the problem of monopoly capitalism to "a question of the morals of banks: if bankers are good men, then they will grant loans (not large loans, apparently) to deserving veterans (those who are willing to work hard) without demanding collateral" (111). Indeed, the film's focus was itself a political evasion, for the "veterans' problem" was "not an issue, or at any rate it is a false issue, since nobody is against the veterans and since they do not constitute a social group, except temporarily and very vaguely" (110).

Despite the similarities of their criticisms, however, Warshow, unlike Baldwin, did not attack the film because he thought it did not adequately address the inequalities between rich and poor in postwar America. Rather, he attacked the film because it focused on the material world rather than the individual's subjective experience of it and thus contributed to the Stalinization of American culture. He alleged that Wyler was more interested in faithfully recreating the claustrophobic atmosphere of the American small town than in exploring the psychology of his characters. He attributed the film's success to "the unusual care that has been devoted to the reality of the surface" (108). Wyler allegedly wanted to create a world that was "so real in detail as to be accepted, more or less continuously and unreservedly, as truthful, and so complete and self-contained as to engage the spectator's full attention and discourage any tendency to look beyond the fixed boundaries" (107). This attention to physical detail extended to the characters, each of whom Wyler tried to represent as realistically as possible. Warshow claimed that Wyler wanted each of the characters to appear "as uncomplicated and predictable as he [sic] might appear to be (but probably would *not* be) if he were a real person on any real street" (109). But Wyler's attention to physical detail ultimately undercut the film's realistic representation of life in small-town America. The characters were unbelievable because they were not psychologically complex. Warshow suggested that "what you see always has a certain interest because it is so recognizable, but what you see is all there is; each character announces himself immediately and in full, each situation is immediately and completely understood" (109). Thus *The Best Years of Our Lives* failed as a film because it limited its focus to the

material world, and the psychological motivations of the characters   **51**
remained a mystery.

Warshow stated his objections to modes of representation that slighted the individual's subjective experience of the material world most explicitly in "The Movie Camera and the American," an essay on the film version of Arthur Miller's play *Death of a Salesman* (1952), which first appeared in *Commentary* in 1952. Miller was an outspoken critic of the assault on basic civil liberties during the postwar period (the right to free speech, the freedom of association) and refused to name names when he was subpoenaed to appear before the House Un-American Activities Committee in 1956. Consequently, anti-Stalinist intellectuals tended to regard him as an unreconstructed Marxist whose plays had been influenced by the cultural politics of the Popular Front, and Warshow was unrelenting in his criticisms of him, comparing him unfavorably to Odets and other politically committed playwrights.[26] He objected in particular to Miller's representational practices, claiming that they amounted to "a mechanical realism which hides a fundamental reluctance to give the real world its due" (121). Miller treated the real world as though it existed independently of the individual and could be measured quantitatively. For this reason, he was guilty of "the characteristic error of American writers" (123). He undercut the realism of his plays by assuming that he could achieve universality by suppressing the particularities of the material world. Whereas in *Death of a Salesman* he was careful to mention the brand names of Willy Loman's kitchen appliances, he never specified the items Loman peddled as a salesman. Moreover, like Wyler and McCarey, he avoided exploring the psychology of his characters. Warshow described Loman as "Andy Hardy broken on the wheel of social criticism" (121). Lacking psychological complexity, Loman was "more a concept than a human being" (124). Miller's refusal to explore Loman's psychology deprived *Death of a Salesman* of its critical edge. Despite his intentions, Miller continually slighted "the claims of the material world" (134), for he did not understand that the individual experienced reality subjectively.

Warshow was even more critical of the film version of Miller's play. He suggested that it suffered from the "exaggerated respect that Hollywood sometimes offers to a recognized work of art" (122) and was not properly cinematic. It was shot almost entirely in close-up and thus failed to take advantage of the "greater mobility of the medium" (122).

Moreover, although most film versions of Broadway plays were better than their originals because they reduced "the amount of undistinguished dialogue" (122), the film version of *Death of a Salesman* barely deviated from Miller's script. Still, Warshow thought the film version was in some respects superior to the play. Despite its fidelity to Miller's script, the film version did not slight the "claims" of the material world. Its use of the close-up, though excessive, brought Frederic March, the actor who played Willy Loman, "so close and clear that his own material reality begins to assert itself outside the boundaries that are supposed to be set by his role" (124). Indeed, March gradually replaced Loman as the focus of the spectator's attention. Imposing his own personality on the character of Willy Loman, March infused a subjective element into the film missing from the play. The spectator lost interest in Loman as s/he became aware of "the spectacle of the aging movie star attempting to express what he believes is to be found in the play, exposing to inspection the bags under his eyes, the unpleasing sag of his thin mouth, as if to insist at whatever cost that he is engaged in a serious enterprise" (124). In other words, the film did not slight the "claims" of the material world because March's performance communicated the experience of aging as it really was. The film was no longer about Willy Loman's inability to achieve the American dream but about Frederic March's loss of stardom. For this reason, the film rendered the social criticism of the play concrete and personal: Miller's interest in the material world was no longer abstract.

Still, Warshow thought the film was seriously flawed because the psychological motivations of the characters remained a mystery, and he compared it unfavorably to a low-budget production, *I Want You* (1952), which had been a box-office failure. Despite the fact that it did not try to engage in a materialist critique of American society, Warshow claimed that *I Want You* recreated the atmosphere of the postwar period more faithfully than Miller's play did because it did not slight the "claims" of the material world. Warshow admired the film for its portrayal of its characters. While their motivations were not psychologically complex, the characters were human beings rather than concepts. They supposedly had a "common-sense relation to reality" (133) and operated under the assumption that their "inner psychological conflicts are of no practical relevance so long as they can be kept under control" (133). Thus the film did not try to establish a relation between their experiences and their identities as social beings. Although, like *The Best Years of Our Lives*, the film meticulously recreated small-town life in the postwar period, it was not a populist melodrama and did not have a political agenda: it did not try to show that the inequalities between rich and poor could be solved in the private sphere. Rather, it belonged to that tradition of "famous American materialism which, if it limits our understanding of other peoples and of ourselves, also offers some protection against the murderous 'spiritualities' of ideology; perhaps one of the American virtues is that our slogans so often ring hollow" (133). In this way, Warshow tried to identify an American tradition of historical materialism that was not linked to the Marxist conceptual apparatus and that had not emerged from the cultural politics of the Popular Front. He claimed that *I Want You* was more materialist in its representation of American society than either *The Best Years of Our Lives* or the film version of *Death of a Salesman* because its focus on the material world was supposedly not ideological, and it did not try to show that the individual's experience of reality was a reflection of her/his identity as a social being.

I have dwelt at such length on Warshow's critique of the representational system of American popular culture because I wanted to show that it was part of a project undertaken by anti-Stalinist intellectuals in the postwar period to reclaim "reality" from Popular Front intellectuals. Like other Cold War liberals, Warshow sought to shift attention from the material world to the individual's subjective experience of it by defining reality in such a way that it did not lend itself readily to a Marxist analysis. He tried to show that the individual's relation to reality was highly mediated and could not be adequately explained by the Marxist conceptual apparatus because it lacked a fully developed theory of subjectivity. He shared Trilling's assumption that reality existed independently of the individual and could not be measured quantitatively. This did not mean, however, that Warshow was interested in addressing the complex relation between the individual's subjective experience of the material world and her/his identity as a social being. Like Trilling, he privileged modes of representation that psychologized reality. Such modes supposedly communicated experience as it really was because they encouraged the individual to con-

54   ceive of her/his lived relations to the world as originating in her/himself rather than in concrete historical circumstances. Although Warshow praised Clifford Odets as the poet of the Jewish middle class, he was in general critical of writers who approached reality from the perspective of their identities as social beings. He admired Odets because Odets was able to communicate the experience of being Jewish, despite the fact that he wrote as a Jew. Odets did not try to show that his experiences were a reflection of his identity as a Jew. In this way, Warshow privileged modes of representation that were conducive to maintaining the postwar settlement. In psychologizing reality, such modes discouraged Americans from linking their subjective experience of the material world to their identities as social beings. Americans consented freely and spontaneously to the postwar settlement because they tended not to think of their experiences as reflecting their race, class, gender, and/or sexual orientation.

In the chapters that follow, I will try to establish a link between a group of films Hitchcock made in the 1950s and this privileging of modes of representation that psychologized reality. I will argue that Hitchcock's representational practices were complicit with the project undertaken by Cold War liberals to reclaim reality from Popular Front intellectuals. Hitchcock's highly psychologized representations of reality in the films I will be discussing encouraged the spectator to conceive of her/his lived relations to the world as originating in her/himself rather than in conditions specific to the postwar period. Like the cultural criticism we have examined, these films treated reality as a purely subjective construction. Reality did not exist independently of the individual but was subjectively experienced; consequently, it did not lend itself readily to a materialist critique. These films privileged a psychoanalytic understanding of male and female subjectivity. They narrativized the male and female Oedipal trajectories and in so doing suggested indirectly that the most useful categories for understanding the individual's lived relations to the world were psychoanalytic. I will try to show that this privileging of a psychoanalytic understanding of male and female subjectivity was conducive to maintaining the postwar settlement because it discouraged the spectator from linking her/his experiences to her/his identity as a social being. The films we will examine tried to insert the spectator into a fixed, stable subject position that contained the construction of her/his subjectivity across a **55** multiplicity of contradictory discourses. The spectator of these films no longer participated in a plurality of contending social formations but became part of a united cultural front rooted in a shared understanding of the world.

2

RECONSTRUCTING HOMOSEXUALITY

Hitchcock and the Homoerotics of

Spectatorial Pleasure

A curious freemasonry exists among underground workers and sympathizers [of the Communist party]. They can identify each other (and be identified by their enemies) on casual meeting by the use of certain phrases, the names of certain friends, by certain enthusiasms and certain silences. It is reminiscent of nothing so much as the famous scene in Proust where the Baron de Charlus and the tailor Jupien suddenly recognize their common corruption.
—Arthur Schlesinger, Jr., *The Vital Center*

Set in Washington, D.C., Alfred Hitchcock's *Strangers on a Train* (1951) abounds with images of the federal government. In shot after shot, the dome of the Capitol building appears in the background brilliantly lit up, and the Jefferson Memorial provides the setting for a suspenseful encounter between the all-American hero, Guy Haines (Farley Granger), and the murderous villain, Bruno Anthony (Robert Walker). The function of these monumental backdrops is not readily apparent. Although national monuments often figure prominently in Hitchcock's films, they usually have an obvious connection to the plot. In the climactic scene of *North by Northwest* (1959), for example, the American agent Eve Kandall (Eva Marie Saint) dangles perilously from Mount Rushmore. Her suspension from the monument translates into visual terms the Cold War conflict at the heart of the film: Mount Rushmore stands for the democratic principles at stake in the recovery of the microfilm stolen by the Communist spies. But the images of the federal government in *Strangers on a Train* bear no obvious relation to the plot. There are no Communist spies conspiring to overthrow the American government in it, only a psychopathic killer who tries to blackmail a champion tennis player into committing murder. Why, then, does the film abound with images that constantly remind the spectator that the film is set in the nation's capital?

In a cursory but suggestive reading of *Strangers on a Train*, Alain Marty provides a possible explanation for the film's constant reminders of its own setting. Although Marty does not specifically discuss the film's recurrent use of national monuments or the significance of its setting in the nation's capital, he links the film to the anti-Communist hysteria unleashed by the McCarthy hearings. He suggests that the film registers "the more or less unconscious preoccupations of public opinion in the 1950s."[1] Stressing the subject's often-unconscious engagement with the discursive practices that structure its relation to the world, he argues persuasively that the film encodes Hitchcock's own paranoia about Communist infiltration of the American government. But despite Marty's attempt to historicize the film by locating it in the Cold War politics of the 1950s, he never specifically engages with the film's topographical referent, its setting. The film emerges from his reading as a kind of mythical allegory. He argues that the film tries to show that "American society must be purged from top (Bruno) to bottom (Miriam) whatever the social cost" (124). Even the all-American Guy Haines must prove himself before he can assume his rightful place in the ruling class, for he undergoes a series of tests "like a medieval knight" (121). Marty's reading, in other words, inadvertently reproduces the reductive categories of Cold War political discourse. It represents the Cold War as a struggle between good and evil, heroes and villains.

Despite its hasty retreat to political allegory, however, Marty's Althusserian reading of *Strangers on a Train* represents a welcome departure from the rigid psychoanalytic approach to classical Hollywood cinema that has dominated Hitchcock criticism. This approach tends to ignore the historical specificity of male subjectivity, its construction in relation to historically specific institutions, discourses, and practices. Raymond Bellour, for example, in a series of textual analyses deeply indebted to Lacanian theories of the cinematic apparatus, has argued somewhat abstractly that Hitchcock's Oedipalized narratives constantly restage the subject's entry into the Symbolic order.[2] He claims that because Hitchcock's films are constructed along an Oedipal trajectory, they insert the male spectator into a fixed, stable subject position. The hero's sadistic pleasure in the woman's fragmented body supposedly guarantees the coherence and totality of his own and therefore allows him to return her look without fear of

58   castration. Moreover, Bellour argues that these films restage the mirror phase as defined by Lacanian psychoanalysis. Because the spectator misrecognizes the hero's bodily coherence as his own, he eludes the threat of castration signified by the image of the woman on the screen.

Feminist film critics have been quick to point out the limitations of this narrow approach to Hitchcock's films. They have shown that Bellour's use of psychoanalysis elides the differences between male and female subjectivity.[3] For if, as Bellour claims, voyeurism and fetishism are the dominant codes of Hitchcock's films, then the only position of subjectivity they make available to the female spectator is a masochistic one. While some feminist film critics accept the argument that spectatorial pleasure is, in Mary Ann Doane's words, "indissociable from pain," others argue that the female spectator's subjective engagement with the filmic text is more complicated.[4] Teresa de Lauretis, for example, claims that the female spectator identifies with the active and desiring male subject as well as with the passive and fetishized object of his gaze.[5] Tania Modleski also emphasizes the female spectator's shifting identifications. She suggests that Hitchcock's films narrativize the female as well as the male Oedipal trajectory and therefore allow for the limited expression of a specifically female desire.[6]

Feminist film critics, then, have not so much rejected the model of filmic pleasure proposed by Lacanian theories of the cinematic apparatus as they have expanded it to include the production of an active and desiring female subject. For although they conceive of the process of identification as a sexually differentiated one, they follow Bellour's example in proposing a monolithic view of male subjectivity. They assume that the male spectator is not only heterosexual but unequivocally so and limit the possibility of occupying multiple identificatory positions to the female spectator.[7] Consequently, they tend to see the male spectator's insertion into a fixed, stable heterosexual subject position as inevitable. But in stressing the fixity of the male spectator's identification with the hero, they overlook the polymorphous sexualities circulating through the filmic text. As I will show, an alternative reading of psychoanalytic theory suggests that we should regard the male spectator's identification with the hero of the classical text as fluid and unstable. Moreover, their application of psychoanalysis to

Hitchcock's Oedipalized narratives seems circular. For Hitchcock's films have an ideological investment in ratifying a psychoanalytic understanding of male subjectivity. One of the ways in which Hitchcock's films try to contain the play of sexualities circulating through the cinematic apparatus is by narrativizing the male Oedipal trajectory. In identifying with the hero, the male spectator becomes complicit with the production of his own Oedipalized subjectivity. Obviously, Hitchcock's films must engage the male spectator libidinally if they are to insure his submission to their discursive structure.[8] The male spectator must first desire his own Oedipalization before he will consent to it. Yet by relying on the process of identification as their primary mode of address, Hitchcock's films threaten to disrupt their own ideological project.

Imported from psychoanalytic discourse, the concept of identification has remained largely unexamined in Lacanian film theory. Although psychoanalytically oriented film theorists emphasize the importance of identification in the construction of the male heterosexual subject, they ignore the concrete historical forces that condition it, and they oversimplify the role Freud assigned to it in the male Oedipal trajectory. Freud conceived of identification as a defense against the boy's homosexual object cathexis with the father. In *The Ego and the Id*, he defines identification as a melancholic structure that compensates the boy for his loss of the father as an object choice. Freud argues that the boy frequently adopts a "feminine attitude" toward the father during the pre-Oedipal phase and fantasizes about taking the place of the mother. But in order for him to resolve the Oedipus complex, he must renounce these fantasies. Unless he represses his attachment to the father and fixes his affections on the mother, he will retain the polymorphous sexuality of the pre-Oedipal phase. He reconciles himself to this loss by incorporating the father into his ego, which reinforces his primary identification with the father. Freud explains that in assuming the features of the lost object, the ego "is forcing itself, so to speak, upon the id as a love-object and is trying to make good the id's loss by saying: 'Look, you can love me too I am so like the object.' "[9]

Insofar as this psychoanalytic model of identification clarifies the primary mode of address of classical Hollywood cinema and its codes, it suggests that rather than inserting the male spectator into a fixed, stable heterosexual subject position, Hitchcock's films return him to

60   the polymorphous sexuality of the pre-Oedipal phase. For, according to Freudian theory, the male spectator's identification with the hero of the classical text involves the repression of a potentially destabilizing homosexual object cathexis: he unconsciously desires the hero of the classical text, or else he would not identify with him. Identification acts as a defense against a homosexual object cathexis. The culturally sanctioned prohibition of homosexuality requires the male spectator to abandon his object relation to the hero. To compensate for this loss, he incorporates the hero into his ego: he does not desire the hero, he is the hero. But this does not mean that he wholly relinquishes his homosexual object choice. Rather, it continues to exist in his unconscious, where it becomes a potential obstacle to the formation of a fixed heterosexual identity. The melancholic structure of identification guarantees the preservation of the object relation to the hero in the unconscious. Thus, in addressing the male spectator as a subject, cinematic discourse establishes a homosexual object relation between him and the hero that it must then repress. As the primary mode of address of classical Hollywood cinema, identification restages the male spectator's feminine attitude toward the father during the pre-Oedipal phase and thereby encourages the formation of a polymorphous, rather than a fixed, heterosexual identity. Obviously, Hitchcock's films must limit the effects of this aspect of identification if they are to insert the male spectator into an Oedipalized subject position.

To show how Hitchcock's films contain the potentially disruptive effects of their own mode of address, I will follow Alain Marty's lead and situate *Strangers on a Train* in relation to the Cold War politics of the 1950s. But whereas Marty links *Strangers on a Train* to the wave of anti-Communism unleashed by the McCarthy hearings, I will focus on the Cold War construction of "the homosexual" as a security risk. This shift in focus has several advantages. First, it furthers recent attempts to historicize the spectatorial subject. I will show that the spectator's subjective engagement with Hitchcock's film was determined by a multiplicity of discursive practices, political as well as medical, that defined homosexuality as pathological. Second, emphasizing the homophobic politics of the postwar period will clarify the paranoia about male heterosexuality encoded in the film. At the same time that it tries to insert the male spectator into an Oedipalized subject position, *Strangers on a Train* represents the achievement of a fixed heterosexual identity as virtually impossible. I will argue that this paranoia is directly related to Cold War fears that "the homosexual" was indistinguishable from "the heterosexual" and had infiltrated all levels of American society. Finally, locating the film in its historical context will shed more light on the heterosexual panic of the period. In particular, it will clarify the significance of the juridical construction of "the homosexual" as a security risk. Because this construction involved the appropriation of a medical model of same-sex eroticism, it resulted in a virtually unprecedented alliance between juridical and medical discourses. To counteract the pioneering attempts of gay men and women to define themselves as an oppressed minority culture, the government appealed to medical evidence supposedly demonstrating that homosexuals and lesbians had no outward characteristics or physical traits that distinguished them from heterosexuals; but because this evidence acknowledged the resistance of sexuality to containment through representation, it called into question the fixity of male and female heterosexual identities. Thus I will use *Strangers on a Train* to examine the relation between the politics of spectatorship and the crisis over national security. I want to show that in the 1950s the construction of male and female subjectivity was conditioned by the identification of homosexuality and lesbianism as threats to national security.

The Kinsey Reports and the Homosexualization of the American Male

On 28 February 1950, John Peurifoy, a State Department official, made a revelation that would not only intensify allegations that the employment practices of the Truman administration recklessly endangered national security but also precipitate a juridical crisis that threatened to undermine the federal government's power to regulate same-sex practices.[10] Under sharp questioning by the Senate Appropriations Committee, Peurifoy disclosed that the State Department had recently dismissed several employees on charges of homosexuality. Republican leaders, already engaged in a campaign to discredit the Truman administration over its national security policies, seized the opportunity to embarrass the president further. Exploiting Peurifoy's disclosure, they accused the president of tolerating homosexual employees in the federal government. Senator Joseph McCarthy charged that the State Department had reinstated a homosexual despite the growing crisis over national security. Suddenly, homosexuals were said to pose as great a threat to the government as members of the Communist party. When the chief officer of the District of Columbia vice squad testified before a Senate committee that thousands of "sexual deviates" were employed by the federal government and had been arrested for "cruising" in the city's parks, Senator Kenneth Wherry, the Republican floor leader, demanded a full-scale Senate investigation. How could thousands of "sexual deviates" with police records be employed by the federal government without the federal government knowing it?

It would be difficult to exaggerate the significance of the ensuing investigation undertaken by the Senate Appropriations Committee into same-sex behavior. To begin with, the discovery that there were "deviates" who could "pass" as heterosexuals and escape detection led to a redefinition of homosexual and lesbian identities. The report issued by the Senate Appropriations Committee disputed the popular stereotypes of the effeminate homosexual and the masculine lesbian. Many of the legal and medical "experts" who testified before the committee claimed that there were "no outward characteristics or physical traits" that positively identified homosexuals and lesbians.[11] Thus effeminate men or masculine women were not necessarily homosexual or lesbian: "The fact is that many male homosexuals are very masculine in their physical appearance and general demeanor, and many female homosexuals have every appearance of femininity in their outward behavior" (2–3). This testimony encouraged the medicalization of the juridical discourse on sex. For if the federal government could not identify homosexual and lesbian employees, how could it regulate their behavior? Moreover, even if it could identify them, how could it legally expel them when, except for their sexual orientation, they appeared "normal"? To support its claims that lesbians and gay men did indeed constitute a security risk, the committee appealed to a medical model of same-sex eroticism. It tried to show that homosexuals and lesbians were by definition emotionally unstable and should therefore "be considered as proper cases for medical and psychiatric treatment" (3). This meant that even those gay men and women who seemed "normal" should be expelled from the government. They were as emotionally unstable as more stereotypical **63** homosexuals and lesbians and were therefore just as vulnerable to the "blandishments of the foreign espionage agent" (5). If the government could not expel "passing" lesbians and gay men on the basis of their behavior, it could on the basis of their psychological profile. Indeed, their very "normalcy" was a sign that they were disturbed.

How do we account for the juridical construction of "the homosexual" and "the lesbian" as security risks? Historians of American sexuality generally agree that Alfred Kinsey's reports on male and female sexuality, published in 1948 and 1953, respectively, forced Americans to reexamine the established norms of male and female sexual behavior.[12] Widely discussed in the news media, Kinsey's reports contained startling findings that seemed to confirm psychoanalytic theories that stressed the instability of sexual identities. The incidence of same-sex behavior among the men and women interviewed for the reports was unexpectedly high. Among the men, for example, 50 percent admitted to being aroused by members of their own sex, 37 percent reported having had at least one post-adolescent homosexual experience leading to orgasm, and 4 percent claimed to be exclusively homosexual. Perhaps the most startling of Kinsey's findings was that "persons with homosexual histories are to be found in every age group, in every social level, in every conceivable occupation, in cities and on farms, and in the most remote areas of the country."[13] The high incidence of homosexuality led Kinsey to conclude that homosexual behavior was an "inherent physiological capacity" (659–60) that could not be suppressed and should therefore be tolerated.

Although historians of American sexuality may be right in claiming that the Kinsey reports eventually undermined the restrictive norms of male and female behavior in postwar America and therefore helped to make possible the sexual liberation movements of the 1960s, their most immediate impact was to exacerbate the emergent heterosexual panic. Kinsey's findings that the sexual identities of most Americans were fluid and unstable only reinforced fears that homosexuals and lesbians had infiltrated the federal government and threatened to subvert it from within. For if Kinsey was correct, if homosexuality and lesbianism did indeed constitute an "inherent physiological capacity" that could not be contained, then gay men and women would have little difficulty converting straight employees to their "perverted" prac-

64　tices. The knowledge that many "normal" men and women had once been so converted, even if they were not now engaging in same-sex practices, made this vulnerability to sexual conversion seem even more acute. The report issued by the Senate Appropriations Committee claimed that "one homosexual can pollute a Government office" (20). In other words, the continued employment of lesbians and gay men by the federal government threatened to result in a homosexualization of American society. The report cited legal and medical evidence supposedly showing that homosexuals and lesbians "will frequently attempt to entice normal individuals to engage in perverted practices. This is particularly true in the case of young and impressionable people who might come under the influence of a pervert" (4).

Kinsey's reports, then, inadvertently contributed to the growing juridical crisis over the politics of sexual practice. Confronted by the evidence of widespread homosexual and lesbian activity among men and women from all walks of American life, the government appealed to the psychiatric discourse on same-sex eroticism, lest Kinsey's findings encourage greater tolerance of homosexuals and lesbians. The Senate Appropriations Committee was especially determined to counteract the evidence suggesting that there was little to distinguish gay men and women from straights except for their sexual orientation. Although it accepted the finding that male homosexuals could be masculine, it continued to associate male homosexuality with effeminacy. It defined the masculine homosexual as doubly pathological. Dividing the male homosexual population according to categories of behavior drawn from heterosexual courtship patterns, it claimed that the active gay man "exhibits no traces of femininity in his speech and or mannerisms which would disclose his homosexuality. This active type is almost exclusively attracted to the passive type of homosexual or to young men or boys who are not necessarily homosexual but who are effeminate in general appearance or behavior" (3). Thus the committee continued to rely on the stereotype of the effeminate gay man to categorize homosexual behavior. It implied that the effeminate gay man, whose behavior corresponded to the stereotype, was more "normal" than the masculine gay man. The masculine gay man, on the other hand, could avoid detection. Because he was active rather than passive, his masculinity supposedly did not correspond to his sexual orientation. In this way, the committee tried indirectly to recuperate

Kinsey's findings for the continued medicalization of same-sex eroticism. It tried to show that lesbians and gay men who did not correspond to the stereotypes were even less normal than those who did.

This is not to suggest that Kinsey's findings were solely responsible for the postwar crisis over the government employment of an indeterminate group of gay men and women who could pass as straight.
The emergence of politicized gay and lesbian communities in large urban areas also contributed to the juridical construction of "the homosexual" and "the lesbian" as security risks. For it was in the postwar
period that middle-class gay and lesbian professionals in cities such as
Los Angeles and New York first began to define themselves as members of an oppressed minority. Rejecting the medicalization of same-
sex behavior, these gay and lesbian professionals pioneered a minoritarian, or subcultural, model of same-sex eroticism. For them, gay
men and women were not "sick" but different. They constituted an
oppressed minority culture that extended beyond the bars and bath-
houses that had traditionally provided urban gay men and women
with a sense of collective identity and that encompassed all aspects of
their lives, including their careers. The pseudonymous Donald Web-
ster Cory, for example, in *The Homosexual in America* (1951), argued that
homosexuals and lesbians shared more than a common sexual identity. They were members of an oppressed minority whose rights had
been systematically violated by the American government: "Our minority status is similar, in a variety of respects, to that of national,
religious and other ethnic groups; in the denial of civil liberties; in the
legal, extra-legal and quasi-legal discrimination; in the assignment of
an inferior social position; in the exclusion from the mainstream of life
and culture."[14]

The Mattachine Society, the first homosexual and lesbian rights
group founded in the postwar period, similarly emphasized the common history of oppression uniting gay men and women. As former
members of the Communist party, the founders of the society, Henry
Hay, Bob Hull, and Chuck Rowland, were committed to theorizing
homosexual and lesbian oppression from a Marxist perspective. They
felt that gay men and women who passed as middle-class heterosexual
professionals were victims of false consciousness and did not realize that they were oppressed, despite their wealth and privilege.
When the society began to recruit members in 1950, it established

consciousness-raising groups that encouraged the participants to see themselves as members of an oppressed minority regardless of their status as professionals. Not surprisingly, Hay, Hull, and Rowland encountered significant opposition to their essentialist claims about distinct lesbian and gay identities. Even those members who were sympathetic to their claims hesitated to embrace their position. They worried that the attempt to define distinct lesbian and gay identities would only isolate them further from mainstream American life. But the majority of newly recruited members simply rejected the idea that they were fundamentally different from heterosexuals. Although they agreed that they had certain interests in common with other homosexuals and lesbians, they insisted that the only thing that distinguished them from heterosexual professionals was their sexual orientation. After a protracted struggle with Hay, Hull, and Rowland, these members assumed leadership of the society and stated categorically that "the sex variant is no different from anyone else except in the object of his [sic] sexual expression."[15]

Historians of the homophile movement usually explain the struggle over how to define lesbian and gay identities within the Mattachine Society in terms of a "retreat to respectability."[16] For these historians, the members of the Mattachine Society who opposed the founders wanted to be accepted into, rather than excluded from, mainstream American society; thus they were unwilling to challenge existing social structures. Yet this explanation oversimplifies the resistance the founders encountered to their essentialist claims. For the divisions within the society's membership suggest that lesbian and gay professionals occupied a multiplicity of competing subject positions in postwar America. The lawyers, doctors, and other middle-class professionals recruited by Hay, Hull, and Rowland resisted the argument that they were essentially different from heterosexual professionals because that argument failed to describe their own lived experience. Unless their mannerisms corresponded to the stereotype of the effeminate gay man or masculine lesbian, they could pass as straight. Consequently, they did not experience the disjunction between their personal and their professional lives as a contradiction. Thus to claim that the rejection of a minoritarian model of same-sex eroticism in the early 1950s constituted a form of false consciousness and/or denial is to minimize the extent to which the relation between homosexuals and lesbians and their sexuality was overdetermined in **67** postwar America. The members who eventually gained control of the Mattachine Society had no interest in radically challenging existing social structures, because those structures allowed them to practice their sexuality without seriously endangering their professional status.

The emergence of a minoritarian model of same-sex eroticism in the postwar period also left its mark on the report issued by the Senate Appropriations Committee. By invoking contemporary psychiatric discourse, the committee tried indirectly to contain the attempts of middle-class gay men and women to define themselves as members of an oppressed minority. It insisted that homosexuality and lesbianism constituted aberrant psychological conditions. It stated that because they suffered from arrested sexual development, homosexuals and lesbians could be cured of their "perverted" practices. It cited medical evidence supposedly showing that gay men and women responded to psychiatric treatment and could be cured "if they [had] a genuine desire to be cured" (3). In this way, the report defined gay men and women as "sick" or recalcitrant heterosexuals who refused to grow up; in so doing, it indirectly countered the argument that lesbians and gay men were systematically oppressed by society. If lesbians and gay men felt alienated from mainstream America, that was because they were maladjusted; their problems were personal rather than political and best remedied in a doctor's office. Thus the federal government interpreted the homophile movement's essentialist claims regarding gay and lesbian identities as an indication of just how "abnormal" they were. The medical model of same-sex eroticism defined homosexuality and lesbianism as developmental disorders rather than as categories of identity similar to other categories of identity such as race, gender, and nationality.

Thus the discursive construction of "the homosexual" and "the lesbian" in the postwar period was marked by an extended ideological struggle among competing political interests. On the one hand, the juridical discourse appropriated the medical model of same-sex eroticism to justify the government expulsion of homosexuals and lesbians; on the other hand, middle-class lesbian and gay professionals began to reject the pathologizing of same-sex practices and to define themselves as members of an oppressed minority with their own culture and traditions. The problem with the first of these constructions was that it appropriated rather than disputed Kinsey's findings. To justify its claims that even gay men and women who appeared "normal" constituted a security risk, it invoked medical "findings" supposedly showing that all human sexuality was fluid and polymorphous. For this reason, it left heterosexuals in a vulnerable and embattled position. In stating that heterosexuals were incapable of resisting the sexual advances of gay men and women, it encouraged heterosexual panic. The problem with the second of these constructions was that it assumed it had a potential constituency in all gay men and women. It failed to consider the multiplicity of subject positions available to middle-class lesbian and gay professionals in postwar America and took for granted that there was a connection between an individual's politics and her/his sexual identity. Many of the members recruited by the Mattachine Society were just as susceptible to anti-Communist propaganda as more mainstream Americans and had no desire to theorize their oppression from a Marxist perspective that seemed to conflict with the nation's security interests. Rather than making a connection between the anti-Communism and homophobia sweeping the nation, these members threw their support behind the federal government and its campaign to rid American society of Communist influence. They introduced resolutions to require loyalty oaths and to establish a committee to investigate members suspected of Communist sympathies. These members saw themselves primarily as vulnerable middle-class professionals whose entitlement was threatened by the growing influence of the Communist party. Their identities as members of an oppressed minority were secondary to their identities as patriotic Americans.

A question remains, however. Why would the federal government appeal to scientific findings that encouraged heterosexual panic? What did it gain by acknowledging the resistance of sexuality to containment through representation? The codification of lesbian and gay identities according to a medical model of same-sex eroticism might, after all, have reassured heterosexuals of the fundamental differences between them and "passing" homosexuals and lesbians. It claimed that all gay men and women were sick, whether they appeared "normal" or not. But the government invoked scientific findings that questioned the stability of all sexual identities, gay or straight. It wanted to justify the expulsion of passing gay men and women by claiming that

they might pervert straight employees if allowed to continue working for the government. Thus at the same time that the government
claimed that lesbians and gay men were fundamentally different from
straights, it also argued that male and female heterosexual identities
were unstable. Yet it was precisely for this reason that the medicalization of contemporary juridical discourse provided a particularly effective mechanism of social control. For it allowed the government to
do more than regulate the behavior of an indeterminate group of
lesbians and gay men. Scholars generally agree that the postwar years
were a period of almost unprecedented social and sexual upheaval.
Returning soldiers often had difficulty readjusting to civilian life, and
many women resented the loss of wartime jobs.[17] Moreover, many
homosexuals and lesbians came out for the first time during the war
and, upon their return home, settled in urban centers where they
established gay and lesbian communities.[18] The juridical construction
of "the homosexual" and "the lesbian" helped to contain these dramatic shifts in attitudes and behaviors. It not only politicized the
sexual practices of an indeterminate group of gay men and women by
linking them directly to the growing crisis over national security, but
also coerced heterosexuals into policing their own behavior. Suddenly,
there was a connection between an individual's politics and her/his
sexual identity. Membership in the Communist party and other leftist
political organizations indicated that the individual was not only unpatriotic but sexually perverted as well. Thus if an individual's sexual
orientation could no longer be determined by her/his lack of conformity to the norms of male and female behavior, then it could be by
her/his politics.

Hitchcock and the Heterosexualization
of Spectatorship

Hitchcock's *Strangers on a Train* participated in these attempts to contain the political and sexual upheavals of the postwar period through
the deployment of homophobia. Based loosely on a Patricia Highsmith
novel of the same name, it identified individual conformity to the
political and sexual norms sanctioned by the state as an act of supreme
patriotism. In Highsmith's blatantly homophobic novel, a fledgling

architect, Guy Haines, befriends Charles Bruno, a spoiled mama's boy from Long Island, on a train while traveling from New York to Texas. Over drinks in the dining car, Guy tells Bruno that he is returning home to Texas to divorce his wife, Miriam, who is pregnant with another man's baby. When he mentions that Miriam might refuse to give him a divorce and thereby jeopardize his first architectural commission, Bruno proposes that they exchange murders. Bruno will murder Miriam, if Guy will murder Bruno's father. Throughout the scenes on the train, Guy becomes increasingly uncomfortable with Bruno's flirtatious behavior. When Bruno suggests that they spend a couple of days together in Santa Fe, Guy snaps: "Pick up somebody else."[19] But it is not until Bruno makes his murderous proposal that Guy becomes truly alarmed by his familiarity. When he leaves Bruno's compartment, he regrets that he has left behind his volume of Plato, Highsmith's not-so-subtle clue that he is latently homosexual: "He didn't like the idea of its spending the night in Bruno's room, or of Bruno's touching it and opening it" (32). Although Guy rejects Bruno's proposal unequivocally, Bruno ignores his protestations and kills Miriam when he discovers that she has indeed refused to give Guy a divorce. He then blackmails Guy into killing his father by threatening to implicate him in Miriam's murder.

Although Hitchcock's film retains the basic outline of Highsmith's novel, it makes several important changes. Rather than a fledgling architect, its Guy Haines is a champion tennis player who intends to enter politics after his final match at Forest Hills. His girlfriend, Ann (Ruth Roman), is not a wealthy socialite but the daughter of a powerful senator, and he resists Bruno's attempts to blackmail him into murdering his father. But the film's most significant change is in translating the action from New York and Connecticut to Washington, D.C. The film's setting in the nation's capital casts the homosexual subplot in a wholly new light. The encounter between the strangers on the train has a political resonance lacking in the novel, for it narrativizes the "homosexual menace" as defined by contemporary juridical discourse.[20] To begin with, it translates into visual terms the juridical crisis precipitated by the discovery that gays and lesbians could look and behave like straights. The Guy Haines of Hitchcock's film certainly does not look homosexual. In his dark wool tweeds and V-neck sweater, he appears too clean-cut and all-American to threaten national security. Yet it is he who initiates the meeting with Bruno: he accidentally kicks Bruno while crossing his legs. Moreover, Hitchcock's scenarization of the encounter on the train immediately identifies Guy as a potential security risk. Bruno recognizes Guy because he has seen his picture in the society pages of the newspaper. (Bruno apparently does not read the sports pages, which is probably meant as another indication that he is a homosexual.) It is common knowledge that Guy wants to divorce Miriam (Laura Elliot) and marry Ann in order to further his political ambitions. Thus the meeting between him and Bruno exposes him to the threat of blackmail.

The juridical discourse of the postwar period made Hitchcock's attempts to represent Guy and Bruno as homosexuals extremely problematic. As we saw above, the report issued by the Senate Appropriations Committee claimed that lesbians and gay men could pass as straight and avoid detection. But if lesbians and gay men could pass, how could they be distinguished from heterosexuals at the level of cinematic representation? One of the ways in which Hitchcock tries to resolve this dilemma is by adhering to the stereotype of the effeminate gay man. His representation of Bruno seems to insist that there *are* outward characteristics and physical traits that positively identify homosexuals. The famous opening shots of the film in which the camera tracks Guy's and Bruno's feet as they rush from opposite sides of Union Station immediately identify Bruno as outside mainstream American society. In marked contrast to Guy, who wears dark wool trousers and wing-tipped shoes, Bruno wears striped trousers and a pair of saddle shoes. Moreover, Bruno's unsolicited confessions about himself on the train suggest that he is overly dependent on his mother. He explains to Guy that his monogrammed tie clip is a gift from his mother. A later shot of him lounging in a silk robe in the richly appointed living room of his father's estate while his mother manicures his nails only reinforces the impression that he is a mama's boy who is insufficiently masculine.

But the growing crisis over the government employment of an indeterminate group of gay men and women who passed as straight problematized Hitchcock's use of the stereotype of the effeminate gay man to identify Bruno as homosexual. As we saw above, the report issued by the Senate Appropriations Committee disputed the stereotype of the effeminate gay man: effeminate mannerisms did not necessarily indicate that a man was homosexual. Thus Hitchcock tries to secure his representation of Bruno as "the homosexual" of contemporary juridical discourse by invoking a medical model of same-sex eroticism. The film encourages a psychoanalytic interpretation of Bruno's behavior by stressing his emotional dependence on his mother (Marion Lorne). Bruno appears to suffer from an unresolved Oedipus complex. His fantasies of replacing the father threaten to become a reality, and thus he remains outside the law. Moreover, the film tries to show that his mother is responsible for his arrested sexual development, which is recontained in his final "arrest" by the state at the end of the film. She encourages his emotional dependence on her by constantly mediating between him and his father. The shot of her manicuring his nails is especially incriminating. She meticulously prepares his hands for the murder and thus is complicit with it.[21]

Hitchcock's film, then, uses the psychoanalytic categories of contemporary juridical discourse to secure its representation of Bruno as the emotionally unstable homosexual who threatens to subvert the federal government from within. Bruno first tries to pervert Guy and then to implicate him in Miriam's murder when he refuses to abide by the terms of their "agreement" on the train. Hitchcock condenses this scenarization of the homosexual menace into one of the film's most powerful images. At one point in the film, the camera tracks Guy as he walks toward the Jefferson Memorial with a police detective. When Guy suddenly turns his head and looks outside the frame, the camera follows the direction of his gaze and pans the Jefferson Memorial. The composition of this shot immediately focuses our eye on Bruno. Unlike the other figures in the shot, he stands near the center of the frame motionless and looking straight into the camera. He has apparently been following Guy and now watches him from the steps of the memorial. Although Bruno is dwarfed by the memorial's massive columns and seemingly endless rows of steps, the stark contrast between his dark silhouette and the gleaming white marble makes the government appear vulnerable and unprotected. Bruno is a blight on the nation's political system. His menacing presence on the steps of the memorial amounts to blackmail. It reminds Guy, the would-be senator, that he cannot expose Bruno as Miriam's murderer without incriminating himself. This scene is especially powerful because it is shot from Guy's point of view. The spectator shares Guy's shock of recognition when Guy realizes that Bruno is watching him. The dizzying movement of the camera as it pans the memorial (repeated when Guy's taxi pulls away from the steps) only reinforces this shock: the spectator's look is momentarily dislocated. In this way, the film positions the spectator as "the heterosexual" of contemporary juridical discourse who is supposedly threatened by the homosexual menace. Like Guy, the spectator is susceptible to blackmail because her/his sexual identity is unstable.

But Hitchcock's representation of Bruno as "the homosexual" is more complicated than this implies. According to the report issued by the Senate Appropriations Committee, it is the homosexual or lesbian employee who is susceptible to blackmail, not the "normal" individual whom he or she perverts. In Hitchcock's film, however, it is Guy, not Bruno, who is the potential security risk; he is the one who is compromised by their encounter on the train. In this respect, the film complicates the homophobic categories of contemporary political discourse. Whereas the report issued by the Senate Appropriations Committee tried to show that homosexuals and lesbians frequently seduced impressionable young men and women who were their co-workers, Hitchcock's film makes little distinction between Guy and Bruno. To be sure, Guy would never murder Miriam himself, but he clearly desires her death and allows Bruno to "seduce" him. For example, after he learns that Miriam has decided not to give him a divorce, he calls Ann from the train station and tells her that he "could strangle her [Miriam's] little neck." A train passes as he speaks, recalling Bruno's murderous proposal.

Moreover, he seems to indicate his consent to the terms of Bruno's proposal when he accidentally leaves his lighter in Bruno's compartment. Marked A to G, the lighter is the film's substitute for the volume of Plato in Highsmith's novel and functions as a signifier of the instability of Guy's sexual identity. Originally a token of Ann's love for him, it now becomes a token of his love for Bruno. In the context of his encounter with Bruno, the *A* engraved on the lighter is ambiguous. It stands not only for Ann but also for Bruno (whose last name in the film is Anthony). Thus the markings can be interpreted to mean that Guy would consider Miriam's murder a token of Bruno's love for him (Anthony to Guy). After all, Miriam's death would enable Guy to marry Ann and achieve his political ambitions. This is certainly how

Bruno interprets the markings on the lighter. After Guy leaves his compartment, Bruno examines the lighter before pocketing it and says, "Crisscross." Bruno's comment could of course merely refer to the crossed tennis rackets engraved on the lighter, but "crisscross" is also the term he uses to describe the exchange of murders. Bruno, then, has some justification for interpreting the lighter to mean that Guy has accepted the terms of his proposal. Yet Guy leaves the lighter in Bruno's compartment not to indicate his consent to the exchange of murders so much as to redefine their relationship. As I noted above, the A is ambiguous. It stands for Ann as well as for Bruno, which opens up the possibility of interpreting the markings on the lighter in a different way. Guy would accept Miriam's murder as a token of Bruno's love for him because it would "normalize" the relationship by triangulating it through Ann.[22] In making it possible for Guy to marry Ann, Bruno would in a sense be giving Ann to Guy (A to G) as well as making her into a guy. Reduced to an object of exchange between the two men, Ann would become a substitute for Bruno. In other words, Guy uses the lighter to redefine the terms of their "agreement." He proposes that he and Bruno exchange Ann rather than the murders.

In this respect, *Strangers on a Train* goes further than the federal government in attempting to police male same-sex behavior. The report issued by the Senate Appropriations Committee distinguished sharply between "latent" and "overt" homosexuals. It limited its investigation to overt homosexuals, or homosexuals who openly engaged in same-sex practices, and ignored those who "knowingly or unknowingly have tendencies or inclinations toward homosexuality and other types of sex perversion, but who, by the exercise of self-restraint or for other reasons, do not indulge in overt acts of perversion" (2). It refused, in other words, to pathologize traditionally accepted forms of male same-sex eroticism such as those in which two men mediated their desire for each other through the exchange of a woman. Rejecting this position, Hitchcock's film insists that homosexual desire is homosexual desire, whether it involves the exchange of a woman or not. For Guy remains outside the law, despite his attempt to normalize his relationship with Bruno. In shot after shot, Guy's actions mimic Bruno's, thereby reducing him to Bruno's double. The crosscuts that link the two men in the film repeat formally the crisscross that links them in the plot. A shot of Bruno looking at his watch crosscuts to one of Guy looking at his. In the scene in which Bruno informs Guy that he has strangled Miriam, the composition of the shots expresses Guy's complicity with the murder visually. The camera shows him and Bruno standing next to each other behind the bars of a wrought-iron gate that casts its shadows across their bodies. Close-ups of his face as he listens in horror to Bruno's description of Miriam's death alternate with close-ups of Bruno talking excitedly. The shot/reverse shot structure of this sequence makes Guy and Bruno seem virtually interchangeable: Guy too belongs behind bars. Guy's doubling of Bruno culminates in the scenes of Guy's tennis match at Forest Hills. Shots of Bruno frantically searching for Guy's lighter, which he has accidentally dropped down a sewer, are crosscut with shots of Guy desperately trying to beat his opponent. In these scenes, Guy seems to have become Bruno. He has more in common with Bruno than with himself: he is active rather than passive. Guy's determination to win the match surprises the tennis announcer. Guy usually plays with a "watch-and-wait" strategy, but his desire to win has made him uncharacteristically "grim and determined."

In representing Guy as Bruno's double, the film encourages the spectator to interpret his behavior psychoanalytically. Guy's doubling of Bruno recalls the mirror phase as defined by Lacanian psychoanalysis. According to Lacan, during the mirror phase, the subject exchanges a fragmented bodily image for a coherent, unified one when it recognizes its own image in a mirror or in another body (usually the mother's). This exteriorization of the subject, its projection outward, enables the subject to conceive of the body as finite rather than as continuous with the mother, and thus establishes a boundary between inside and outside: the subject becomes an object that can be incorporated and mimicked. Applying Lacan's account of the mirror phase to Guy's doubling of Bruno suggests that it is one of the preconditions for Guy's entry into the Symbolic order. In mimicking Bruno's actions, Guy achieves a relatively unified and coherent identity. Guy must first project himself outward before he can master his transgressive desires. Recognizing himself in Bruno enables Guy to displace those desires onto him. He does not desire Miriam's death, Bruno does; he does not desire Bruno, Bruno desires him. Moreover, in mimicking Bruno's actions, Guy shows that he has relinquished the polymorphous sexuality of the pre-Oedipal phase. Guy's doubling of

Bruno recalls the Freudian model of identification described above. It indicates that he no longer desires Bruno but identifies with him. The culturally sanctioned prohibition of homosexuality forces Guy to renounce Bruno as an object choice, and he compensates for his loss by incorporating Bruno into his ego. He no longer adopts a "feminine attitude" toward Bruno but begins to act like him. He is determined to beat his opponent in the tennis match because he wants to prevent Bruno from planting the lighter at the scene of the murder.

Hitchcock's film, then, follows the example of contemporary juridical discourse in privileging a psychoanalytic understanding of male subjectivity. It tries to show that in order for the male subject to achieve a fixed heterosexual identity, he must successfully negotiate the Oedipus complex. For if Guy must pass through the mirror phase before he can enter the Symbolic order, so too must he elude the threat of castration signified by Miriam and her transgressive sexuality. Mary Ann Doane has shown that glasses worn by women in classical Hollywood cinema indicate an active looking "or even simply the fact of seeing as opposed to being seen."[23] Although Doane stresses the epistemological rather than the sexual implications of such looking, her analysis still seems applicable to Miriam, whose glasses signify plenitude rather than lack. Miriam represents the sexually "deviant" woman demonized by Cold War political discourse because she resists confinement to the private sphere. Not only does she continue working when she no longer needs to, but she refuses to restrict her sexuality to the privatized space of the nuclear family. The subject of her own desire, she circulates freely among men. She returns the male gaze rather than submitting to it passively and refuses to become an object of Guy's desire and his alone. The scenes in which Bruno follows her at the amusement park are constructed in such a way as to excuse her murder. Because they are shot almost wholly from Bruno's point of view, the spectator identifies with Bruno, who is both attracted to and repelled by her. Although she has come to the park with two other men, she seems to want Bruno to pick her up. She constantly looks to see if he is still following her. When she buys an ice cream cone, she turns toward him and licks it suggestively, staring straight into the camera. In this way, the film tries to suggest that she is "asking for it." Because her sexuality is castrating, she deserves to die. In other words, we are meant to accept her death as a precondition for

Guy's entry into full masculinity as signified in the Symbolic order.
Significantly, when Bruno informs Guy that he has strangled Miriam,
he gives her glasses to him as though they were a kind of trophy or
prize; in so doing, he returns her look to him. Her cracked glasses are
the mark of her castration and thus guarantee Guy's totality and
coherence. He can now return her look without fear of castration.

This is not to suggest that Guy achieves a fixed, stable heterosexual identity. In narrativizing the postwar crisis over the politics of
sexual practice, Hitchcock's film follows the example of contemporary
juridical discourse and represents all human sexuality as polymorphous. Despite Guy's determination to prevent Bruno from planting
the incriminating lighter at the scene of the murder, he continues to
adopt a "feminine attitude" toward him. He never makes a choice
between Ann or Bruno; rather, the choice is made for him. He continues to mimic Bruno's actions even in the final shots of the film. He
pursues Bruno through the amusement park just as Bruno once pur-
sued Miriam. Moreover, in these shots, Bruno is clearly the one in
control of the action. He nearly overwhelms Guy during their struggle
on the merry-go-round, and Guy only retrieves the lighter when the
merry-go-round crushes Bruno to death.[24] Bruno's death, then, functions as a kind of deus-ex-machina conclusion to Guy's Oedipal journey. Bruno is a powerful figure who constantly threatens to seize
control of the narrative. He is more charismatic than the all-American
Guy, and his potentially destabilizing presence can only be contained
by his violent expulsion from the diegesis, just as the potentially
destabilizing presence of homosexuals and lesbians could only be
contained by their violent expulsion from the government. Rather
than Guy resolving his Oedipus complex, it is resolved for him. This
becomes apparent in the final shot of the film in which we see Guy and
Ann sitting on a train. Guy's Oedipal journey seems to have come to
an end, for he appears to have entered the Symbolic order. Ann is
sitting in the place where Bruno sat when he proposed exchanging
murders with Guy, and thus she seems to have replaced him as an
object of Guy's desire. Yet when a priest leans over to ask Guy if he is
Guy Haines the champion tennis player, Guy, about to reply yes, has
second thoughts and quickly changes places. In concluding in this
way, the film stresses the instability of Guy's Oedipal resolution.
Although Guy's Oedipal journey seems to have come to an end, he

remains susceptible to, if not allured by, the "homosexual menace." He cannot even trust a representative of the very institution that sanctions monogamous heterosexuality.

In this way, Hitchcock's film ratifies the findings of the Senate Appropriations Committee. It shows that straights are indeed susceptible to blackmail. Because their sexual identities are fluid and unstable, straights are incapable of resisting the sexual advances of gay men and lesbians. But whereas the report issued by the Senate Appropriations Committee argued that the expulsion of lesbians and gays from the government would counteract the "homosexual menace," Hitchcock's film questions whether the threatened homosexualization of American society can be prevented. Guy's relationship with Bruno is normalized only when Bruno is crushed to death by the merry-go-round.[25] The crisis over the government employment of gay men and women who pass as straight appears to justify extreme measures. Miriam's murder and Bruno's death are both necessary to counteract Guy's threatened homosexualization. In what is perhaps the most famous shot of the film, we see Miriam's murder reflected in her own glasses, which have fallen to the ground. Here the camera reappropriates Miriam's look. The act of seeing belongs to the camera, not to her. As a woman, she is meant to be seen rather than to see. But with this shot the film also implicates itself in the production of a female subject who is desired rather than desiring. In reappropriating Miriam's look, the film endorses her castration (and by implication the castration of all women who dare to resist confinement to the private sphere). As I have already noted, the film seems to suggest that the stability of American society depends on the female subject restricting her sexuality to the privatized space of the nuclear family. The desiring female subject signifies plenitude rather than lack and therefore threatens the male subject with castration: she refuses to become an accessory to his Oedipal trajectory. Hitchcock's film, in other words, attributes the homosexual menace not to the gay men and women who were employed by the federal government and passed so much as to those American women who positioned themselves as subjects rather than as objects of desire. Miriam's unwillingness to occupy a passive position in relation to desire forces Guy to consent to Bruno's murderous proposal. Guy's inability to contain Miriam's desire within the domestic sphere signifies his castration. Thus if the female subject persists in occupying an active position in relation to desire, she must be forcibly subjected to the logic of male heterosexual desire.

That *Strangers on a Train* does indeed attribute the crisis over national security to those American women who refused to restrict their sexuality to the domestic sphere rather than to the gay men and women who supposedly constituted a security risk is perhaps most obvious in its representation of Ann's sister, Barbara (Patricia Hitchcock). Barbara bears a close physical resemblance to Miriam, which Bruno notices when he first meets her at one of Guy's tennis matches. Barbara's glasses remind him of Miriam, and he is momentarily transported to the scene of the murder. The camera cuts from a shot of Bruno looking at Barbara to a shot of her returning his gaze. A shot of the lighter then appears, superimposed over Barbara's image. But Barbara's resemblance to Miriam is more than physical, for, like Miriam, she positions herself as a subject rather than as an object of desire. Although she is not as promiscuous as Miriam, she occupies an active position in relation to desire, constantly flirting with the detective assigned to follow Guy. Thus she threatens to become like Miriam, a woman she describes as a "tramp," implying that she deserved to die, and must be forcibly subjected to the logic of male heterosexual desire. The similarities between her and Miriam become obvious even to her in the scene in which Bruno nearly strangles Mrs. Cunningham to death at Senator Morton's party. When Bruno realizes that Barbara is watching him, he becomes delirious and begins to strangle Mrs. Cunningham in earnest; Barbara's presence reminds him of the murder, and he thinks he is strangling Miriam rather than Mrs. Cunningham. Barbara feels as though Bruno were strangling her and becomes terrified. When Ann asks her what happened, she stammers, "His hands were on her neck. . . . Ann, he was strangling me!" Thus Bruno's nearly fatal strangling of Mrs. Cunningham should be seen as a warning. In positioning herself as a subject of desire, Barbara, like Miriam, is "asking for it" and must be forced to occupy a passive position in relation to desire. Unless she relinquishes her position as a subject of desire, Barbara will end up like Miriam.

In representing Bruno's nearly fatal strangling of Mrs. Cunningham as a warning that admonishes Barbara to relinquish her position as a subject of desire, the film inadvertently shows that the juridical construction of "the homosexual" and "the lesbian" functioned primarily as a mechanism for containing the political and sexual upheaval of the postwar period. Ironically, Bruno becomes an agent of the very discourses that constructed homosexuality and lesbianism as threats to national security. Although the film represents Bruno as "the homosexual" of Cold War political discourse who supposedly threatened to subvert the government from within, it uses him to enforce the psychosexual norms of the 1950s. Not only does he "punish" Miriam for daring to occupy an active position in relation to desire, but he also enables Guy to elude the threat of castration by strangling Miriam. Moreover, he forces Barbara to relinquish her position as a subject of desire by warning her that she threatens to end up like Miriam. In using Bruno to enforce the psychosexual norms of the 1950s, the film shows that the construction of "the homosexual" as a security risk provided the government with a mechanism for insuring that women restricted their sexuality to the domestic sphere. Miriam's refusal to occupy a passive position in relation to desire prevents Guy from successfully negotiating the Oedipus complex, and thus he threatens to become like Bruno. Unable to elude the threat of castration, he occupies the position of "the homosexual" of contemporary juridical discourse: his encounter with Bruno has left him vulnerable to the threat of blackmail. But Ann's willingness to restrict her sexuality to the domestic sphere helps to reclaim him for the Symbolic order. By positioning herself as an object rather than as a subject of desire, she insures that he does not become like Bruno.

Ultimately, then, *Strangers on a Train* suggests that the solution to the crisis over the politics of sexual practice lay not in the expulsion of gay men and women from the government so much as in a stricter regulation of female behavior. Hitchcock's film tries to show that it was not the gay men and women employed by the government who threatened national security, but those American women who refused to restrict their sexuality to the domestic sphere. I argued above that the shot of Miriam's murder reflected in her glasses seems to acknowledge the film's complicity with the production of a female subject who is desired rather than desiring. In reappropriating Miriam's look (and by implication the look of the female spectator), the film returns the scopophilic pleasures of the cinematic apparatus to the male heterosexual spectator. Now I would like to argue that this moment of self-reflexivity calls attention to the operations whereby the film tries to insert the spectator into a fixed, stable subject position. The spectator does not see Miriam's murder directly. Her glasses act as a mirror in which her castration becomes visible (and by implication the castration of the female spectator by the cinematic apparatus). In this respect, the shot acknowledges the film's complicity with the specular logic of the mirror phase as defined by Lacanian psychoanalysis. The film structures the spectator's gaze according to a specific mode of apprehension. In subjecting the spectator to this mode of apprehension, it restages her/his entry into the Symbolic order. It provides the spectator with the categories of seeing through which s/he becomes visible not only to her/himself but to other spectators as well. In this way, the film insures that the spectator will be satisfied that s/he has been adequately reflected on the screen. The spectator's subjective engagement with the film virtually guarantees the production of Oedipalized male and female subjects less vulnerable to the "homosexual menace." Because of the film's narrativization of the contemporary crisis over national security, the spectator submits to the specular logic of its mode of address and recognizes her/himself reflected on the screen. Like the characters with whom s/he identifies, the spectator is susceptible to the homosexual menace and therefore willingly acquiesces to her/his heterosexualization, which becomes the ultimate patriotic act.

But this moment of self-reflexivity also indicates a crisis in the film's own system of representation. The film must call attention to its own operations, lest the spectator not realize that s/he is meant to see her/himself reflected in the characters on the screen. Moreover, the film must supplement its own operations by invoking other discursive practices. To guarantee the heterosexualization of the spectator, it enlists the contemporary juridical construction of "the homosexual." But why would Hitchcock's film distrust the logic of its own specular regime? Apparently, the proliferation in the postwar period of competing constructions of same-sex eroticism threatened to disrupt the discursive structure of classical Hollywood cinema. As we saw above, the process of identification involves the repression of a potentially destabilizing homosexual object cathexis between spectator and hero. The male spectator must first desire the hero before he can identify with him. The widespread paranoia with respect to male heterosexual identities in postwar America rendered this aspect of identification extremely problematic. By encouraging the male spectator to identify

82   with the hero, Hitchcock's film threatened to reinforce his sexual instability.[26] Attempts to redefine gay men and women as members of an oppressed minority only added to this crisis in cinematic representation. Constructed across a multiplicity of competing discourses, the spectator might reject the subject position made available to her/him by the film. Thus, by invoking the homophobic categories of Cold War political discourse, the film tried to contain the political and sexual indeterminacy of the spectator. It appropriated the discourses that inserted the subject into Cold War politics and therefore all but guaranteed the spectator's heterosexualization. Even gay men and women committed to depathologizing same-sex eroticism had difficulty resisting appeals to their patriotism.

3

RESISTING HISTORY

Rear Window and the Limits of the Postwar Settlement

This is not to say that the Communist "interest" is a legitimate one, or that the Communist issue is irrelevant. As a conspiracy, rather than as a legitimate dissenting group, the Communist movement is a threat to any democratic society.—Daniel Bell, "Interpretations of American Politics"

We've become a race of Peeping Toms.—Stella in *Rear Window*

In the preface to *An End to Innocence* (1955), his first critical work, Leslie Fiedler registers his misgivings about publishing a book of literary criticism in which so many of the essays are political. He sees himself as primarily a "literary person," and when he writes of politics, he does so only reluctantly.[1] But because he has lived through a crisis in liberalism that seems to him "a major event in the development of the human spirit" (1, xxiii), he feels justified in addressing issues not ordinarily considered literary. Indeed, although he lacks a specialized knowledge of politics and is only an indifferent researcher, he believes his training as a literary critic makes him peculiarly well qualified to analyze recent political events. For the very reason that he is primarily a "literary person," he can subject events such as the Rosenberg trial to a "close reading" (1, xxii). His training in the "newer critical methods" (1, xxiii) enables him to provide an analysis of the contemporary crisis in American culture that does not scant ambiguity or paradox but rather gives "to the testimony of a witness before a Senate committee or the letters of the Rosenbergs the same careful scrutiny we have learned to practice on the shorter poems of John Donne" (1, xxiii).

Why would Fiedler believe that close reading, a critical practice most closely associated at the time he was writing with *Scrutiny* and *Kenyon Review*, journals famous for emphasizing the autonomy of the text, was the best critical tool for analyzing the crisis in liberalism? Did he understand the newer critical methods, or did he mistakenly think they were compatible with a materialist understanding of culture? His "close readings" of political events suggest that he did indeed understand the newer critical methods. For despite its tendency to interpret the text in isolation from its historical context, close reading *was* the best critical tool for him to use. He had no interest in providing a materialist critique of postwar American culture; rather, he wanted to show that materialist criticism could not adequately explain the American situation. On the one hand, his analysis of the crisis in liberalism seems to acknowledge the historicity of the subject, its construction by a plurality of already existing discourses that guarantee its insertion into history; on the other, it seems to deny the subject's discursive construction in a specific historical context. He stresses the incoherence of political identities, their fracturing by changing historical conditions. In "Hiss, Chambers, and the Age of Innocence," for example, originally published in *Commentary* in December 1950, he reduces history to the Freudian uncanny. The subject experiences its insertion into history as the return of the repressed. Despite our attempts to forget our political past, "like some monumental bore, it grabs us by the lapels, [and] keeps screaming into our faces the same story over and over again" (1, 3). The subject, in other words, can never escape history. Although it tries to repress the past, the past returns, like the uncanny, to remind it of its own historicity.

Yet the subject's insertion into history is always uneven. Indeed, its very historicity disconnects it from its political past, which is why it experiences its political past as uncanny. Although Fiedler claims that the subject must accept its own connection to the past to achieve "moral adulthood" (1, 4), he argues that "it is a painful thing to be asked to live again through events ten years gone, to admit one's identity with the person who bore one's name in a by now incredible past" (1, 4). History, in other words, actually prevents the subject from constructing a coherent political identity. The subject feels disconnected from its political past because, historically, it is. The network of discourses in which the subject is constructed is constantly shifting, and thus its political identity remains fractured, incoherent: "It is hardest of all to confess that one is responsible for the acts of the past, especially when such acts are now placed in a new and unforeseen context that changes their meaning entirely" (1, 4). For Fiedler, then, the subject's very historical production cuts it off from history. Society's constantly changing historical conditions militate against the achievement of a fixed, stable political identity.

Fiedler's theorization of the subject as both produced by and cut off from history is crucial to his reading of Alger Hiss's perjury trial and its significance for liberalism. He accuses Hiss of refusing to acknowledge his own insertion into history. By insisting that he was innocent, Hiss "failed all liberals, all who had, in some sense and at some time, shared his illusions (and who that calls himself a liberal is exempt?), all who demanded of him that he speak aloud a common recognition of complicity" (1, 23). Hiss's denial under oath that he had committed treason implied not only that his commitment to the Popular Front was historically justified, but also that liberals should remain faithful to their "illusions." In the altered historical conditions of postwar American society, however, such a position was no longer acceptable. Although Hiss could perhaps justify his former Stalinization because of the Depression, his continuing allegiance to the Communist party, indicated by his refusal to admit his guilt, was incompatible with America's economic recovery. The Popular Front critique of American culture had become irrelevant. Thus, in claiming that he was innocent, Hiss denied America's changing historical conditions, and in denying America's changing historical conditions, he refused to acknowledge his own shifting relation to discourse.

To establish Hiss's resistance to his own insertion into history, a resistance that allows him to remain loyal to the legacies of the New Deal, Fiedler compares him to Henry Julian Wadleigh, one of Whittaker Chambers's former contacts at the State Department and a witness at Hiss's trial. He considers Wadleigh, with his disheveled appearance and acquired Oxford accent, a "comic version" (1, 7) of Hiss. Like Hiss, Wadleigh confessed his guilt and declared his innocence at the same time. Although he readily admitted passing secret documents to Chambers while he was an employee at the State Department, he denied that his activities had betrayed American interests. Showing no sign of contrition, he claimed that history justified his actions. In so doing, he ignored his own historicity. He refused to believe that the altered conditions of postwar American society no longer justified fellow traveling: "Wadleigh has learned nothing. He cannot conceive of having done anything *really* wrong. He finds in his own earlier activities only a certain excessive zeal, overbalanced by good will, and all excused by—Munich" (1, 7). In maintaining his innocence, in other words, Hiss, like Wadleigh, refused to see the way in which the Cold War radically altered the meaning of his political identity. Although his fellow traveling in the 1930s could perhaps have been excused because of the European appeasement of Hitler, the Cold War placed his commitment to the Popular Front in a new and unforeseen context that in retrospect rendered it treasonous.

Fiedler sees Hiss's and Wadleigh's resistance to history, their unwillingness to accept their shifting construction as political subjects, as symptoms of the crisis in liberalism. According to Fiedler, prominent leftist intellectuals exerted an influence over public policy during the New Deal that far exceeded their numbers, and McCarthy's exposure of many of them as Communists threatened to discredit their legacies. Fiedler is prepared to accept that liberal intellectuals in the 1930s were justified in affiliating themselves with the Communists because they could assume that the Communists shared their moral values, those of the "old Judeo-Christian ethical system, however secularized" (1, 22). Subsequent political events, however, demonstrated that the Communists "had ceased to subscribe to a political morality universally shared, whatever its abuses, until 1917" (1, 22). As a result, liberal intellectuals now had a moral obligation to confess their former fellow traveling. For only by confessing it could they reclaim the New Deal and its social welfare programs for the postwar settlement. This does not mean, however, that admitting their complicity with the Stalinization of American culture in the 1930s would be a way of connecting with their past; rather, it would be a way of exorcising a part of their history better left behind them. Fiedler claims that "the Hiss case marks the death of an era, but it also promises a rebirth if we are willing to learn its lessons" (1, 24). Confessing their own participation in the Stalinization of American culture would be tantamount to acknowledging that their relation to discourse had shifted because of America's economic recovery: they were no longer Stalinized leftist subjects but subjects of the Cold War consensus.

The structure of Fiedler's essay repeats formally his argument that the open acknowledgment of the ties between the liberals and the Communists during the 1930s would lead to a "rebirth" of liberalism. By waiting to admit his own liberalism until the end of his essay, he enacts the very break with the past he is proposing as a solution to the liberal crisis. He carefully conceals his liberalism throughout "Hiss, Chambers, and the Age of Innocence" and claims to be providing an "unbiased look" (1, 9) at the proceedings of the House Un-American Activities Committee and its investigation of Hiss. In so doing, he seems to deny his own insertion into history. In stating that his reading of Hiss is "unbiased," he places himself above history. He supposedly does not have a vested interest in claiming that the trials of fellow travelers such as Hiss threaten to damage liberalism irreparably. At the same time, however, by acknowledging his own liberalism at the end of the essay, he implies that there is no escaping history. History resembles the Freudian uncanny: regardless of our attempts to repress it, it inevitably returns. Fiedler can no longer conceal his liberalism but must admit it. Still, he confesses his own history of fellow traveling as a way of putting it behind him. Because he accepts that America's growing prosperity refuted the Popular Front critique of American culture, he can provide an "unbiased look" at the significance of Hiss's trial for liberalism. In a sense, he *is* above history. His recognition that his own relation to discourse has shifted renders him immune to ideology, which is why he can subject Hiss's trial to a close reading.

Despite its emphasis on America's changing historical conditions, Fiedler's close reading of Hiss's perjury trial seeks to discredit the sort of materialist critique of American culture favored by Popular Front intellectuals. His claim that Hiss, in committing perjury, denied his own historicity as a subject, allows him to substitute psychological for historical categories of analysis. History supposedly does not adequately explain Hiss's continuing Stalinization. Hiss could never acknowledge that postwar American prosperity contradicted the Marxist analysis of the capitalist relations of production because to do so would have been to change "the whole meaning of his own life, turned what had perhaps seemed to him his most unselfish and devoted acts, the stealing of State Department documents, into shameful crimes—into 'treason'!" (1, 11). It does not occur to Fiedler that Hiss's continuing allegiance to the Popular Front reflected deeply held political convictions, or that, as a political agent, he *chose* to remain committed to a materialist critique of American culture. Rather, Hiss's history of involvement with the Communist party could only represent the acting out of a barely repressed Oedipal drama: "It was as if Alger

Hiss had dedicated himself to fulfilling, along with his dream of a New Humanity, the other dream his father had passed on to him with his first name—from rags to riches" (1, 14). Fiedler makes a similar argument about Chambers, whose Stalinization as a Popular Front intellectual, he claims, was also psychologically rather than ideologically motivated. According to him, Chambers discovered "in the revolution an answer to the insecurity and doubt which had brought his brother to suicide, [and] himself to months of despair and near paralysis" (1, 15). Ultimately, then, Fiedler acknowledges the historicity of the subject only to deny it. Psychology rather than history provides the most adequate explanation for Hiss's and Chambers's discursive construction as Popular Front intellectuals.

I have been discussing "Hiss, Chambers, and the Age of Innocence" in such detail because I want to argue in what follows that Fiedler's denial of history and the psychologizing of political behavior it enabled were crucial to the establishment of the postwar settlement known as the Cold War consensus. I intend to show that Fiedler's essay participated in an extended ideological struggle among liberal intellectuals for hegemonic control over the postwar settlement.[2] Liberal intellectuals had exerted hegemonic control over the American political system since the 1930s. Until the rise of McCarthyism, they had succeeded in containing within the parameters of their own thought the reasoning and calculation of all forms of political opposition. Because of the success of the New Deal, even conservatives took for granted the need for limited government intervention in the economy. McCarthyism, however, threatened to undermine this hegemonic control by exposing many of the intellectuals responsible for the New Deal as Communists or fellow travelers. Suddenly America under the New Deal appeared no different from the Soviet Union. The public repudiation of their former ties to communism offered liberal intellectuals a solution. By distancing themselves from the more extreme elements of the American Left, they could remain loyal to the legacies of the New Deal without alienating large segments of the American electorate. Liberal intellectuals, in other words, constantly needed to renew the hegemony of the social welfare state in order for it to remain hegemonic. This meant that they had to enter into vigorous debate not only with the conservative opposition but with the more radical elements of the ruling liberal coalition because the exposure of those elements by the American right threatened to discredit the achievements of the New Deal.

But liberal intellectuals not only had to contest and contain all forms of political opposition, including those within their own ruling coalition, they also had to gain control over the way in which Americans thought and lived their relations to the world.[3] The postwar settlement needed to occur on a cultural as well as a political level in order to win the free and spontaneous consent of the American people. Thus the liberals had to extend their hegemony beyond the political sphere to the cultural realm. For the postwar settlement to remain hegemonic, it needed to operate unconsciously, to determine, without appearing to do so, a definition of reality to which Americans would consent freely and spontaneously because it seemed to go without saying. This meant that the liberals had to limit the fund of interpretive possibilities available to the American people for understanding their own lived experience. For only by establishing the authoritative descriptions of American culture would they gain control over the discursive construction of the postwar subject. ·

That they were largely successful in accomplishing this I will show by examining Hitchcock's *Rear Window* (1954) in relation to the postwar settlement. I will argue that Hitchcock's film tried to recuperate the cinematic apparatus from its contamination by the emergence of the national security state. The series of repressive legislative acts that established the national security state authorized the appropriation of the cinematic apparatus and its technology for internal security purposes.[4] Hitchcock's film openly acknowledges the taint of this appropriation. Its hero, the photojournalist L. B. Jeffries, or "Jeff" (James Stewart), deploys the techniques of the national security apparatus to spy on the neighbors of his Lower East Side apartment complex. To be sure, he lacks the listening devices, hidden cameras, and microfilm of the FBI and the CIA, but his telephoto lens allows him to scrutinize even the remotest corners of his neighbors' apartments and to discover their most carefully guarded secrets. Yet in admitting its complicity with the government persecution of suspected Communists, homosexuals, lesbians, and other "undesirables," *Rear Window* was simply adopting Fiedler's strategy in "Hiss, Chambers, and the Age of Innocence." It readily admits that its technology facilitated the systematic repression of basic civil liberties (the right to free speech, the freedom of association) as a way of reclaiming that technology for the postwar settlement. Implicit in the film's "confession" of its own tainted procedures is a critique of McCarthyism. The film pathologizes Jeff's constant surveillance of his neighbors by suggesting that he suffers from an arrested sexual development. Alluding to the McCarthy witch hunts in this way enables the film to repudiate its own fellow traveling. Although it cannot deny that in the past the cinematic apparatus lent its technology to the national security state, it can recuperate that technology for the liberal consensus by indirectly attacking the government surveillance of suspected Communists, homosexuals, and lesbians as a form of psychopathology.

Liberal Pluralism and
the Denial of Political Agency

In a postscript to "McCarthy and the Intellectuals," an essay originally published in *Encounter* in August 1954 but included in *An End to Innocence*, Fiedler identified McCarthy's hearings on the army as one of the low points of the postwar period. Although the hearings irreparably damaged McCarthy, they failed to result in an official censure of his conduct, and administration officials shamefully tried to mollify him. When Secretary of the Army Stevens finally stood up to the Wisconsin Senator, he displayed, according to Fiedler, only a "last-minute, useless kind of courage" (1, 85). But what bothered Fiedler most about the hearings was that they were televised. Their coverage on television implicated the entire nation, not just those directly involved, in the "whole ignoble affair" (1, 85). According to Fiedler, television elicited from the American people a voyeuristic curiosity about the political process. Americans did not watch the hearings out of a sense of civic duty but because they wanted to see McCarthy make a spectacle of himself. Thus they were complicitous with the shameful proceedings: "It was not only that nobody directly involved in the circus managed to perform with distinction or tact, but that even those not directly implicated, the nation itself, sat transfixed for weeks before their television receivers in a voyeuristic orgy" (1, 85). Television, in other words, threatened to transform American politics into a spectacle in which politicians "preened for the cameras" (1, 85).

Fiedler's argument that television threatened to reduce American politics to a form of entertainment was typical of the liberal critique of postwar American culture. Liberal historian Richard Hofstadter, for example, in "The Pseudo-Conservative Revolt," his contribution to *The New American Right* (1955), a collection of essays on the postwar crisis in liberalism edited by Daniel Bell, warned that television threatened to erode the distinction between the public and private spheres traditional to pluralistic democracies.[5] Televised coverage of committee hearings enabled the American people to feel as though they were directly participating in them. According to Hofstadter, the use of television has "brought politics closer to the people than ever before and [has] made politics a form of entertainment in which the spectators feel themselves involved."[6] For this reason, television threatened to undermine, rather than strengthen, the democratic process. Although it seemed to involve the American people more directly in the democratic process, it encouraged them to treat the public sphere as an extension of the private. Hofstadter claimed that because the McCarthy hearings had been televised, politics "had become, more than ever before, an arena into which private emotions and personal problems can be readily projected" (52). For Hofstadter, then, television promoted the privatization of the public sphere. It supposedly encouraged the American people to regard the political process as a form of entertainment intended for their own private consumption.

Hofstadter's claim that television facilitated the privatization of the public sphere suggests that what he and other liberal intellectuals were afraid of was not so much that television might transform American politics into a spectacle but that American politics as a form of spectacle was changing because of television.[7] After all, American politics had always been a form of spectacle.[8] Structured according to a propagandistic model of communication, it had positioned the voter as a spectator. The political public sphere rarely fostered rational, enlightened debate about the common good, as the liberals implied when they attacked television, but tended to depend on the skillful manipulation of public opinion through the careful control of information. As the primary mode of mass communication in postwar America, however, television threatened to disrupt this communicative model by enabling the American people to actively interpret rather than passively receive political messages. Televised coverage of committee hearings undermined the traditional model of political communication in that it broke down the structural separation between the source of the political message and its intended recipient. Because television created the illusion that the American people were participating directly in the McCarthy hearings, it allowed them to see themselves as the producer rather than the consumer of the political message. In projecting their personal problems onto the political arena, they were giving meaning to what they saw, producing their own texts, and interpreting them according to their own lived experience.

Daniel Bell's introduction to *The New American Right*, "Interpretations of American Politics," explains more fully why liberal intellectuals were afraid that the privatization of the public sphere through television would erode the democratic process. Bell argued that the privatization of the public sphere had led to an "ideologizing" of American politics, or a reduction of American politics to a series of divisive and irresolvable ideological conflicts. Traditionally, the American political process had been pragmatic rather than ideological. It had enabled competing special interest groups to reach a consensus through bargaining: "The saving glory of the United States is that politics has always been a pragmatic give-and-take rather than a series of wars-to-the-death" (27). But the tendency of Americans to project their personal problems onto the political arena had radically transformed the political process. The privatization of the public sphere through television encouraged Americans to confuse political with moral issues. Ironically, although Americans had become more relaxed in the area of traditional morality, they had become "moralistic to an extreme in politics" (20). As a result, the American political process was no longer a pragmatic "give-and-take." It had shifted from "specific interest clashes, in which issues can be identified and possibly compromised, to ideologically-tinged conflicts which polarize the groups and divide the society" (27). This development supposedly threatened to destroy the democratic process: "The tendency to convert issues into ideologies, to invest them with moral color and high emotional charge, invites conflicts which can only damage a society" (27).

Although contributors to *The New American Right* agreed with Fiedler that the most appropriate categories for understanding political behavior were psychological rather than historical, unlike him, they were interested in developing a materialist understanding of postwar American culture. They related McCarthyism and the "ideologizing" of the political process directly to the economic prosperity of the postwar period. At the same time, however, they carefully distinguished their materialism from that of the Stalinized intellectuals who had been exposed by McCarthy. Sociologists David Riesman and Nathan Glazer, for example, in "The Intellectuals and the Discontented Classes," argued that in periods of economic prosperity "ideology tends to become more important than economics" (66) in determining political behavior. In "Social Strains in America," sociologist Talcott Parsons simply dismissed Marxist categories as not applicable to American economic structures: "The United States of course has a class structure; but it is one which has its primary roots in the system of occupational roles, and in contrast to the typical European situation it acts as no more than a brake on the processes of social mobility" (121). These rejections of Marxist theory and its explanatory powers served primarily as disclaimers. By arguing that the category of class could not adequately explain the structure of American society, the contributors to Bell's collection of essays made clear that they were working within a liberal rather than a Marxist intellectual tradition and thus were not fellow travelers.

But in carefully distinguishing their critical practice from that of the Popular Front, they were also adopting Fiedler's strategy in "Hiss, Chambers, and the Age of Innocence." Like Fiedler, they sought to recuperate liberalism from its association with the Stalinization of American culture in the 1930s. In claiming that Marxist categories were not applicable to American society, they repudiated their former ties to the Communist party. Parsons readily conceded that there had been a great deal of Communist infiltration of American society in the 1930s when "considerable numbers of the intellectuals became fellow-travellers" (130). But because of the economic prosperity of the postwar period, the Stalinization of leftist intellectuals could no longer be justified. The Communist party had supposedly "drastically repudiated the procedures of constitutional democracy" (131), and thus liberal intellectuals who remained committed to a materialist critique of American culture were truly enemies of the state. Moreover, America's economic recovery rendered the Marxist critique of the capitalist relations of production irrelevant. American prosperity required new categories of analysis, categories that could explain the continuing disaffection of large segments of the American population, despite the nation's growing prosperity. Parsons complained that the fellow traveling of liberal intellectuals rendered liberalism vulnerable to attack from the American Right. Citing the Popular Front, the American Right could attack liberalism "on the grounds that association with Communist totalitarianism makes anything liberal suspect" (132). Here Parsons tried to reclaim the liberal intellectual tradition for a materialist critical practice that could explain America's continuing social tensions without recourse to the category of class. Recourse to the category of class would only prove that liberalism had indeed been irreparably damaged by its history of fellow traveling.

Contributors to *The New American Right*, then, tried to develop a materialist critique of American culture that remained faithful to the liberal intellectual tradition at the same time that it retrieved that tradition from its tainted past. For them, the most important factor in American society was the desire for status; only the desire for status could adequately explain McCarthyism and the scapegoating of ethnic and religious minorities. Seymour Martin Lipset, for example, in "The Sources of the 'Radical Right,'" claimed that whereas leftist political movements committed to economic reform usually gained strength during periods of unemployment and economic depression, status politics predominated "in periods of prosperity, especially when many individuals are able to improve their economic position" (168). According to Lipset, the material prosperity of immigrant families in periods of economic recovery rarely translated into social acceptance. More-established American families felt threatened by the economic success of immigrant families and therefore refused to accept them into the middle and upper classes. Compounding this rejection was the tendency of well-to-do immigrants to misunderstand the class structure. They viewed "the status hierarchy as paralleling the economic structure; they believe that one need only move up the economic scale to obtain the good things of the society. But, as they move up economically, they encounter social resistance" (193). For this reason, they tended to become ardent supporters of McCarthy whose populism appealed to their resentment of the more privileged sectors of American society.[9]

The problem with this critique was that it still had recourse to the category of class. On the one hand, contributors to Bell's collection claimed that in American society class and status existed independently of each other; on the other hand, they inadvertently showed that they were directly related. Well-to-do immigrant families felt entitled to a higher social status because, economically, they belonged to the middle and upper classes; more-established American families tried to exclude well-to-do immigrants from the middle and upper classes because such immigrants lacked social status. Bell's contributors, in other words, denied that class and status were intimately connected, despite the evidence provided by their own examples. Their definition of class was too narrow; they conceived of class as a purely economic category. Still, their materialism required them to conceive of class in purely economic terms. Limiting their definition of class to the purely economic enabled them to separate America's economic and social systems. By establishing the existence of a status hierarchy independent of and not parallel to the economic ladder, they could focus on the social, rather than the economic, structures of American society. In this way, they provided an analysis of American culture more faithful to the liberal intellectual tradition. Although their critical practice was materialist, it considered the social the most important category for understanding American culture. They were clearly not working within the Marxist intellectual tradition, because they assumed that the social system functioned independently of the economic system.

Moreover, by isolating American social and economic structures from each other, they avoided the economic determinism of the Popular Front. Focusing on the status hierarchy rather than the economic ladder allowed them to psychologize political behavior. Despite their materialism, they argued that psychology rather than material conditions ultimately determined political behavior. McCarthyism and the scapegoating of religious and ethnic minorities could best be explained psychologically. In periods of economic prosperity, when the possibility of social mobility was greatest for religious and ethnic minorities, the desire for status could supposedly become pathological. Richard Hofstadter claimed that because immigrant families were "unable to enjoy the simple luxury of assuming their own nationality as a natural event, they are tormented by a nagging doubt as to whether they are really and truly and fully American" (48). Compounding this "nagging doubt" was the resistance they encountered as they climbed the economic ladder. Rejected by the middle and upper classes, they supposedly developed "an enormous hostility to authority, which cannot be admitted to consciousness, [and which] calls forth a massive overcompensation which is manifest in the form of extravagant submissiveness to strong power" (47). Hofstadter's tendency to reduce McCarthyism to a form of psychopathology was typical of the contributors to Bell's collection. Talcott Parsons also felt that the most useful categories for understanding McCarthyism were psychological rather than economic or political. He claimed that in periods of dramatic structural change such as the one America was experiencing, irrational behavior in the form of political extremism was inevitable: "There will tend to be conspicuous distortions of the patterns of value and of the normal beliefs about the facts of situations. These distorted beliefs and promptings to irrational action will also tend to be heavily weighted with emotion, to be 'overdetermined' as the psychologists say" (127).

In substituting psychological for historical categories of analysis, contributors to *The New American Right* were following the same trend as Fiedler in *An End to Innocence*. In "Afterthoughts on the Rosenbergs," originally published in *Encounter* in 1953, Fiedler argued that the Rosenbergs should have been pardoned.[10] Although he had no doubt they were guilty, he felt they deserved clemency on humanitarian grounds: "Under their legendary role, there were, after all, *real* Rosenbergs, unattractive and vindictive but human" (1, 33). Indeed, the real tragedy of their case was that they seemed to deny their own humanity. They allegedly defined their identities solely in political terms: "For even at the end the Rosenbergs were not able to think of themselves as real people, only as 'cases,' very like the others for which they had helped fight" (1, 38). For this reason, Fiedler thought they provided an especially graphic example of the tensions in American society between the public and private spheres: "In the face of their own death, the Rosenbergs became, despite themselves and their official defenders, symbols of the conflict between the human and the political, the individual and the state, justice and mercy" (1, 33). Fiedler's series of binary oppositions is revealing. He wanted to open up a space in American culture in which politics could not intervene, and thus he needed to reify the distinction between the public and private spheres. His argument required him to exclude politics from the network of discourses in which the subject was constructed. The subject of the Cold War consensus had to see its "humanity" in constant and irresolvable conflict with the state. Fiedler suggested indirectly that the subject's political identity was purely a function of its relation to the state, and that it entered into this relation only when exercising its rights as a citizen. Thus its political identity was an artificial construct of the democratic process rather than an extension of its "real" humanity and could never exhaust its subjectivity, as the Rosenbergs mistakenly believed.

To establish their hegemony over the postwar settlement, the contributors to *The New American Right* similarly needed to reify the distinction between the public and private spheres. They agreed with Fiedler that the subject's political identity was operative only when it entered into direct relation to the state. They felt that the privatization of the public sphere through television encouraged the subject to see its political identity as an extension of its own personal history. As a form of mass communication, television constructed a subject whose political behavior was psychologically motivated. By denying political agency in this way, their analysis of postwar American culture enabled them to oversee the postwar settlement. They provided a vision of American society in which the political process remained free of the "taint" of ideology. Pluralistic democracies not only tolerated ethnic and religious diversity, but also strictly maintained the distinction between the public and private spheres. Thus liberal Democrats would never permit any one special-interest group to dominate, or to claim a monopoly of, the political system, as the Republicans had under McCarthy's leadership.

Rear Window and the Psychopathology of Surveillance

Alfred Hitchcock's *Rear Window* participated in this extended ideological struggle among liberal intellectuals for establishing their hegemony over the postwar settlement. It helped to perform the necessary cultural work by extending the Cold War consensus beyond the political system to the cultural realm. Critics usually interpret *Rear Window* as Hitchcock's critique of the voyeuristic economy of the filmic system.[11] Jeff's constant scrutiny of his neighbors through his telephoto lens reduces spectatorial pleasure to a form of voyeurism. Jeff represents the spectator, transfixed by the events in the apartment complex opposite his window, which acts as a kind of screen. The spectator readily identifies with Jeff because, like him, s/he is immobilized in a chair and must limit her/his activity to looking. Consequently, s/he feels complicit with Jeff's transgressive desires. Because the spectator derives pleasure from looking at the images on the screen, s/he too must be fixated at an infantile stage of psychosexual development. Although it seems to me that *Rear Window* does indeed conceive of spectatorial pleasure as a form of fetishistic scopophilia, this reading does not adequately explain why the film would want to discredit the cinematic apparatus. In particular, it fails to identify the historical conditions that would have made the film's critique of its own system of representation possible. Critics who use *Rear Window* to substantiate Lacanian theories of the cinematic apparatus conflate Hitchcock's critique of spectatorial pleasure with their own.[12] For the film does not so much critique the voyeuristic economy of the cinematic apparatus as try to retrieve the cinematic apparatus from its contamination by the emergence of the national security state.

The emergence and consolidation of the national security state had reduced voyeurism to a surveillance practice. In appropriating the technology of the filmic system, the national-security apparatus politicized voyeuristic pleasure. According to the specular logic of the national security state, voyeurism was no longer a private form of erotic pleasure but a mode of political behavior intended to expose potential enemies of the state. In mobilizing spectatorial pleasure for its own purposes, the national security state virtually guaranteed that the individual would not so much watch others for erotic pleasure as scrutinize them for any indication of political and/or sexual deviance that conflicted with the nation's security interests. The cinematic apparatus was directly implicated in this politicization of voyeuristic pleasure. The filmic text allowed the spectator to legitimately engage in voyeurism in a public space. Consequently, it facilitated the appropriation of spectatorial pleasure by the national-security apparatus. In a sense, voyeurism had already become a form of public pleasure

through the institutionalization of the filmic system as a narrative form
that encouraged the spectator's total absorption in the diegesis.[13] But
the filmic system contributed to the politicization of voyeurism in
other ways. Like television, it threatened to undermine the structural
separation between the source of the message and its intended recipient critical to propagandistic models of communication. Every aspect
of the cinematic apparatus, from the darkened auditorium to the
placement of the projector behind the spectator, conspired to make the
spectator confuse her/himself with the characters on the screen.[14] In so
doing, it collapsed the distinction between the public and private
spheres. The spectator mistakenly saw her/himself as the producer
rather than the consumer of the images projected on the screen. For
this reason, filmic discourse helped to insert the spectator into a Mc-
Carthyite, rather than a liberal, subject position.

But the filmic system was even more directly implicated in the
politicization of voyeuristic pleasure. For in the early 1950s, Hollywood studios produced a series of low-budget, Cold War propaganda
films such as *I Was a Communist for the FBI* (1951) and *My Son John* (1952)
that justified the politicization of the private sphere.[15] These films
encouraged the spectator to scrutinize her/his psyche for any indication of sexual and/or political deviance that might throw doubt upon
her/his loyalty. The "enemy within" was not limited to the Communists, homosexuals, and lesbians who had supposedly infiltrated the
federal government; it also included the individual's own psyche. As
the site of unconscious, potentially transgressive desires, the psyche
constantly threatened to betray the individual and, by extension, the
nation's security interests. Ironically, such films politicized privacy as a
way of preserving it. Although obviously it would be absurd to reduce
Hitchcock's cinematic practices to the crude propaganda of *My Son
John* or *I Was a Communist for the FBI*, they were nevertheless complicit
with Hollywood's attempt to legitimate the national security state
through the use of the cinematic apparatus. As I showed in chapter 2,
Strangers on a Train exploited the voyeuristic economy of the filmic
system for the purposes of internal security. It tried to conscript the
spectator for the national security state by addressing her or him
libidinally and showed that s/he could derive voyeuristic pleasure
from clandestinely observing and exposing homosexuals and lesbians

who "passed" as heterosexuals. Thus it legitimated the right of the state to regulate the sexual practices of all Americans, whether homosexual or heterosexual, in the name of national security.

Hitchcock's representation of spectatorial pleasure as a form of fetishistic scopophilia in *Rear Window* acknowledges the corruption of voyeuristic pleasure by the national-security apparatus. In suggesting that cinematic viewing was merely another form of surveillance, *Rear Window* tries to repudiate Hitchcock's own contaminated practices as a director, practices that implicated him, however indirectly, in the government persecution of suspected Communists, homosexuals, and lesbians. But the film also seems to want to reclaim voyeurism as a private form of erotic pleasure. It conflates voyeurism with the surveillance practices of the national security state in order to show that voyeuristic pleasure had become corrupt. Its representation of filmic pleasure directly implicates the filmic system in the rise of McCarthyism. It suggests that the national security state had successfully mobilized voyeuristic desire for the clandestine scrutiny and subsequent exposure of potential enemies of the state. The film's emphasis on the psychopathology of spectatorship implies that the specular logic of the filmic text helped to create the conditions for McCarthyism. Because of its voyeuristic structures, the filmic text constructs a spectatorial subject who is fixated at an infantile stage of psychosexual development and who, therefore, derives pleasure from violating the privacy of others. As a photojournalist, Jeff is a representative subject of the mass media. His spying on his neighbors is merely an extension of his photojournalism. Scrutinizing their activities through his telephoto lens acts as a substitute for his lack of photo assignments during his convalescence and suggests that his work as a photojournalist has paved the way for his transformation into a Peeping Tom. He has simply transferred the pleasure he derives from looking at the world through his camera to scrutinizing his neighbors' most private activities.

In other words, rather than representing the voyeuristic economy of the filmic text as necessarily corrupt and corrupting, Hitchcock's film tries to show that under the scopic regime of the national security state, voyeurism had become a surveillance practice. Jeff's voyeuristic practices are rooted in the establishment of a national-security apparatus that legitimated the use of the camera for intruding on the privacy

of others. His abuse of voyeuristic pleasure is directly related to a set of **101**
specific social conditions in which privacy had become politicized. In
shot after shot, the film tries to restore voyeuristic pleasure to the
private sphere by stressing the autonomy of the camera's look. Because the camera's look exists independently of Jeff, the spectator is
ultimately responsible for determining its structure. Jeff does not always see what the camera sees. When Lars Thorwald (Raymond
Burr), for example, leaves his apartment with a woman the morn-
ing after he has murdered his invalid wife, the camera moves back
through Jeff's apartment window and shows him asleep in his wheelchair, thereby suggesting that the camera can operate independently
of Jeff: the structure of its look does not depend on him. Even from the
very beginning, the film emphasizes the independence of the camera's
look from Jeff's corrupt use of it by constantly shifting between objective and subjective point-of-view shots. In the opening sequence, for
example, the camera pans the courtyard of Jeff's Lower East Side
apartment complex and briefly introduces us to each of his neighbors:
Lars Thorwald, a jewelry salesman, and his nagging invalid wife; Miss
Torso, a dancer who practices her sexually suggestive dance routines
in front of her window; a middle-aged, alcoholic musician suffering
from composer's block; a middle-aged couple who sleep on the fire
escape; and Miss Lonely Heart, a middle-aged spinster unable to find
the man of her dreams. It then moves back through Jeff's apartment
window and shows Jeff asleep in his wheelchair, sweating profusely in
the ninety-degree heat. Here the film makes a point of not adopting
Jeff's point of view. But if Jeff has not been controlling the camera's
look, then the spectator has: the pleasure s/he has derived from looking at Jeff's neighbors has not been mediated by Jeff. In this way, the
opening shots try to distinguish the voyeuristic economy of the filmic
text from the scopic regime of the national security state by returning
voyeuristic desire to the spectator's own psychical structures.

In relating Jeff's corrupt use of the camera to the rise of McCarthyism, the film tries to show that voyeuristic desire can be rehabilitated
for the postwar settlement. At the same time that the film acknowledges the contamination of its own voyeuristic economy by the scopic
regime of the national security state, it tries to construct alternative
forms of voyeuristic pleasure that are not political. For example, although Jeff's girlfriend, Lisa Fremont (Grace Kelly), derives pleasure

from observing Jeff's neighbors, she does not treat them as objects of public scrutiny but identifies with them. Indeed, she initially resists observing them because she does not want to violate their privacy and tells Jeff that his interest in their activities is "diseased." She only becomes interested in them when she discovers Miss Lonely Heart and Miss Torso, women with whom she can identify.[16] Whereas Jeff watches Miss Lonely Heart with amused detachment, Lisa identifies with the lonely spinster when she pretends to entertain a lover. When Jeff tells Lisa that she has nothing in common with Miss Lonely Heart, she replies: "Oh! You can see my apartment from here . . .?" She apparently knows what it is like to spend evenings alone fantasizing about the man of her dreams. She has a similar reaction to Miss Torso. When Jeff derisively compares Miss Torso to a "queen bee with her pick of the drones," Lisa defends her, for she knows how she would feel in a similar situation: "I'd say she's doing a woman's hardest job— juggling wolves." She feels sure that Miss Torso does not love any of the men she is entertaining in her apartment, even the "prospering looking one" she allows to kiss her on the balcony. When Jeff asks her how she can be so sure, she says, "You *said* it resembled my apartment, didn't you?"

In "Visual Pleasure and Narrative Cinema," an essay that continues to shape discussions of the libidinal economy of classical Hollywood cinema, Laura Mulvey has argued that Lisa does not truly become an object of Jeff's desire until she breaks into Lars Thorwald's apartment.[17] As she frantically searches the apartment for the murdered Mrs. Thorwald's wedding ring, Jeff observes her through his telephoto lens, thereby treating her as one of his neighbors: she is no longer an active subject of desire who aggressively pursues him but an object he masters through scrutinizing her. Although Mulvey is quite right to call attention to the intensification of Jeff's desire for Lisa in this scene, she misinterprets its significance. Jeff's fetishistic and scopophilic pleasure in looking at Lisa through his telephoto lens as she searches for the incriminating ring is important not so much because it allows him to master her as because it indicates an important shift in the voyeuristic structure of his gaze. Looking at Lisa through his telephoto lens not only intensifies his voyeuristic pleasure but also returns it to the private sphere. His interest in his neighbors' activities is no longer "diseased" but personal. In placing Lisa in danger, Thorwald's sudden return works to reconfigure Jeff's interest in him. Jeff can no longer observe Thorwald's murderous activities through his telephoto lens without becoming directly involved in them, because they now threaten Lisa. This shift in his way of looking becomes apparent even earlier in the film when Miss Lonely Heart is assaulted by a man she has picked up in a bar and brought back to her apartment for a drink. At first Jeff watches in fascination, but then abruptly turns away ashamed. Echoing Tom Doyle (Wendell Corey), the detective Jeff has asked to investigate Thorwald, Jeff says, "[Tom] might have gotten hold of something when he said it's pretty private stuff going on out there." For the first time in the film, Jeff is unable to use his camera to maintain a distance between himself and his neighbors. He looks away in shame because he feels complicit with the assault and can no longer treat Miss Lonely Heart as an object for his own private consumption; that is to say, he realizes that he too has violated her by constantly observing her through his telephoto lens.

Thus the structure of Jeff's voyeurism gradually shifts over the course of the film. Although he continues to derive pleasure from observing his neighbors, he no longer treats them as objects of public scrutiny but begins to connect with them by identifying with them. This shift in the organization of his look is perhaps most apparent in the film's climactic scene. There he tries to defend himself from Thorwald, who has entered his apartment to confront him, by popping the flash of his camera in Thorwald's face. But this recourse to his camera fails. Though momentarily blinded by the flash, Thorwald recovers his sight and manages to push Jeff out his apartment window into the very space he has refused to enter except through his telephoto lens. Jeff can no longer maintain a distance between himself and his neighbors through his camera but is as much a part of the apartment complex as they are. Indeed, he is no different from them, Thorwald included, because his methods of exposing Thorwald place him equally outside the law. He constantly encourages Doyle to violate Thorwald's constitutional rights and refuses to believe that Doyle cannot legally search Thorwald's apartment or open the trunk he has sent to his wife in upstate New York without a search warrant. He does not understand that even criminals have rights but seems to feel that suspicion alone should provide sufficient grounds for Thorwald's arrest. Here the film's critique of the McCarthyite subject resembles Fiedler's in

"Afterthoughts on the Rosenbergs." Jeff's observations of Thorwald reduce him to a "case." As a subject of the mass media, Jeff refuses to acknowledge Thorwald's "humanity"; he does not realize that as a private individual he has an obligation to show mercy even to murderers. Ironically, when Doyle tells him that Thorwald must have gone to the train station with his wife because he later told the building superintendent he had, Jeff dismisses the report as "a secondhand version of an unsupported story by the murderer himself." He does not seem to realize that his own story is second hand and unsupported, or that in systematically violating Thorwald's constitutional rights, he too is guilty of breaking the law.

The shot/reverse shot structure of the film's climactic scene visually expresses Jeff's problematic relation to the law. Shots of Jeff sitting in his wheelchair in the dark directly facing Thorwald are crosscut with shots of Thorwald standing in the doorway obscured by shadows. Because all we see is Jeff's darkened silhouette, he and Thorwald seem virtually indistinguishable; indeed, Jeff looks even more sinister and menacing than Thorwald. Although it is true that Thorwald has murdered his wife and should be exposed, Jeff, in relentlessly pursuing him, has violated his "humanity." We even experience a moment of sympathy for Thorwald when he desperately pleads with Jeff: "Say something. . . . Tell me what you want from me." Here the film reveals the "real" Thorwald under the murderer and in so doing tries to insert the spectator into a liberal subject position. It forces her/him to acknowledge that Thorwald is not a "case" but a human being who deserves her/his compassion, despite what he has done. Moreover, the shot/reverse shot structure of this scene enacts formally the reversal of Jeff's voyeuristic relation to Thorwald in the plot. Jeff is no longer scrutinizing Thorwald; rather, Thorwald is scrutinizing him. It is *his* mysterious behavior that is now open to question: why has he been observing Thorwald through a telephoto lens, writing him anonymous notes, and surreptitiously telephoning him to arrange secret meetings? The structure of this scene, in other words, locates Jeff outside the law by establishing a resemblance between him and the very murderer he has been trying to expose. Like Thorwald, he has been caught in the act of breaking the law and must now confess his guilt.

In trying to reprivatize the voyeuristic economy of spectatorial pleasure, Hitchcock's film demonstrates its support for the postwar settlement. The film's emphasis in the climactic scene on Jeff's resemblance to Thorwald indirectly ratifies the liberal critique of postwar American culture. Jeff's constant surveillance of his neighbors collapses the distinction between the public and private spheres. The ability of his telephoto lens to penetrate even the remotest corners of his neighbors' apartments makes privacy impossible because it reduces even their most intimate activities to a form of entertainment for his own private consumption. That is to say, there is no aspect of their personal life free from public scrutiny. In exposing their privacy to public scrutiny in this way, Jeff politicizes the private sphere. In the context of the McCarthy witch hunts, his surveillance of his neighbors' activities is a political act. A McCarthyite rather than a liberal subject, he inappropriately takes on the role of the state in trying to expose Thorwald. He does not seem to understand that his identity as a neighbor is in direct conflict with his identity as a citizen. Rather, he sees his relation to the state as an extension of his "real" self, a self overly inserted in mass culture.

Like the contributors to *The New American Right*, the film tries to show that the collapse of the distinction between the public and private spheres threatens to "ideologize" American society. One of the consequences of Jeff's politicization of the private sphere is that it polarizes the neighbors who become increasingly suspicious of one another. When the middle-aged couple who sleep on the fire escape discover that their dog has been strangled, the wife angrily accuses the whole apartment complex of having done it. Because they treat one another not as neighbors but as spies, they are all guilty of the dog's death: "Neighbors [should] like each other, [should] speak to each other." Although obviously such a comment is most applicable to Thorwald, the neighbor who strangled the dog, it also pertains to Jeff. Jeff neither likes nor speaks to his neighbors. His only contact with them is through his telephoto lens, and thus he too is complicitous with the "ideologizing" of the apartment complex, despite his refusal to become involved in it except vicariously. He thinks of his neighbors as potentially guilty of the most brutal crimes. But Jeff has done more than contribute to the politicization of the private sphere; he has also facilitated the privatization of the public sphere. His suspicions of Thorwald are psychologically rather than politically motivated. He pursues Thorwald, not because he wants to bring him to justice, but because he derives voyeuristic pleasure from doing so. In other words, he has allowed the scopic regime of the national security state to corrupt his voyeuristic desire. For him, voyeurism is no longer a private form of erotic pleasure but a surveillance mechanism. If he truly wanted to act on behalf of the state, he would prevent his construction as a subject of the mass media from determining his political behavior.

The correlation in the film between Jeff's voyeuristic interest in his neighbors and the McCarthy witch hunts indicates the extent to which progressive liberal intellectuals had succeeded in establishing hegemonic control over the production of the postwar subject. The film seems to share the position of the contributors to *The New American Right* insofar as it suggests that the tensions in American society between the public and private spheres are structurally necessary. It shows that Jeff's subjectivity is always in excess of his identity as a citizen of the state and in so doing tries to insert the spectator into a liberal subject position.[18] At the same time, however, that the film seeks to conscript the spectator for the postwar settlement, it exposes the contradictions in the liberal critique of postwar American culture and its theorization of the subject. In particular, it reveals that the distinction between the public and the private spheres is little more than a structuring fiction of pluralistic democracies. Ironically, according to Hitchcock's film, the only way to restore the distinction between the public and the private spheres is by modeling the private on the public: the private sphere must function as a pluralistic democracy. In this way, the film emphasizes the interpenetration of the public and the private spheres in pluralistic democracies. The private sphere becomes the primary site for the construction of the liberal subject, a subject who consents freely and spontaneously to the postwar settlement because it conceives of liberal democratic principles as based on common sense.

This contradiction in the film's own proposed solution to the postwar crisis is perhaps most obvious in its representation of Jeff and Lisa's relationship. The film structures their relationship according to the pluralistic model of democracy proposed by the contributors to *The New American Right* as a solution to the postwar crisis. The film represents their relationship as a pragmatic "give-and-take" and insists that the only way in which they can contain their differences is by compromising with each other. Basically incompatible, Jeff and Lisa represent competing special interests. They are both equally committed to their careers, Jeff as a photojournalist, Lisa as a model, and thus it does not seem likely they will ever marry. Although Lisa is obviously head over heels in love with Jeff and aggressively pursues him, Jeff refuses to marry her because, as he tells Stella (Thelma Ritter), the insurance company nurse who comes to his apartment every day to massage him, she is "too perfect." He thinks that she could never adapt to the hardships of his photo assignments. Moreover, whereas he wants a wife who would accompany him to out-of-the-way places like Kashmir, she wants him to quit his job at the magazine and open a studio in New York. Despite their differences, however, Jeff and Lisa resist "ideologizing" their relationship and eventually reach a compromise. In watching Lisa search Thorwald's apartment for the incriminating wedding ring, Jeff realizes that she is not "too perfect." If she can face the murderous Thorwald when he returns to his apartment unexpectedly, she can adapt to the hardships of remote places like Kashmir.

By the end of the film, Lisa also demonstrates a willingness to compromise. She no longer urges Jeff to remain in New York with her, but prepares to accompany him on his photo assignments. Her willingness to compromise is most obvious in the final shots of the film. The film ends the way it began, with a pan of the apartment complex. This time, however, the pleasure we derive from observing Jeff's neighbors works to depoliticize the voyeuristic economy of the filmic text. Our interest in them has become wholly personal. We enjoy looking at them because they have finally resolved their problems: Miss Lonely Heart has met and fallen in love with the middle-aged alcoholic musician who no longer suffers from composer's block; the middle-aged couple who sleep on the fire escape has gotten a new dog; and Miss Torso's soldier boyfriend has returned home from the Korean War. Repeating its movement in the opening shots of the film, the camera then moves back through the window of Jeff's apartment and shows Jeff dozing in his wheelchair, with a smile on his face. It then cuts to Lisa, who is lounging on a couch in front of Jeff's apartment window reading the sort of book he would enjoy, *Beyond the High Himalayas*. Slowly panning her, it carefully notes what she is wearing item by item: penny loafers, an old pair of blue jeans, and a red sport shirt, all items Jeff himself might wear on one of his assignments. Here, appropriately enough, Lisa expresses her willingness to make concessions through her clothes: she will accompany Jeff anywhere, even beyond the high Himalayas, if it will make him happy. But she also uses her clothes to show that there are limits to what she will concede. Lest we think she has completely abandoned her interests for Jeff's, the final shot of the film shows her stealing a glance at him to see if he is still asleep and then quickly exchanging the book she has been reading for a copy of *Harper's Bazaar*. Although she is willing to give up her modeling career for Jeff, she insists on maintaining her own separate identity. Fashion has retained its importance for her, as her use of her clothes in this scene makes clear.

The film, then, tries to resolve the postwar crisis by extending the Cold War consensus beyond the political arena to the cultural realm. Its representation of Jeff and Lisa's relationship insists that liberal democratic principles can provide the most effective structures for everyday life. Neither Jeff nor Lisa should try to dominate their relationship. Although they should certainly protect their own interests, they should not press their individual claims too aggressively, because to do so would be to risk "ideologizing" their relationship. Rather, they should try to identify the interests they have in common through bargaining with each other. In this way, their relationship helps to restore the distinction between the public and private spheres. Specifically, it helps to recontain Jeff's voyeurism in the private sphere by depoliticizing it. Lisa's willingness to make concessions returns her to the privatized space of the middle-class nuclear family. In giving up her modeling career, she no longer exposes herself to public scrutiny but becomes an object of private consumption solely for Jeff. The final shots of her lounging on Jeff's couch try to extend this recontainment of voyeuristic pleasure beyond Jeff to the male heterosexual spectator. The fragmentation of her body, its fetishization by the camera, insures that the male heterosexual spectator will also treat her as an object of private consumption. In slowly panning her, the camera allows the male heterosexual spectator to elude the threat of castration signified by her image. Her fragmented body guarantees the totality and coherence of his own, and thus he can return her look without fear of castration.

Here, however, the film contradicts its own critique of McCarthyism and the politicization of the private sphere through the rise of the mass media. For in trying to insert the male heterosexual spectator into a voyeuristic subject position that is not political, it enacts the very collapse of the distinction between the public and private spheres it seeks to reverse. The only way in which the male heterosexual spectator can treat Lisa as an object of private consumption is in the public space of the darkened auditorium. Moreover, because Jeff and Lisa's relationship enacts the Cold War consensus on a private level, it functions as an extension of the public sphere. It guarantees their free and spontaneous consent to the postwar settlement by fostering rational, enlightened debate about their common good. Thus the film ultimately suggests that the political identity of the liberal subject *should* wholly saturate its humanity. For if the subject's humanity did not coincide perfectly with its political identity, it might make political claims based on its identity as a gendered and/or racialized subject. For the liberals to maintain their hegemony over American culture, the liberal subject had to act as a political agent in the private as well as in the public sphere.

I have claimed that Jeff and Lisa's relationship resembles a pluralistic democracy because the film clearly wants us to see it in those terms. I also wanted to show that the film's representation of their relationship as a sort of pluralistic democracy suggests that the liberals had extended their hegemony over the political arena to the cultural realm. The film accepts unequivocally the applicability of liberal democratic principles to all aspects of American life. Now, however, I want to argue that the pragmatic "give-and-take" of Jeff and Lisa's relationship is one-sided. Lisa gives more than she takes. To be sure, Jeff finally agrees to marry her, but only after she has proven to him that she can make the necessary adjustments to his career as a photojournalist. Here the film inadvertently makes visible the political double bind in which the postwar settlement placed women and other historically disenfranchised groups. Lisa must not press her claims *as a woman*. Whereas Jeff, as a man, has a right to both a sexually satisfying marriage and a highly successful career, she does not. For her to insist otherwise would be to confuse her identity as a woman with her political identity. In claiming that she too has a right to a highly successful career, she would be acting as a feminist. Yet not to press her claims is already to confuse her identity as a woman with her

110   political identity. She willingly abandons her career because she realizes that as a middle-class married woman in postwar American society she has no right to one. Ultimately, then, Hitchcock's film enacts
the very limits of the liberal consensus. It tries to show that what Lisa
loses in the public sphere (a highly successful career) she gains in the
private (a sexually satisfying marriage), a claim it would hardly make if
she were a man. Thus it is willing to accommodate her interests, but
only within the confines of the privatized space of the middle-class
nuclear family.

4

THE FANTASY OF THE MATERNAL VOICE

The Man Who Knew Too Much and the Eroticization

of Motherhood

The important thing for a mother to realize is that the younger the child the more necessary for him to have a steady, loving person taking care of him. In most cases, the mother is the best one to give him this feeling of "belonging," safely and surely. . . . If a mother realizes clearly how vital this kind of care is to a small child, it may make it easier for her to decide that the extra money she might earn, or the satisfaction she might receive from an outside job, is not so important, after all.
—Dr. Spock, *The Common Sense Book of Baby and Child Care*

In the preceding two chapters, I tried to situate *Strangers on a Train* and *Rear Window* historically by relating them to the rise of McCarthyism and the postwar crisis of liberalism. I wanted to show that Hitchcock's films not only engage issues of gender and sexual identity, as film theorists have long recognized, but also helped to underwrite and consolidate the postwar settlement by ratifying the liberal critique of postwar American culture. My contention was that both films help to clarify the relation between the organization of gender relations in postwar American society and the ongoing crisis over national security. In chapter 2, for example, I used *Strangers on a Train* to argue that the identification of homosexuality and lesbianism as un-American functioned primarily as a strategy for containing resistance to the postwar settlement. The construction of "the homosexual" and "the lesbian" as national-security risks virtually guaranteed that gender and nationality operated as mutually reinforcing categories of identity. Examining *Strangers on a Train* in the context of the McCarthy witch hunts, I claimed that it tried to insert the spectator into a fixed, stable subject position by invoking the homophobic categories of Cold War political discourse. In chapter 3, I used *Rear Window* to call attention to the limits of the postwar settlement. I argued that *Rear Window*

112 tried to depoliticize voyeuristic pleasure by recontaining it within the private sphere and that in so doing it showed that the liberal consensus was experienced differently by individuals who were positioned differently within the social formation (by race, class, and gender). I also argued that its attempt to reclaim the cinematic apparatus from its contamination by the emergence of the national security state was directly related to the debates among Cold War liberals over the relation between the public and private spheres.

In this chapter, I want to continue to situate Hitchcock's films in relation to the postwar settlement, but with the intention of problematizing Hitchcock's status as an auteur. I will argue that the auteur theory, as it was elaborated by American critics and directors in the 1950s, was complicit with the emergence and consolidation of the national security state. My goal is to show that Hitchcock's attempts to establish himself as an auteur were an integral part of his project to underwrite the postwar settlement. I will claim that Hitchcock promoted his reputation as an auteur because he wanted to conceal the relation between his films and the discourses of national security. To substantiate my argument, I will compare the two versions of *The Man Who Knew Too Much*, the only film he remade. I have chosen to focus on these two films because they raise important questions about the unity and coherence of his work as a whole. In comparing the two versions of the film, I will try to show that Hitchcock's system of representation, which has become virtually synonymous with the textual system of classical Hollywood cinema as a whole, is not as homogeneous and monolithic as critics working within an auteurist tradition of film criticism have claimed.[1] Such critics usually argue that Hitchcock remade *The Man Who Knew Too Much* because he supposedly did not get it "right" the first time. For this reason, they tend to analyze the 1934 version of the film from the perspective of the remake and ignore its embeddedness in historically specific practices and institutions. William Rothman, for example, dismisses the original as a seriously flawed version of the remake. He claims that the "weaknesses of [the original] can be summed up by saying that it has no male figure who is [the heroine's] equal and does not acknowledge the implications of this imbalance."[2] Stressing the differences between the original and the remake, he argues that the remake provided Hitchcock with the opportunity to redress the "imbalance between husband and wife" that supposedly mars the original.[3]

Ina Rae Hark similarly ignores the historical specificity of the original by treating it as part of a directorial corpus. Although she quite rightly rejects Rothman's misogynistic argument that the lack of a male character who is the heroine's equal necessarily represents an imbalance in the original, she too analyzes it from the perspective of Hitchcock's work as a whole. Like Rothman, she argues that Hitchcock remade *The Man Who Knew Too Much* because the implications of the "imbalance" between the hero and the heroine continued to bother him.[4] To support her claims, she cites the following remarks Hitchcock made to François Truffaut when Truffaut asked him to explain his reasons for remaking the film: "Incidentally, there is an important difference between the two versions of *The Man Who Knew Too Much*. In the British version the husband remains locked up, so that the wife carries the action by herself in Albert Hall and till the end of the picture."[5] These comments are purely descriptive and tell us little about Hitchcock's reasons for remaking the film. They are clearly meant to promote his reputation as an auteur by positioning him as the punctual source of the film's meaning. Yet Hark interprets them as evidence of his dissatisfaction with the film's original version. She uses them to argue that he wanted to remake *The Man Who Knew Too Much* because it supposedly relinquished patriarchal authority to the mother and constituted a "document of male incompetence."[6] Moreover, she claims that he wanted to make a version of the film that would be more representative of his work as a whole because it corresponded to the "customary double plot" of the spy films modeled after *The Thirty-Nine Steps* (1936).[7]

I have discussed these readings in such detail not because I want to single them out as particularly egregious examples of recent critical approaches to the original version of *The Man Who Knew Too Much*, but because they seem to me to exemplify the problems with Hitchcock criticism in general.[8] Critics tend to ignore the historical specificity of Hitchcock's films and focus instead on their thematic unity and coherence. Although in the wake of poststructuralist theory auteurist approaches to film have become deeply problematic, critics continue to attribute to Hitchcock's films a monolithic, homogeneous system of representation that installs him as the stable point of authorial origin.[9] Consequently, they tend not to see Hitchcock as a subject in history, constituted in and through discourse, but rather attribute to him an unproblematic authorial agency. This approach to Hitchcock's corpus has serious limitations. To begin with, determining who is speaking in classical Hollywood cinema is notoriously difficult.[10] After all, part of the project of the Hollywood film is to deny the materiality of its textual system by concealing its function as a signifying practice. The so-called impression of reality of the cinematic apparatus virtually guarantees the spectator's total absorption in the diegesis. Moreover, the textual system of the Hollywood film is highly conventionalized and exceeds individual directors. For this reason, it tends to persist from one directorial corpus to another. To guarantee their legibility, individual films must conform to the conventions governing the production of meaning in the film industry. Consequently, the classical system tends to suppress or absorb the authorial traces of individual directors.

But there is a more serious problem with an approach that analyzes Hitchcock's films from the perspective of his work as a whole. For in stressing the thematic unity and coherence of his films, such an approach becomes complicit with his attempts to deny the historical specificity of his textual practices. As I noted above, Hitchcock promoted his reputation as an auteur by encouraging a teleological understanding of his work that stressed the continuity of his development as a director. He encouraged this understanding in a variety of ways. For example, he appeared briefly in each of his films, beginning with *The Lodger* (1926). These appearances functioned as a kind of authorial signature and were clearly meant to identify him as the stable point of textual origin.[11] Moreover, he encouraged the auteurist approach to his films promulgated by the critics associated with the French film journal, *Cahiers du Cinema,* in the 1950s.[12] These critics identified him as one of the few Hollywood directors who had successfully resisted the studio system and "authored" his films. In this way, Hitchcock tried to deny the extent to which his utterance had been determined by the conditions governing the mass production and consumption of Hollywood films in the postwar period. His films were supposedly not subject to the constraints of the film industry but were an expression of his own personal world view. This is not to deny that there is some justification for treating Hitchcock as the originating agency of his films. His careful supervision of each stage of production and the continuity of his artistic and technical collaborations allowed him to exercise considerable artistic control over his films, especially in the 1950s when he began working for Paramount Studios.

Still, this does not mean that his films were not subject to the conditions that governed the film industry in the 1950s. Nor does it mean that his textual practices can be understood in isolation from the dominant construction of social reality in the postwar period. On the contrary, Hitchcock's attempts to leave his signature on his films indicate the extent to which his textual practices were complicit with the surveillance practices of the national security state. In promoting his reputation as an auteur, Hitchcock tried to deny the historicity of his subjectivity, its construction across a multiplicity of conflicting discourses. In particular, he tried to position himself as a unified and coherent subject who occupied the Oedipalized subject position inscribed in his films. I have chosen to focus on the differences between the two versions of *The Man Who Knew Too Much* because I want to foreground the historicity of Hitchcock's subjectivity, its construction in relation to the discourses of national security. I will argue that Hitchcock spoke from a position within a network of discourses that placed considerable constraints on his utterance. This network was not limited to the textual system of classical Hollywood cinema but included the discourses that regulated the construction of male subjectivity at the particular historical moment in which he made his films. Moreover, this network was not fixed but constantly shifting. It was the site of intense ideological struggle and thus remained highly unstable throughout the period in which he worked as a director. For this reason, the libidinal economy of his films did not always correspond to Hollywood's regime of pleasure but frequently resisted it.

I will try to establish the relation between the historicity of Hitchcock's subjectivity and his textual practices by examining the two versions of *The Man Who Knew Too Much* in their historical contexts. Rather than reading the original as part of a directorial corpus, I will stress its relation to historically specific structures of domination and oppression. My goal is to show that Hitchcock's authorial system was not monolithic but responded to changes in historical circumstances. Because I want to show that Hitchcock did not always speak from a position within the textual system of classical Hollywood cinema but frequently resisted its operations, I will focus on the differences between the two versions of the film. I will try to explain these differences by locating them in Hitchcock's shifting relation to discourse. I will argue that the remake resists the textual operations of the classical system more than the original does, and that it reverses the hierarchy of sound established in the original in conformity with classical norms. Whereas the original tries to maintain the primacy of the image by subordinating auditory pleasure to visual pleasure, the remake disregards the primacy of the image and foregrounds auditory pleasure at the expense of visual pleasure. I will claim that this reversal is directly related to the remake's participation in a system of representations that was specific to the postwar period and that helped to underwrite the postwar settlement. This system stressed the importance of the bond between mother and child during the child's earliest years and in so doing discouraged women from pursuing careers outside the home. The remake is organized around a fantasy of the maternal voice that restages the spectator's primordial listening experience. In the remake, the maternal voice functions as a kind of sonorous envelope that wraps the child in a blanket of comforting sound. This fantasy enables the remake to stress the importance of the bond between mother and child during the child's earliest years. The remake exploits the auditory traces of the spectator's pre-Oedipal relations with the mother by staging an imaginary return to infantile plenitude and bliss. In so doing, it tries to insure the spectator's inscription within the discourses of national security.

The Problem of the Speaking Woman:
Hitchcock and the Advent of Sound

Because I will focus primarily on the different ways in which Hitchcock uses sound in the two versions of *The Man Who Knew Too Much*, I want to discuss briefly the set of conventions governing the incorporation of sound technology in classical Hollywood cinema. The advent of sound threatened to disrupt the textual operations of the classical system by undermining the primacy of the image, and the film industry developed a number of textual strategies for insuring that the sound track remained subordinate to the image track.[13] The incorporation of sound technology promised to enhance the perceptual intensity or impression of reality created by the cinematic apparatus. Unlike objects that become two-dimensional when represented by a photographic image, sound remains three-dimensional even after it has been recorded.[14] For this reason, its incorporation in the classical system added a spatial dimension to the two-dimensional screen, which significantly increased the spectator's absorption in the diegesis. This was important because it reinforced the organization of spectatorship that governed the reception of Hollywood films. One of the ways in which the film industry tried to anticipate and standardize the consumption of its products was by providing the spectator with an ideal vantage point from which s/he could enter the fictional world of films.[15] This explains the increasing reliance during the silent era upon linear narrative and the use of characters whose motivations were psychological. Such strategies insured that the consumption of films did not depend upon the historical specificity of individual spectators, their race, class, and sexual orientation, but upon their absorption in the diegesis.[16] The advent of sound promised to contribute to the increasing standardization of the consumption of films. By enhancing the impression of reality created by the cinematic apparatus, the use of sound reinforced and solidified the spectator's identification with the characters on the screen; in so doing, it helped to contain or neutralize the potentially disruptive effects of her/his participation in a multiplicity of different social formations and made individual acts of consumption more predictable.

At the same time, however, that the incorporation of sound promoted the mass marketing and consumption of Hollywood films by contributing to the homogenization of the audience, it also undermined the classical system by challenging the primacy of the image. To begin with, the three-dimensionality of recorded sound called attention to the two-dimensionality of the photographic image. In restoring speech to the body, the synchronization of voice and image added to the illusion of physical presence and visual depth created by the cinematic apparatus. Thus the perceptual intensity of the classical text became dependent upon the sound track. Moreover, whereas in silent film intertitles were used sparingly and signification depended almost entirely upon the image, in sound film the synchronization of voice and image was used to solidify the spectator's identification with the characters and was crucial to the production of meaning.[17] Consequently, it threatened to disrupt the classical system of representation. Although synchronization promised to reinforce the primacy of the image by containing sound within the diegesis and identifying its source, it nevertheless undermined the representation of women as objects of visual pleasure. The use of intertitles in silent film encouraged the fetishization of the female body by separating it from the female voice. The female body in silent film could be easily appropriated by the male gaze because the use of exaggerated gestures and facial expressions to compensate for the lack of sound constituted a moment of display reminiscent of the "cinema of attractions."[18] But by restoring the female voice to the female body, synchronization provided the female body with an imaginary unity and coherence it lacked in silent film and therefore rendered its appropriation by the male gaze more difficult.

One of the ways in which the film industry tried to insure that the female body continued to function as a fetish object was by applying synchronization unequally to male and female characters.[19] In classical Hollywood cinema, female characters are more bound by the image than are the male characters. They are deprived of verbal and auditory mastery and often have difficulty speaking. Their voices remain contained within the diegesis and are rarely allowed to function independently of their bodies. Only male characters are allowed to speak from the privileged position of the disembodied voice-over.[20] The film industry also tried to contain the threat posed by synchronization by subordinating the female voice to the female body. In the classical text, the female voice has an intractable materiality that exceeds signification. It has a distinctive timbre or tonal quality that anchors it firmly to the body. Female characters in classical Hollywood cinema often speak with a regional or foreign accent, and are reduced to uttering inarticulate cries and screams. As a result, their voices are what Kaja Silverman describes as "thick with body."[21] The sounds they emit seem to issue from the body rather than from the mind. In this way, the film industry insured that the incorporation of sound technology reinforced rather than undermined the representation of the female body as an object of visual pleasure. By applying synchronization unequally to the male and female characters, the classical text facilitated the appropriation of the female body by the male gaze. Whereas the male characters in classical Hollywood cinema are associated with meaning, the female characters are associated with nonmeaning and thus are more easily objectified.

Kaja Silverman tries to explain the corporealization of the female voice in classical Hollywood cinema in purely psychoanalytic terms.[22] She argues that the conventions governing the use of sound in the classical text subordinate the female voice to the female body in order to insure that the female voice functions as an acoustic mirror that reassures the male spectator of his bodily unity and coherence. Silverman's argument is compelling because, unlike most theories of the cinematic apparatus indebted to Lacanian psychoanalysis, it conceives of male subjectivity as continually at risk rather than as monolithically phallic. Still, it seems to me that the conventions governing the representation of the female voice in classical Hollywood cinema can also be explained historically. The subordination of the female voice to the female body can also be seen as a strategy for containing the emergence of the New Woman in the 1920s.[23] The incorporation of sound technology by the film industry coincided with the disruption of the traditional organization of gender relations following World War I. This disruption included the integration of women into the work force, which eroded the gender-specific division of labor; the shift to a consumer-oriented economy, which increased the social and economic importance of women; and the emergence of the New Woman. Although the New Woman was not as sexually liberated as her image suggested, her emergence nevertheless helped to erode the Victorian double standard. Because she insisted on controlling her own sexuality, the New Woman was especially threatening to the traditional organization of gender relations.

The film industry was partially responsible for the disruption of the traditional organization of gender relations following World War I because it contributed to the emergence of the New Woman. Hollywood was one of the few institutions in American society that acknowledged women's increasing social and economic importance. The film industry facilitated women's integration into the newly emergent consumer culture by producing films addressed specifically to them.[24] These films positioned them as subjects rather than as objects of desire. They provided them with an institutional opportunity to transgress the prohibitions against female scopophilia and in so doing challenged the patriarchal organization of the look. Intended primarily as vehicles for matinee "idols" such as Rudolphe Valentino and Ramon Navarro, these films were organized around the exhibitionistic display of the male body and had more in common with the cinema of attractions than with the emerging classical paradigm; consequently, they placed the female spectator in an unmistakably fetishistic and voyeuristic subject position. This is significant because fetishism and voyeurism were institutionalized in classical Hollywood cinema as specifically male perversions. Indeed, in the classical text, female characters who derive pleasure from looking are usually coded as sexually deviant. The conventions developed by the film industry for governing synchronization helped to contain the eroticization of the female gaze. By subordinating the female voice to the female body, the classical system instituted a regime of pleasure that reinstalled fetishism and voyeurism as primarily male perversions. The corporealization of the female voice reduced female characters to objects of visual and auditory pleasure and thus repositioned the female spectator as an object of desire.

Before turning to the two versions of *The Man Who Knew Too Much* and the different ways in which they incorporate sound, I want to clarify this discussion of sound technology by examining briefly Hitchcock's first "talkie," *Blackmail* (1929). Focusing on *Blackmail* will enable me to establish the textual strategies Hitchcock developed for containing the threat sound technology posed to the classical system. I have chosen to discuss *Blackmail* not only because it was Hitchcock's first talkie, but because it combines the techniques of both silent and sound film. Hitchcock had already made a silent version of *Blackmail,* and he incorporated footage from it in the sound film. The sound version of the film opens with a chase sequence taken from the silent version. Shot in a quasi-documentary style, the sequence shows the apprehension, interrogation, and incarceration of a criminal. Hitchcock's incorporation of the sequence seems meant to invite comparisons between the film's silent and sound versions. The only sounds we hear during the chase sequence are the accompanying musical score and an occasional sound effect. Its placement at the beginning of the sound version seems intended to establish the primacy of the image track before synchronization is introduced. It demonstrates the ability of silent film to construct a linear narrative largely from images and with the minimal use of sound. When the long-awaited dialogue is finally introduced, it is poorly dubbed and almost inaudible. The camera tracks the hero, Frank (John Londgen), and the Chief Inspector (Harvey Braban) as they walk down a corridor in Scotland Yard discussing the events recorded in the opening sequence. Because they are shot from behind, we cannot see their faces, which makes it almost impossible to follow their conversation: we cannot determine which of them is speaking. For this reason, the sequence frustrates our desire to see and hear them speak. Moreover, it establishes our desire to follow their conversation as a kind of auditory voyeurism. In tracking them from behind, the camera places us in the position of eavesdroppers and suggests that synchronization threatens to pervert the faculty of hearing by sexualizing it.

In other words, Hitchcock's first talkie tries to contain the threat the advent of sound posed to the classical system of representation by establishing a hierarchy in which auditory pleasure is subordinated to visual pleasure. It stigmatizes auditory pleasure as a perversion by positioning the spectator as an eavesdropper who derives pleasure from overhearing the private conversations of others. This desire to maintain the primacy of the image helps to explain Hitchcock's decision to dub the voice of the heroine, Alice.[25] The actor who played Alice, Anny Ondra, spoke with a heavy Czech accent, and Hitchcock decided to have her mouth her part while another actor, Joan Barry, spoke the words off screen. Critics usually explain this decision by arguing that Hitchcock wanted to represent Alice as realistically as possible, but this explanation does not seem wholly satisfactory. The decision to dub Alice's voice detracts from rather than enhances the film's reality effect. After all, it does not seem likely that a Chelsea shopgirl would have spoken with Barry's educated accent, and the disturbing effect of watching Ondra hesitate each time she speaks hinders the spectator's absorption in the diegesis by impeding her/ his identification with Ondra. The decision to cast Ondra in the part rather than, say, Barry also hindered the spectator's perceptual placement within the film's narrative space. Unlike Barry, Ondra was a silent-screen star well known to audiences for her roles in other films, and her presence hindered the spectator's identification with Alice. On the one hand, the casting of a star like Ondra should have encouraged the spectator's absorption in the diegesis by mobilizing more sustained structures of identification.[26] Spectators were already psychically invested in identifying with the characters Ondra played in her films because of their familiarity with her life off screen. On the other hand, her stardom exerted a kind of centrifugal force that counteracted the spectator's perceptual placement within the film's narrative space. Spectators knew that Ondra spoke with a heavy Czech accent and that the voice of her character had been dubbed.

In casting an actor whose voice had to be dubbed, however, Hitchcock virtually guaranteed that the spectator's auditory drive remained subordinated to her/his scopic drive. Because of her difficulty speaking, listening to Alice is not as pleasurable as watching her, and the film's representation of her has more in common with the cinema of attractions than with the emerging classical paradigm and its indirect mode of address. The film tries to establish a visual rather than an auditory relation between the spectator and Alice's body. For example, in the scene in which the artist (Cyril Ritchard) tries to rape her, Hitchcock has her undress behind a screen in the artist's studio. Although the screen prevents the artist from looking at her, she remains wholly visible to the camera. The split-screen effect of this sequence reinforces the exhibitionistic display of her body and places the spectator in an explicitly voyeuristic position in relation to her. The spectator is allowed to see what the artist is forbidden to see. In other words, the sequence has the structure of a peep show. The split-screen effect intensifies the spectator's voyeuristic relation to Alice by making the spectator feel as though s/he were engaging in a forbidden activity because s/he can see what the artist is prevented from seeing. This exhibitionistic display of Alice's body reinforces the hierarchy established in the silent chase sequence at the beginning of the film in which the soundtrack is subordinated to the image track. The libidinal economy of the sequence encourages the spectator to watch Alice rather than listen to her. Consequently, it discourages the spectator from identifying with her, despite her perilous situation. She has been reduced to a spectacle and no longer functions as a point of identification for the spectator.

This is not to ignore the extent to which Alice functions as an object of auditory as well as visual pleasure in this sequence. Precisely because her voice is not wholly anchored to her body, it has the

potential to become detached from it and to function independently as **123**
a spectacle. The film's textual system corresponds to the classical
paradigm in that it subordinates Alice's voice to her body. The attempted rape corporealizes Alice's voice by reducing her to uttering
involuntary and inarticulate cries. At the same time, however, her
voice becomes wholly detached from her body. The attempted rape
takes place off screen behind the draperies of the artist's bed. Thus we
hear, but do not see, Alice scream repeatedly, "Let me go!" In this way,
the film establishes a hierarchy in which Alice is more bound by the
image than are the male characters. In conformity with the classical
system, the film applies the synchronization of voice and image unequally to the male and female characters. Although Alice's voice is
allowed to function independently of her body in this sequence, it
remains corporealized. The inarticulate cries she emits are involuntary
and clearly issue from her body. Moreover, by refusing to anchor her
voice firmly to her body, the film deprives her of the illusion of bodily
unity and coherence it gives to the male characters through the use of
synchronization. As a result, her image lacks the physical presence
and visual depth of the other images, which are more evenly syn-
chronized. Her voice constantly threatens to become detached from
her body, as it does in this sequence, and thus she does not seem as
"real" as they do.

Where the film's incorporation of sound technology deviates from
the classical paradigm is in calling attention to the inequalities of its
own system of representation. Indeed, the film does not try to conceal
Alice's subordinate position in relation to sound technology but acknowledges it as a form of patriarchal oppression. The film thematizes
Alice's difficulty speaking and in so doing readily admits that in applying synchronization to the male and female characters unequally, it
deprives her of verbal mastery. Hitchcock stresses the consequences of
Alice's difficulty speaking by showing that it places her in a subordinate position in relation to her lover, Frank. As a representative of the
law, Frank does not lack verbal mastery but speaks authoritatively.
From the very beginning, Alice has difficulty asserting herself verbally.
In the scene in the tea room, for example, she cannot decide whether
to accompany Frank to the film *Fingerprints*. At first she agrees, but
then changes her mind when she sees the artist. When Frank gets
angry, she changes it back again. Frank becomes so frustrated by her

equivocation that he decides to go to the film without her. Her lack of verbal mastery becomes even more pronounced following the attempted rape. Assigned to investigate the artist's murder, Frank gains control of her speech. When she tries to confess her guilt, he prevents her from speaking, exclaiming peremptorily, "For God's sake, be quiet, Alice!" Moreover, he begins to speak for her. When Tracy (Donald Calthrop), the man who tries to blackmail Alice, asks Frank, "Why can't you let her speak?" Frank replies, "You mind your own business. In any case, she'll speak at the right moment." Thus Hitchcock traces Alice's subordinate position in relation to Frank directly to her difficulty speaking. Frank's ability to speak authoritatively as an officer of the law allows him to dominate her verbally. Frank prevents her from confessing to the murder by commanding her to remain silent and by speaking for her. Consequently, she is unable to prevent the police from pursuing Tracy to the roof of the British museum, where he plunges to his death, falsely accused of the artist's murder.

The extent to which Alice's difficulty speaking places her in a subordinate position is perhaps most apparent in the scene in which the artist tries to rape her. Like Frank, the artist gains control of her speech by dominating her verbally. He demonstrates his ability to do so when he plays the piano for her and sings a song called "Young Miss of Today" that is meant to refer to her. This song alludes to the emergence of the New Woman, which it celebrates. The artist clearly welcomes the erosion of the Victorian double standard because it legitimates his own sexual promiscuity. The song begins, "They say you're a wild, an awful child, Miss of Today," but the refrain repeats the phrases "there's no harm in you, Miss of Today" and "you're absolutely great, Miss of Today." The artist confuses Alice with the New Woman and sings the song as a kind of tribute to her. When he finishes singing the song, he tells her, "And that's a song about you, my dear." In this way, he places Alice in a subordinate position in relation to him. He uses the song to construct an image of her that is purely a projection of his own desire. Although she obviously has nothing in common with the sexually promiscuous woman described in the song, Alice is forced to accept the song as a description of her own sexually liberated behavior. Because she has difficulty asserting herself verbally, she is unable to resist the image the artist has constructed of her until it is too late. Indeed, she does not seem to realize that he has mistaken her for a typical Miss of Today, because she does not consider herself sexually promiscuous and has not accompanied him to his studio in order to have sex with him. When she does finally assert herself verbally, the artist simply ignores her, telling her, "Don't be silly, Alice." According to the patriarchal logic of the film, her actions speak louder than her words. In accompanying the artist to his studio, she identifies herself as a New Woman because she positions herself as a subject of desire.

In stressing the ability of the male characters to dominate Alice verbally, the film implicates the classical system in the subordination of women. The artist functions as a kind of diegetic surrogate for Hitchcock. Like the artist, Hitchcock tries to control Alice's speech. As we saw above, he refuses to allow her to speak with her own voice. He wanted her to conform to an image of femininity that corresponded to the spectator's expectations, and so he decided to dub her voice. Ironically, however, in so doing, he undermined rather than furthered his attempts to control the image she projected on screen. Her difficulty speaking constantly reminds the spectator that she is composed of parts from different women (Anny Ondra's body, Joan Barry's voice) and therefore does not correspond to a "real" woman but is purely a construction. This link between Hitchcock and the artist constitutes a powerful indictment of the classical system. It suggests that the subordination of the female voice to the female body in the classical text constitutes a form of rape. In conformity with the conventions governing the use of sound, Hitchcock applied the synchronization of voice and image unevenly to Alice. In so doing, he deprived her of the illusion of bodily unity and coherence and promoted the fetishization of her image by the male spectator. Because her voice is not wholly anchored to her body and constantly threatens to become detached from it, it has the potential to function independently as a fetish object. For this reason, Hitchcock's refusal to allow Alice to speak with her own voice implicates him in the artist's attempt to rape her. Like the artist, he does not listen to her when she speaks but tries to make her conform to an image of femininity that does not suit her.

This is not to exaggerate Hitchcock's indictment of the classical system and the way in which it applied synchronization unequally to male and female characters. At the same time that Hitchcock implicates himself in the artist's attempt to rape Alice, he also tries to align the female spectator's desire with the film's libidinal economy by indicating that Alice is partially responsible for the attempted rape. The film is organized around a paranoid fantasy about the impact of the emergence of the New Woman on the film industry. Hitchcock seems to question his own ability to anticipate and control the film's reception. He stresses the construction of female subjectivity in relation to the consumer culture of the 1920s. His constant allusions to the New Woman draw attention to the female spectator's newly emergent position as a subject of desire and imply that the eroticization of the female gaze threatened to disrupt the classical system of representation. In positioning women as subjects of desire, the film and advertising industries discouraged them from identifying with female characters who functioned primarily as objects of visual and auditory pleasure. For this reason, it was unlikely that they would submit passively to Hitchcock's attempts in *Blackmail* to position them as objects rather than as subjects of desire. One of the ways in which Hitchcock tried to prevent them from resisting their perceptual placement within the film's narrative space was by suggesting that in accompanying the artist to his studio, Alice was "asking for it." In the scene immediately following the attempted rape, the soundtrack plays a reprise of the song "Miss of Today" and in so doing obliquely suggests that there is not much difference between Alice and the sexually promiscuous women described in it. Although Alice clearly murders the artist in self-defense, she insists on controlling her own sexuality and therefore is partially responsible for the rape. That is to say, she resembles the woman described in the song because she refuses to cede control of her body to Frank and openly defies his authority.

This emphasis on the construction of female subjectivity in relation to the consumer culture of the 1920s establishes a link between Hitchcock and Frank. Indeed, like the artist, Frank functions as a kind of diegetic surrogate for Hitchcock. Frank's relationship with Alice parallels Hitchcock's relationship with the female spectator. Consequently, it can help us to clarify the relation between Hitchcock's refusal to allow Alice to speak with her own voice and the institutionalization of female forms of fetishism and voyeurism. Underlying Frank's desire to control Alice's speech is a desire to control her sexuality. He associates her attempts to assert herself verbally with her attempts to position herself as a subject of desire. Although he knows that she murdered the artist in self-defense, he considers her complicit with the attempted rape. Merely because she is present in the artist's studio, she is an accessory to the crime. After all, in accompanying the artist to his studio, she openly defied Frank's authority, and Frank prevents her from confessing to the murder because he is afraid that she will implicate him as well as herself in the attempted rape. His inability to control her sexuality calls into question his authority as a representative of the law. At the same time, however, the attempted rape allows him to gain control of her body. The attempted rape makes Alice regret that she accompanied the artist to his studio and thus guarantees that she will never again defy Frank's authority. In other words, the blackmail referred to in the film's title is the attempted rape, which coerces Alice into ceding control of her body to Frank. Frank's function as a kind of diegetic surrogate for Hitchcock helps to clarify the film's ideological project. Hitchcock uses the attempted rape to discourage the female spectator from positioning herself as a subject of desire. The incorporation of sound technology threatened to reinforce the construction of female subjectivity in relation to the consumer culture of the 1920s, and by implicating Alice in the attempted rape, Hitchcock encourages the female spectator to reject her newly emergent position as a subject of desire. He tries to show that women who position themselves as subjects of desire are "asking for it" because they make themselves vulnerable to rape and other forms of sexual violence.

I have dwelt on *Blackmail* at such length because I want to clarify Hitchcock's use of sound by situating it historically. I have tried to show that Hitchcock deprived Alice of the illusion of bodily unity and coherence the synchronization of voice and image gave to the male characters because he wanted to contain the eroticization of the female gaze promoted by the advertising and film industries. In the original version of *The Man Who Knew Too Much*, Hitchcock continued to try to contain the construction of female subjectivity in relation to the consumer culture of the 1920s by subordinating the female voice to the female body. Like Alice, Jill (Edna Best), the heroine of the original, tries to position herself as a subject of desire. But whereas Alice lacks verbal mastery and has difficulty speaking, Jill occupies a masculine position in relation to language. She constantly engages in witty repartee and tries to dominate her husband, Bob (Leslie Banks), verbally. When the film opens, she has not yet committed herself to her family; indeed, she seems to resent the constraints her marriage places on her sexuality. She refuses to cede control of her body to Bob and constantly flirts with Louis Bernard (Pierre Fresnay), an undercover agent for the British Foreign Office who is masquerading as a champion skier. She also seems to resent her responsibilities as a mother and jokes about disowning her daughter, Betty (Nova Pilbeam). When Betty interrupts a clay pigeon–shooting contest in which Jill is competing, Jill turns to Bob and says "Your child's going to cost me the match. . . . If I lose, I'll disown it forever." When Jill loses the contest, she blames Betty for preventing her from concentrating and says to her opponent, only half-jokingly, "Let that be a lesson to you. Never have children."

Jill's wish to disown Betty soon becomes a reality when Betty is kidnapped by some spies who are plotting to assassinate a European statesman named Ropa. Bob and Jill learn of the plot when one of the spies, Jill's opponent in the clay pigeon–shooting contest, shoots Louis. Before he dies, Louis tells Jill to retrieve from his hotel room a note that he has hidden inside his shaving brush indicating when and where the assassination is supposed to take place. The spies kidnap Betty to prevent Bob and Jill from revealing the contents of the note to the British Foreign Office. By inhibiting her speech, the kidnapping serves as a kind of punishment for Jill's masculine relation to language. The film represents her verbal mastery as a violation of the hierarchical structure of the patriarchal family. She uses her verbal skills to place Bob in a subordinate position in relation to her. Whereas she occupies a masculine position in relation to language, he occupies a feminine one. He does not know how to respond to her verbal sallies. In the scene in which Louis is killed, for example, Jill tries to make Bob jealous by flirting with Louis. She stages a conversation with Louis in which she complains about Bob as a lover and speaks loudly enough so that Bob will overhear her. But rather than responding verbally, Bob merely chokes on his drink. In other words, by inhibiting Jill's speech, the kidnapping establishes a relationship between her and Bob that is more in keeping with the hierarchical structure of the patriarchal family. The kidnapping places her in a position in relation to language that is more appropriate to her gender.

She no longer tries to dominate Bob verbally, but acknowledges her subordinate position as a speaking subject.

The original version of *The Man Who Knew Too Much* addresses the construction of female subjectivity in relation to the discourses of the advertising and film industries more explicitly than does *Blackmail*. It links Jill's refusal to acknowledge her subordinate position in relation to Bob directly to issues of female spectatorship. Jill constantly violates the codes that traditionally governed female spectatorship. She refuses to occupy the position of the passive and compliant female spectator. As we have seen, she insists on competing in the shooting contest rather than watching it from the sidelines. Although in so doing she performs before an audience, her participation in the contest does not reduce her to a spectacle. Rather, it phallicizes her by establishing her skills in a traditionally masculine sport. Even when she loses the contest, she refuses to occupy the position of the passive and compliant female spectator. She joins Bob and Betty in the audience and begins talking excitedly, thereby disrupting the contest. The other spectators must turn around and ask her to be quiet so that her opponent can concentrate. She similarly defies the codes that traditionally governed female spectatorship when she flirts with Louis. Although her flirtation with Louis constitutes an exhibitionistic display meant to attract Bob's gaze, it places Bob in the traditional position of the female spectator. She makes a spectacle of herself not so much to incite Bob's desire as to flaunt her identity as a subject of desire. Despite their marriage, she refuses to cede control of her body to Bob. For example, in the scene described above, she allows Bob to overhear her conversation with Louis because she wants him to know that she does not accept the hierarchical structure of the patriarchal family. She resents the constraints the institution of marriage places on her sexuality, and, in staging the conversation with Louis, she makes clear her identity as a subject rather than as an object of desire.

The film similarly emphasizes the construction of Betty's subjectivity in relation to the discourses of consumption addressed specifically to women. Like Jill, Betty resists the codes that traditionally governed female spectatorship. In the opening sequence, she too refuses to watch the sports events passively from the sidelines and undermines the traditional distinction between spectator and performer. The film begins with her disrupting the downhill skiing competition. She darts onto the slope to retrieve her dog, which has jumped out of her arms. Louis, who is skiing down the slope, must fall in order to avoid hitting her, and he crashes into the spectators, thereby involving them directly in the performance. As we saw above, Betty also disrupts the shooting contest in order to ask Jill for permission to stay up late. She seems to want to occupy the positions of spectator and performer simultaneously and competes with Jill for the audience's attention. She refuses to remain a spectator and joins Jill on the platform, as though she too were competing in the contest. In stressing Jill's and Betty's refusal to occupy the traditional position of the female spectator, Hitchcock calls attention to a potential crisis in the classical system. He tries to show that the very textual strategies the film industry had developed for mass marketing its products threatened to disrupt its system of representation. According to Hitchcock, the eroticization of the female gaze had made it more difficult to anticipate and control the reception of the classical text. Fetishism and voyeurism were no longer specifically male perversions but could be legitimately engaged in by women. Both Jill and Betty reject the position traditionally occupied by the female spectator and try to position themselves as subjects of desire. In this way, Hitchcock suggests that the discourses of the advertising and film industries hindered rather than promoted the female spectator's absorption in the diegesis. Given their newly emergent positions as subjects of desire, the women in the audience were unlikely to submit passively to the film's attempts to interpellate them into an ideological position.

In serving as a kind of punishment, the kidnapping reverses the construction of Jill's subjectivity in relation to the discourses of consumption addressed specifically to women. Jill functions increasingly as an object, rather than a subject, of desire. The kidnapping places her in the position traditionally occupied by the female spectator. It forces her to acknowledge her subordinate position in the hierarchical structure of the patriarchal family. She begins to occupy a position in relation to language not unlike Alice's in *Blackmail*. Because the kidnapping has inhibited her speech, she no longer tries to dominate Bob verbally, but accepts his authority to speak for the family. In the scene in which Bob shows her the note written by the kidnappers, she becomes speechless and faints. When she does assert herself verbally, she does so as a mother who wants to protect her daughter's life, not as a verbally adept woman who openly defies patriarchal authority. When the man from the British Foreign Office tries to persuade Bob to reveal the contents of the note by telling him that Ropa's assassination could lead to another world war, she prevents Bob from speaking and exclaims, "Our child comes first, she must come first!" Jill's loss of verbal mastery culminates in the scenes at Albert Hall. There the subordination of her voice to her body becomes complete: she is reduced to uttering an inarticulate cry. Although she has prevented Bob from revealing the contents of the note, she thwarts the assassination attempt by screaming. In so doing, she relinquishes control of her voice to the state. She allows the state to determine when and how she speaks. In this way, she renounces her position as a subject of desire. She shows that she is willing to sacrifice her interests to those of the state.

In other words, the scenes at Albert Hall point to the reconstruction of Jill's subjectivity in relation to the codes that governed female spectatorship before the emergence of the discourses of mass consumption. She functions in these scenes primarily as an object of visual and auditory pleasure. These scenes perform virtually the same function as the silent chase sequence at the beginning of the sound version of *Blackmail*. Relying on the techniques of silent film, they demonstrate the ability of the classical text to construct a linear narrative wholly from images and without the use of synchronization. We see, but do not hear, Jill, who must resort to the exaggerated gestures and facial expressions of the silent film star to communicate her anguish and indecision. The sound track functions primarily as a supplement to the image track. The rising tension of William Walton's "Storm Cloud Cantata" adds to the suspense of the sequence and helps to communicate Jill's anguish and indecision. The scenes at Albert Hall also indicate a shift in Jill's relation to patriarchal discourse by positioning her as a passive and compliant female spectator. Because she does not want to endanger Betty's life by thwarting the assassination attempt, she no longer defies the codes that traditionally governed female spectatorship and passively watches the performance. Shot after shot shows her looking first at Ramon (Frank Vosper), the man who was her opponent in the shooting contest and who has been hired by the spies to assassinate Ropa, and then at Ropa. The dizzying movement of the camera as it cuts from one to the other and back again communicates visually her anxiety in trying to decide whether to disrupt the performance. The image eventually goes out of focus, indicating her total absorption in the performance. She has allowed the rising tension of the cantata to overwhelm her perceptions. When she finally disrupts the performance, she does so in a way that does not conflict with her position as a passive and compliant female spectator. In screaming, she acts as a kind of proxy for the state and acknowledges its authority to control her voice. In the scenes at Albert Hall, then, she no longer tries to position herself as a subject of desire but functions as an object of visual and auditory pleasure.

The reconstruction of Jill's subjectivity in relation to the discourses that traditionally governed female spectatorship is perhaps most obvious in the film's climactic scene in which she rescues Betty by shooting Ramon. What is interesting about this scene is that we do not actually see her shoot Ramon. The camera cuts from a long shot of Betty and Ramon standing on the roof of the building in which the spies are holed up to a close-up of Jill's face. We hear a gunshot as the camera cuts to another long shot of Betty and Ramon in which we see Ramon fall from the building. The camera then cuts to a medium shot of Jill holding the gun, which is smoking. In other words, the film does not actually show her shooting Ramon but indicates it. The editing of this sequence is striking because it differs significantly from the editing of the sequence in which Jill competes in the shooting contest. In that sequence, the camera shows Jill taking aim and shooting. The differences between the editing of the two sequences calls attention to the shift in Jill's relation to patriarchal discourse. In showing Jill taking aim and shooting, the earlier sequence indicates her desire to usurp patriarchal authority. We see Jill engaging in a traditionally masculine activity that phallicizes her. Thus one of the effects of the editing of the later sequence is to dephallicize Jill by cutting to a long shot of the building where the spies are just when she is about to shoot Ramon. It avoids showing her engaging in an activity that conflicts with her identity as a wife and mother because she no longer resists the hierarchical structure of the patriarchal family but accepts her place in it. What distinguishes this sequence from the earlier one is that she uses her skills as a marksman to fulfill her responsibilities as a mother, not to compete in a traditionally masculine sport. She no longer desires to usurp patriarchal authority but submits to the constraints her responsibilities as a mother place on her sexuality.

Like *Blackmail*, then, the original version of *The Man Who Knew Too Much* establishes a hierarchy of sound in which the female characters are more bound by the image than are the male characters. We do not actually see Jill shoot Ramon because showing her engaging in a traditionally masculine activity would contradict her function as an object of visual and auditory pleasure. Her agency as a character is limited to the fulfillment of her responsibilities as a wife and mother. Because the Albert Hall sequence is crucial to establishing this hierarchy of sound, I want to return to my earlier comments about it and amend them. I argued that the sequence performs the same function as the silent chase sequence at the beginning of *Blackmail* in that it establishes the primacy of the image by demonstrating the ability of the classical text to construct a linear narrative wholly from images. Now I want to examine the textual operations whereby the sequence establishes the primacy of the image in more detail. Throughout the sequence, the sound track and the image track compete for control of the film's textual system. The tension and suspense of the sequence depend heavily upon the sound track. Hitchcock prepares us for the sequence when he has Abbott (Peter Lorre) play a recording of Walton's "Storm Cloud Cantata" earlier in the film in order to show Ramon the precise moment in the performance when he can shoot Ropa without the audience hearing the shots. Consequently, throughout much of the sequence, our attention is riveted on the sound track. We listen closely for the moment Abbott has indicated on the recording because we are curious to see if Jill will disrupt the performance before the assassination occurs. In other words, our absorption in the diegesis at this point in the film depends heavily upon the sound track. In gradually building toward a crescendo, the cantata is largely responsible for the tension and suspense we feel throughout the sequence.

Still, the editing of the sequence ultimately guarantees the primacy of the image because it works to subordinate the sound track to the image track. Hitchcock uses a series of rapidly cut shots to indicate that the moment of the assassination attempt is approaching. Shortly before we hear the long-awaited clash of cymbals, the camera cuts from a close-up of Jill's face to a shot of Ropa, then to a shot of the conductor turning the pages of Walton's score, then to a shot of a musician preparing to use the cymbals, and finally to a shot of Ramon aiming his gun in Ropa's direction. Hitchcock intensifies the suspense of this sequence of shots by rapidly repeating them shortly before Ramon shoots. Thus Hitchcock ultimately relies on the image track to indicate the moment when the assassination is supposed to occur. The repetition of shots shortly before Ramon shoots directs our attention away from the sound track to the image track. The role of the sound track has become supplemental rather than primary. Whereas before we were anxious to hear the clash of cymbals, now we are anxious to see it.

One of the ways in which Hitchcock consolidates and maintains this hierarchy of sound is by representing Abbott and Nurse Agnes (Cicely Oates) as the verbal doubles of Bob and Jill. Like Bob, Abbott lacks verbal mastery and occupies a feminine position in the film's hierarchy of sound. He does not speak English fluently and is verbally dependent on Nurse Agnes, who must translate for him. In the film's opening sequence, for example, when Louis crashes into the spectators and knocks him down, Bob asks Abbott if he is alright and he replies, "Better ask my nurse. My English isn't good enough for me to know." His voice only reinforces this feminine position in the film's hierarchy of sound. It has an intractable materiality that exceeds signification. Like the voices of the female characters, it is corporealized. It has a high-pitched, nasal quality that, according to the film's system of signification, connotes femininity rather than masculinity. Nurse Agnes, on the other hand, occupies a position in the film's hierarchy of sound that resembles Jill's. Just as Jill dominates Bob verbally, Nurse Agnes dominates Abbott verbally. She speaks more authoritatively than he does and thus is a more effective leader of the organization of spies. As he did with Jill, Hitchcock emphasizes Nurse Agnes's masculine relation to language by showing her wielding a gun. For example, during the siege at the end of the film, when Ramon defies Abbott's orders and threatens to surrender to the police, she pulls a gun on him and says, "You took this on for our cause and you've got to go through with it." Significantly, it is at this point that she is killed by a stray bullet and permanently silenced. Moreover, like Abbott's voice, hers seems to exceed the gender of her body. But whereas his is corporealized and connotes femininity rather than masculinity, hers is

not wholly anchored to her body and is allowed to function independently of it. Low and husky, it occupies a privileged position in the
film's hierarchy of sound because it is not subordinated to her body
and its tonal quality connotes masculinity rather than femininity.

This becomes apparent in the scenes at the Tabernacle of the Sun
in which she uses her voice to gain control of Clive (Hugh Wakefield),
the friend who accompanies Bob to Wapping in search of Betty's
kidnappers. These scenes are worth discussing in some detail because
of their idiosyncratic use of the voice-off. Hitchcock uses the voice-off
to identify Nurse Agnes's voice as a threat to patriarchal discourse.
Precisely because it exceeds the gender of her body, Nurse Agnes's
voice threatens to disrupt the film's hierarchy of sound. Nurse Agnes
uses her voice to place Clive in the position traditionally occupied by
the female spectator. In these scenes, her voice becomes detached
from her body and threatens to undermine the film's textual system by
reversing its hierarchy of sound. The use of the voice-off in the classical text is usually limited to designating a space that lies beyond the
frame but that remains within the diegesis.[27] That is to say, it indicates
the presence of a speaker who is temporarily not visible in the frame
but who is nevertheless present in the diegesis and who will at some
point be brought back into the film's visual field. For this reason, it is
normally used to reinforce the spatial unity and homogeneity of the
diegesis. It adds to the film's illusion of visual depth and physical
presence by filling out the diegetic space.

Hitchcock's use of the voice-off in the scenes at the Tabernacle of
the Sun does not conform to this set of conventions. He does not use
the voice-off to reinforce the spatial unity of the diegesis but to emphasize the threat Nurse Agnes's voice poses to the film's hierarchy of
sound. Nurse Agnes's voice cannot be contained by her body but
functions independently of it. Consequently, it violates the codes the
film industry had developed for representing the female voice. When
Nurse Agnes begins to address the congregation from the dais, her
voice becomes temporarily disembodied. The camera cuts from a medium shot of her standing at the dais to a long shot of the congregation. As the camera pans the congregation, we hear her ask for volun-
teers who are willing to submit to "a very simple process of control."
Her voice also becomes temporarily disembodied in the scenes in
which she hypnotizes Clive. The camera cuts from a close-up of her to

a close-up of Clive, and we hear her repeat in a low, husky tone, "You are already feeling sleepy, do you hear me?" This use of the voice-off helps to consolidate and maintain the film's hierarchical system of representation in which the sound track is subordinate to the image track. It calls attention to the threat the incorporation of sound technology posed to the primacy of the image. These scenes are organized around a struggle between the auditory and the visual for control of Clive's perceptions. Clive functions in these scenes as a kind of diegetic surrogate for the spectator. Nurse Agnes gains control of him by eroding his power of vision. He becomes vulnerable to the hypnotic power of her voice because he is forced to rely on his hearing as his primary mode of perception. The editing of these scenes stresses the way in which his sense of hearing gradually displaces his sense of sight. The camera cuts from a shot in which he is shown falling asleep to a shot in which Nurse Agnes's image becomes blurred and fades from view. It then cuts to a shot in which we see his monocle fall from his eye, thereby indicating that his sense of hearing has displaced his sense of sight altogether. In this way, these scenes help to consolidate the film's hierarchical system of representation. They identify hearing as an unreliable mode of perception that is no substitute for sight. Hearing becomes associated with a threatening loss of control in which the subject surrenders the ability to perceive reality accurately.

Rehabilitating the Female Voice:
Hitchcock and the Professionalization of Motherhood

Like *Blackmail*, then, the original version of *The Man Who Knew Too Much* maintains the primacy of the image by subordinating the spectator's auditory drive to her/his scopic drive. The use of the voice-off in the scenes at the Tabernacle of the Sun identifies sound as a threat to the classical system, which must be contained. By creating the illusion of bodily unity and coherence for female as well as for male characters, synchronization encouraged the female spectator to position herself as a subject of desire. In the remainder of this chapter, I want to argue that the remake of *The Man Who Knew Too Much* reverses this hierarchy. Whereas the original version of the film subordinates auditory pleasure to visual pleasure, the remake foregrounds auditory pleasure at the expense of visual pleasure. My goal is to show that Hitchcock's textual practices were not monolithic and homogeneous, but flexible; that is to say, they responded to changes in historical circumstances. I want to be quite clear from the beginning that in making this claim, I do not mean to suggest that the female characters are less bound by the image in the remake than they are in the original; nor do I mean to suggest that in the remake the female voice is not corporealized. Rather, I want to show that in the remake, Hitchcock allows the female voice to function independently of the female body without it threatening the hierarchical structure of the patriarchal family. Like those of the female characters in the original, Jo's (Doris Day) voice has an intractable materiality that exceeds signification. At the same time, however, it is meant to evoke the maternal body. Hitchcock uses her voice to envelop the spectator in a comforting blanket of sound that returns her/him to the imaginary plenitude of the primordial listening experience. I will argue that just as Hitchcock developed a system of representation in the original version of the film that was specific to the conditions of the 1930s, he developed a system of representation in the remake that was specific to the conditions of the 1950s. The remake participated in a set of discursive practices that tried to discourage women from pursuing careers outside the home by stressing the importance of the bond between mother and child during the child's earliest years. In the 1950s, when Hitchcock remade *The Man Who Knew Too Much*, the institutionalization of female forms of fetishism and voyeurism did not pose as great a threat to patriarchal discourse as did wives and mothers who resisted confinement to the domestic sphere.

This emphasis on the historical specificity of Hitchcock's textual practices raises important questions about the auteur theory and its relation to the discourses of national security. The major exponent of auteur criticism in postwar America was Andrew Sarris. Sarris carried to extremes the kind of criticism practiced by the critics associated with *Cahiers du Cinema* in the 1950s. In his "Notes on the Auteur Theory in 1962," he elaborated the distinction between auteur and metteur-en-scène originally made by André Bazin. Bazin used the terms to distinguish between directors like Hitchcock who left their signatures on their films and those like Huston who merely adapted the material assigned to them by the studios. Sarris rigidly applied the distinction and used it to construct a map that organized the history of the American film industry. Establishing a kind of pantheon, he ranked Hollywood directors according to the thematic unity and coherence of their films. The Hollywood directors he most admired were those who had supposedly overcome the barriers to artistic self-expression that "plagued" the film industry. Reducing the critical approach of the *Cahiers* critics to a rigid theoretical paradigm, he argued that "the third and ultimate premise of the *auteur* theory is concerned with interior meaning, the ultimate glory of the cinema as an art. Interior meaning is extrapolated from the tension between a director's personality and his material."[28] In suggesting that Hollywood directors were not necessarily bound by the constraints of the film industry, Sarris sought to raise the status of American film as an art form. Indeed, his elaboration of the auteur theory was crudely and unabashedly nationalistic. He was no longer willing to apologize for the commercialism of the American film industry and announced that "after years of tortured revaluation, I am now prepared to stake my critical reputation, such as it is, on the proposition that Alfred Hitchcock is artistically superior to Robert Bresson by every criterion of excellence, and further that, film for film, the American cinema has been consistently superior to that of the rest of the world from 1915 through 1962" (134).

Film scholars usually explain the emergence of the auteur theory, and its elaboration by postwar American critics, as an extension of the romantic conception of the artist to the area of film studies. John Caughie, for example, claims that "the intervention of *auteurism*, its critical revolution, was simply the installation in the cinema of the figure who had dominated the other arts for over a century: the romantic artist, individual and self-expressive."[29] But this explanation ignores the relation between the elaboration of the auteur theory in postwar America and the discourses of national security. For in using the theory to establish a pantheon of Hollywood directors whose work supposedly transcended the conditions that governed the film industry, critics like Sarris engaged in a critical practice that was complicit with the surveillance practices of the national-security state. By suggesting that Hollywood directors were not necessarily bound by the constraints of the film industry, Sarris denied that the mass production and consumption of films were conditioned by concrete historical forces. Although he acknowledged the importance of material conditions, his emphasis on establishing a pantheon of Hollywood directors diverted critical attention from them. For him, the critic's task was not to expose the conditions that governed the film industry but to identify the directors who had left their signatures on their films. Arguing against a critical approach that examined Hollywood films in historical context, he stated, "If directors and other artists cannot be wrenched from their historical environments, aesthetics is reduced to a subordinate branch of ethnography" (133). In other words, the critic's task was not to situate Hollywood films historically but to "wrench" them from their historical context. The Hollywood directors Sarris included in his pantheon had supposedly transcended the ideological conditions that governed artistic production at the particular historical moment in which they worked. In this way, Sarris contributed to the attempts of Cold War liberals to open up a space in American culture in which politics did not intervene. His elaboration of the auteur theory enabled critics to avoid discussing the ideological content of a director's corpus and instead to focus on whether it was stylistically consistent.

To clarify the relation between Sarris's conception of the auteur as an autonomous subject whose artistic production was supposedly not conditioned by concrete historical forces and the surveillance practices of the national security state, I want to stress the differences between the two versions of *The Man Who Knew Too Much*. Examining the remake in the context of a system of representations that was specific to the postwar period will show that Hitchcock's attempts to establish himself as an auteur were ideological in that they denied the historicity of his subjectivity. By installing himself as the originating agency of his films, Hitchcock diverted critical attention from the concrete historical forces that conditioned his artistic production in the postwar period. The films he made in the 1950s supposedly did not contribute to the production of subjects who consented freely and spontaneously to the postwar settlement but rather addressed universal themes that were transhistorical. Comparing the two versions of *The Man Who Knew Too Much* will show that the elaboration of the auteur theory by postwar American critics allowed Hitchcock to deny the construction of his subjectivity in relation to the discourses of national security. Hitchcock's use of sound in the remake of *The Man Who Knew Too Much* differs significantly from his use of sound in the original version of the film because the remake participated in the network of discourses that helped to underwrite and consolidate the postwar settlement. The relation between the remake and the discourses of national security is perhaps most obvious in its representation of Jo as an irresponsible mother who ignores the advice of Dr. Spock and other postwar experts on child rearing and pursues a career outside the home.

One of the most striking differences between the remake and the original is that Jo is a former professional singer who has given up a highly successful stage and recording career for her husband, Ben (James Stewart), who is a doctor from Indianapolis. Unlike Jill in the original version of the film, Jo does not resent the constraints her marriage places on her sexuality; nor does she try to position herself as a subject of desire. Rather, she resists the hierarchical structure of the patriarchal family because she does not see why she cannot combine raising a family and pursuing a career outside the home. She tries to persuade Ben to practice medicine in New York so that she can continue to appear on stage. Her resentment of having to give up her career first surfaces in the scene in the restaurant in Morocco where she quarrels with Ben because he is unwilling to move to New York. Ben clearly feels threatened by her success as a singer. When the Draytons recognize Jo and introduce themselves as fans, Ben responds somewhat defensively by introducing himself and Jo as "Doctor and Mrs. MacKenna." He apparently does not want there to be any confusion about Jo's identity. Jo is no longer Jo Conway, the famous singer who thrilled the Draytons when she appeared on the London stage four years earlier, but Mrs. MacKenna, the wife of a doctor from Indianapolis. Moreover, it becomes apparent in this scene that he has forced her to give up her career. He does not see how she can simultaneously pursue a career and fulfill her responsibilities to him and their son, Hank (Christopher Olsen). When Mrs. Drayton (Brenda de Banzie) expresses her disappointment that Jo does not intend to return to the London stage, Ben explains, "It's just that I'm a doctor, and, you know, a doctor's wife doesn't have much time." But this is just an excuse, and Jo interjects, "What my husband's trying to say is that Broadway musical shows are not produced in Indianapolis, Indiana. Of course, we could live in New York. I hear the doctors aren't starving there, either." But Ben refuses to allow her career to eclipse his and replies, "Well, it's not that I have any objections to working in New

York. It's just that it'd be kind of hard for my patients to come all the way from Indianapolis."

Ben's resentment of Jo's success as a professional singer manifests itself primarily in his attempts to limit the circulation of her voice by returning it to the domestic sphere. As a professional singer, Jo allows her voice to circulate freely as a commodity. Her records enable her fans to own her voice and to listen to it almost endlessly. Ben clearly feels threatened by this aspect of her career and constantly tries to silence her. When she voices her suspicions about Louis Bernard (Daniel Gelin), for example, he dismisses them by saying, "I know this is mysterious Morocco, but we're not going to lose our head, are we?" He similarly refuses to listen to her when they arrive at the hotel and she complains that they are being watched by the Draytons. Although in both cases her suspicions prove to be justified, he dismisses them as hysterical symptoms. Invoking his authority as a doctor, he tries to convince her that she has succumbed to "mysterious" Morocco and lost her head. Moreover, just as Frank in *Blackmail* uses the attempted rape to gain control of Alice's speech, Ben uses Hank's kidnapping to return Jo's voice to the domestic sphere. When the man from the British Foreign Office questions them at the London airport about the kidnapping, Jo tries to persuade Ben to tell him what Louis Bernard said before he died. When Ben refuses, she decides to reveal the contents of the note herself, telling him, "Maybe they could find those people and Hank." But Ben prevents her from speaking by responding angrily, "Maybe! Maybe's not good enough for me, and I don't think it oughta be good enough for you, either." His incriminating tone leaves her speechless, and she breaks down in tears.

This scene is worth commenting on in detail because it contrasts markedly with a similar scene in the original and calls attention to Hitchcock's shifting relation to discourse. Hitchcock's reworking of the scene reflects the remake's participation in the network of discourses that helped to consolidate the postwar settlement by discouraging women from pursuing careers outside the home. In the original, it is Jill who prevents Bob from revealing the contents of the note to the man from the British Foreign Office who questions them about the kidnapping. As we saw above, when the man from the British Foreign Office tries to persuade Bob to reveal the contents of the note by claiming that Ropa's assassination might lead to another world war, Jill intervenes, telling him, "Our child comes first, she must come first!" In this way, Hitchcock indicates Jill's inscription within patriarchal discourse. Jill no longer resists the hierarchical structure of the patriarchal family but accepts her place in it. Although she prevents Bob from speaking and dominates him verbally, she does so to protect Betty, not to usurp patriarchal authority. Indeed, her place in the hierarchical structure of the patriarchal family authorizes her to intervene in the situation. In preventing Bob from speaking, she fulfills her responsibilities as a mother. The scene in the remake differs because Jo's commitment to her family has never been seriously in doubt. She poses a threat to patriarchal discourse, not because she refuses to cede control of her body to Ben, but because she wants to continue her singing career, despite her responsibilities as a wife and mother. Thus Hitchcock's reworking of the scene is rooted in concrete historical circumstances. Hitchcock does not allow Jo to speak in the scene in the remake because she refuses to restrict her voice to the domestic sphere and allows it to circulate freely as a commodity. By preventing her from speaking, Ben gains control of her voice and returns it to the domestic sphere. His incriminating tone deprives her of control of her voice and reduces her to uttering inarticulate cries. This is significant because her voice signifies her resistance to structures that were specific to the postwar period.

Ben's desire to interrupt the uncontrolled circulation of Jo's voice surfaces most fully in the scene in which he sedates her in order to prevent her from reacting hysterically to Hank's kidnapping. In persuading her to take sedatives before telling her about the kidnapping, he forcibly returns her voice to her body. The sedatives deprive her of control of her voice and reduce her to a kind of verbal hysteria. What is telling about this scene is that Ben projects onto Jo his own hysterical reaction to the kidnapping. It becomes apparent in this scene that Ben feels threatened by Jo's voice because it places him in a subordinate position in relation to her. Her success as a singer overshadows his success as a doctor, which is why he refuses to move to New York. He persuades her to take the sedatives by telling her that she has been behaving hysterically: "Now, you've been excited, you've been talking a blue streak, you've been walking in circles." But this description is more applicable to him than it is to her. He is the one who has been talking a blue streak. By projecting his own hysteria onto her, however, he does not have to acknowledge his loss of verbal mastery. Jo is **143** the one who has supposedly lost control of the use of language. Indeed, by forcing her to take the sedatives, he reduces her to his own hysterical state. She loses control of her voice, and the only way in which she can express herself is by uttering inarticulate cries. When he finally tells her about the kidnapping, she cries hysterically and repeats again and again, "I could kill you! You gave me sedatives!" and "I want my boy!" In this way, Ben restricts the circulation of Jo's voice to the domestic sphere. Jo's inarticulate cries subordinate her voice to her body. They attribute to it an intractable materiality that connotes the maternal body. Her verbal hysteria signifies her anxiety as a mother, and she never fully recovers control of her voice until Hank is restored to her in the final scene of the film.

Hitchcock's treatment of Jo in this scene is unusually sympathetic. He encourages the spectator to identify with her anger and sense of violation by shooting the scene almost wholly from her point of view. Consequently, the spectator resents Ben's attempts to restrict the circulation of her voice to the domestic sphere. This does not mean, however, that Hitchcock consistently adopts Jo's point of view or that he is sympathetic to her desire to continue her career, despite her responsibilities as a wife and mother. On the contrary, he helps to underwrite the contemporary discourses of mothering by suggesting that her career as a professional singer conflicts with her responsibilities as a homemaker. In the 1950s, women were encouraged to professionalize their responsibilities as homemakers rather than to pursue careers outside the home.[30] Homemaking became a specialized field of knowledge with its own secondary literature. Rather than rely on their own knowledge of raising children or that of family and friends, women were expected to follow the "expert" advice of Dr. Spock and other trained professionals. Dr. Spock's attitude toward child rearing was typical. In *The Common Sense Book of Baby and Child Care*, originally published in 1946 but revised and reprinted several times in the postwar period, Dr. Spock stressed the difficulties of raising children to be well-adjusted adults and urged young mothers in particular to seek the advice of specialists. Although in the opening chapter he tried to reassure expectant mothers by telling them, "You know more than you think you do" and "don't be afraid to trust your own common sense," he urged them to disregard the advice of family members and to consult their doctors when they had questions about the "proper" methods of raising children.[31]

In treating child rearing as a quasi-professional occupation that required familiarity with a growing body of secondary literature, "experts" like Dr. Spock discouraged women from pursuing careers outside the home. According to the developmental psychology of the postwar period, the child's personality was formed while it was an infant.[32] Consequently, Dr. Spock stressed the importance of the bond between mother and child during the child's earliest years. On the one hand, he urged fathers to become more involved in the raising of their children. He tried to persuade them that "a man can be a warm father and a real man at the same time" (18) and explained that their relations with their children "will have a vital effect on their spirits and characters for the rest of their lives" (18). On the other hand, he discouraged women from working outside the home because he felt that they alone could provide children with the care they needed to grow up well adjusted. Expressing a widely held view in the postwar period, he stated that "in most cases, the mother is the best one to give [the child] this feeling of 'belonging,' safely and surely. She doesn't quit on the job, she doesn't turn against him [sic], she isn't indifferent to him, she takes care of him always in the same familiar house" (570). In other words, the mother had an obligation to devote herself full time to her children because only she could provide them with the constant care they supposedly needed. The father's involvement in the domestic sphere was limited to containing the mother's influence over the children: "If a father leaves [the child rearing] all to his wife for the first two years, she gets to be the expert and the boss as far as the children are concerned. He'll feel more bashful about pushing his way into the picture later" (18).

That Dr. Spock's emphasis on the importance of the bond between mother and child was meant to discourage women from working outside the home becomes clear in the section of *Baby and Child Care* that he devoted to "The Working Mother." Although Dr. Spock realized that many women could not afford to devote themselves full time to their children and that others might want to work outside the home "because they wouldn't be happy otherwise" (570), he warned that mothers who tried to combine raising a family and pursuing a career risked damaging their children psychologically. Rather than urging the government to subsidize child care for working mothers, he argued that "it would save money if the government paid a comfortable allowance to all mothers of young children who would otherwise be compelled to work" (569–70). He discouraged mothers from working outside the home by claiming that children required individual care until the age of three and that finding adequate care for children who were older was virtually impossible. He advised against placing babies in nurseries because "the staff may not have had the expert training in understanding small children to be able to foster their fullest development, spiritually, socially, and physically" (571–72). Enrolling older children in nursery schools and kindergartens was also unacceptable because "the school day may not last until [the mother] can take over, and there is the problem of who is to take care of the child when he [sic] is sick" (572). Dr. Spock implied that mothers who ignored his advice and persisted in working outside the home ran the risk of disrupting their children's psychological development. Admitting that the children of working mothers usually "turn out all right" (569), he also claimed that many "grow up neglected and maladjusted" (569). In the 1950s, the term *maladjusted* was usually a code word for homosexual, and thus it is hardly surprising that so few mothers challenged the gender-specific division of labor by working outside the home. According to the discourses of national security, children who threatened to become homosexual or lesbian also threatened to become Communists or fellow travelers. Thus mothers who worked outside the home were not only irresponsible but also unpatriotic.

Although Hitchcock encourages us to identify with Jo, especially in the scene in which Ben forcibly returns her voice to her body, he clearly expects us to judge her according to this quasi-professional model of motherhood. We know from a comment Mrs. Drayton makes that Jo did not give up her career immediately after Hank was born but continued to appear on stage. Hitchcock stresses the consequences of this failure to follow the advice of the experts. Although Hank seems relatively well adjusted, he does not promise to contribute to the reproduction of the national security state. In the opening scene, he almost causes an international incident when he accidentally removes the veil from an Arab woman's face. The film attributes this violation of patriarchal law to Jo's resistance to the professionalization of motherhood. Joe does not adequately supervise Hank and thus is an irresponsible mother. When Hank accidentally removes the veil from the Arab woman's face, Jo is absorbed in reading a fashion magazine and does not realize that he has wandered off. In this way, the film tries to show that Hank has not been adequately socialized and is failing to develop "normally." Jo has been too busy with her career to bond "properly" with him. Consequently, he does not understand patriarchal law and violates it unwittingly. Indeed, Jo herself does not seem to understand patriarchal law and thus is doubly irresponsible as a mother. Louis Bernard must explain to her the significance of the veil in Muslim culture. The film similarly emphasizes the consequences of Jo's resistance to the professionalization of motherhood in the scene in the Arab market. Ironically, Mrs. Drayton is more solicitous of Hank's welfare than Jo is. When Louis Bernard is stabbed, it is she who runs after Hank and prevents him from becoming involved in the confusion. Jo merely calls after him and remains in the background, safely removed from the commotion.

The film also emphasizes Jo's failings as a mother by suggesting that her resistance to the professionalization of motherhood threatens to disrupt the Oedipal structure of the middle-class nuclear family. Disregarding one of her primary functions as a mother, she tries to undermine Hank's identification with Ben. She competes with Ben for Hank's attention and encourages Hank to identify with her. Indeed, just as Ben seems to expect Hank to follow in his footsteps and become a doctor, Jo seems to expect him to follow in her footsteps and become a singer. Jo's desire to function as a point of identification for Hank surfaces most fully in the scene in which she sings "Que sera, sera" to him as he prepares for bed. Significantly, in the version of the song she has taught him to sing all the authority figures are female. In the first verse, a boy asks his mother if he will be rich and handsome when he grows up; in the second verse, he asks his elementary school teacher (referred to as "she") if he should become a painter or a singer when he grows up. What is striking is that in both cases the boy turns to female authority figures for guidance. In teaching Hank to sing this version of the song, Jo disrupts the Oedipal structure of the middle-class nuclear family. She tries to displace Ben as Hank's primary point of identification. The song instills in Hank a respect for female authority and encourages him to model himself after Jo. Hank receives conflicting messages from Jo, which hinders him from successfully negotiating the Oedipus complex. On the one hand, as a boy, he is supposed to identify with Ben and show an interest in his activities. On the other hand, Jo encourages him to identify with her and show an interest in her activities.

To understand fully the extent to which Jo's desire to function as a point of identification for Hank conflicted with the Oedipal structure of the middle-class nuclear family in the 1950s, it is necessary to return briefly to Dr. Spock's *Baby and Child Care* and examine its discussion of the Oedipus complex. Applying Freudian theory reductively, Dr. Spock argued that it is "normal" for the well-adjusted boy to become romantically attached to the mother. He claimed that when the boy reaches the age of three, he begins to realize that he will grow up and become a man like his father, which gives him "a special admiration for his father and other men and boys. He watches them carefully and works hard to be as much like them as he can, in appearance and behavior and interests" (357–58). According to Dr. Spock, this "special admiration" for the father leads the boy to develop a romantic attachment to the mother. Because of his desire to be like the father, the boy who is developing "normally" supposedly "takes on his father's attitude toward other males and toward women" (358). As a result, he develops an attachment to the mother that resembles the father's. Distorting Freudian theory, which locates the boy's desire for the mother in his pre-Oedipal relations with her, Dr. Spock claimed that when the boy reaches the age of four, he is "apt to insist that he's going to marry his mother when he grows up. He isn't clear just what marriage consists of, but he's absolutely sure who is the most important and appealing woman in the world" (358). To insure that he continues to develop "normally," the mother is supposed to help the boy negotiate this stage of his development by containing his attachment to her. Dr. Spock explained that "Nature doesn't want the attachment to go so far or get so strong that it lasts through life or even through childhood. Nature expects that [the boy] by 5 or 6 will become quite discouraged about the possibility of having [the mother] all to himself" (359). Thus when the boy insists that he is going to marry her, the mother is supposed to act pleased, but she is also supposed to explain that "she's already married and that when he grows up he'll find a girl his own age to marry" (361).

This formulation of the Oedipus complex, which was typical during the 1950s, suggests that Hitchcock was critical of Jo's desire to function as a point of identification for Hank because it conflicted with the Oedipal structure of the middle-class nuclear family. Dr. Spock was particularly censorious of the mother who, like Jo, competed with the father for the boy's attention and encouraged him to develop an interest in traditionally feminine activities. In a chapter devoted to "Special Problems," Dr. Spock warned that the mother who encourages the boy to identify with her not only acts in opposition to Nature but risks doing irreparable harm to him psychologically. The mother who is overly attached to the boy and interferes with his identification with the father supposedly prevents him from negotiating the Oedipus complex successfully. Dr. Spock explained that "if [the mother] succeeds in making her world more appealing to him, easier to get along in, than the world of boys (where he has to make his own way), then he may grow up precocious, with feminine interests" (577–78). This did not mean that the boy should not respect the mother and show an interest in her activities, but the mother should not encourage him to model himself after her. Dr. Spock claimed that "it's all to the good if a mother can spend time and have plenty of fun with her boy, provided she also lets him go his own way, provided she shares in his interests rather than having him share too many of hers" (578). In other words, Hitchcock stresses the irresponsibility of Jo's desire to function as a point of identification for Hank because it supposedly prevents him from negotiating the Oedipus complex successfully. In the scene in which Jo sings "Que sera, sera" to Hank, it becomes clear that she has succeeded in making her world appear more appealing than Ben's. Thus Hank threatens to grow up "precocious," or with an "abnormal" interest in activities such as singing that are traditionally considered feminine.

I have emphasized Hitchcock's representation of Jo as an irresponsible mother who hinders rather than facilitates Hank's negotiation of the Oedipus complex because I wanted to call attention to the remake's participation in the network of discourses that helped to underwrite and legitimate the postwar settlement by discouraging women from working outside the home. The remake helped to consolidate the postwar settlement by suggesting that women who tried to combine raising children and pursuing a career were not only irresponsible but unpatriotic. Rather than promising to contribute to the reproduction

of the national security state, Hank threatens to grow up "maladjusted." This link between the remake and the discourses of national
security helps to explain what is arguably the most important difference between the remake and the original, namely, Hitchcock's decision to make Jo a former professional singer. According to psychoanalytic theory, in the traditionally organized family, the maternal voice
functions as an acoustic mirror that reinforces the child's illusion of
bodily unity and coherence.[33] The maternal voice contributes significantly to the child's perceptual development by organizing the child's
auditory field. In particular, it defines space for the child by identifying
and explaining the world of objects. Moreover, it is generally the first
object the child introjects. The child identifies the mother's voice long
before it identifies her body, and thus her voice continues to mediate
the child's relation to her body. Finally, the mother's voice prepares the
child for its entry into language. The mother organizes the world
linguistically for the child. The child learns to speak by imitating the
sounds emitted by the mother and by modeling its voice after hers. For
this reason, the mother's voice can function as a sonorous envelope or
comforting blanket of sound in which the child experiences an imaginary plenitude and bliss.[34] At the same time, however, the fantasy of
inhabiting a space organized and defined by the mother's voice can
also assume the form of a terrifying miasma of nonmeaning.[35] Because
the child's entry into language depends upon the mother's intervening
agency, her voice constantly reminds the child that it lacks verbal
mastery.

Applying this analysis of the maternal voice and its role in the
child's perceptual development to the remake reinforces Jo's irresponsibility as a mother. According to the patriarchal logic of the remake, Jo
is an irresponsible mother not only because she hinders Hank from
negotiating the Oedipus complex by interfering with his identification
with Ben but because her voice fails to provide Hank with an acoustic
mirror in which he can discover his own identity. As I noted above, Jo's
recording career promotes the fetishization of her voice. Her voice has
become detached from her body and functions independently as a
fetish object. Her records provide her fans with a surplus of auditory
pleasure because they enable them to listen to her voice almost endlessly. Consequently, her voice fails to provide Hank with a comforting
blanket of sound that reinforces his illusion of bodily unity. Hank's

primordial listening experience has little in common with the psychoanalytic paradigm described above. Jo's voice does not connote the maternal body but "Jo Conway," the highly successful singer who has appeared on New York, London, and Paris stages. Thus Hank's relation to her voice is unusually fraught with anxiety. The fantasy of inhabiting a space organized and defined by her voice has the potential to assume the form of a terrifying miasma in which he not only lacks verbal mastery but also must share his access to her body with her fans. Thus Hitchcock's decision to make Jo a former professional singer reinforced the link between the remake and the system of representations that helped to consolidate the postwar settlement by discouraging women from pursuing careers outside the home. The uncontrolled circulation of Jo's voice disrupts Hank's primordial listening experience. Jo has failed as a mother not only because she continued to appear on stage after Hank was born but also because her voice does not provide him with a sonorous envelope in which he can experience an imaginary unity and coherence.

Hitchcock's emphasis on the failure of Jo's voice to provide Hank with a blanket of comforting sound points to another important difference between the original and the remake. I argued above that the kidnapping serves the same function in both versions of the film in that it punishes the heroine for her refusal to acknowledge the hierarchical structure of the patriarchal family. But this ignores Hitchcock's radically different use of sound in the remake. Whereas the kidnapping in the original deprives Jill of verbal mastery and thus places her in a position in relation to language that is more appropriate to her gender, the kidnapping in the remake returns Jo's voice to the domestic sphere and thus leads to its rehabilitation. In the final scene of the film, Jo uses her voice to reestablish her bond with Hank. She tries to discover where the Draytons are holding Hank captive in the embassy by singing "Que sera, sera." Because it is a song that she and Hank have often sung together, it indicates her recognition of the importance of the acoustic bond between them. What is particularly significant about this scene is that her voice is allowed to function independently of her body. In a famous series of shots, the camera "shows" her voice traveling up several flights of stairs, down a long corridor, and into the room where the Draytons are holding Hank captive. Although in this sequence Jo performs before an audience, her voice connotes the maternal body rather than "Jo Conway," the famous recording star. Her performance is wholly for Hank's benefit; indeed, she sings so loudly that the audience becomes uncomfortable and embarrassed. Moreover, her relation to Hank becomes wholly auditory in this sequence. When Hank hears her voice, he immediately recognizes it and cries out, "That's my mother's voice, that's my mother singing." He then begins to whistle "Que sera, sera" in order to indicate his whereabouts. In this way, the remake emphasizes the importance of the acoustic dimension of the bond between Jo and Hank. Throughout the sequence, Jo's voice functions as a sonorous envelope that wraps Hank in a comforting blanket of sound. When Drayton (Bernard Miles) pulls a gun on Ben and Hank and forces them to descend the stairs, Jo's voice can be heard singing "We'll Love Again," a song about two lovers who are reunited after a long separation. The song, which is barely audible on the sound track and therefore borders on meaningless babble, seems meant to reassure Hank that he will soon be reunited with Jo.

I have focused on Hitchcock's idiosyncratic use of Jo's voice in this sequence because I wanted to clarify the differences between the remake and the original, differences that raise questions about the auteur theory, as it was elaborated by postwar American critics, and its relation to the discourses of national security. I have tried to show that Hitchcock's use of sound in the remake differs significantly from his use of sound in the original. Rather than treating the original as part of a directorial corpus, I have tried to situate it in relation to the institutionalization of female forms of fetishism and voyeurism. I have argued that in establishing a hierarchy of sound in which Jill is more bound by the image than are the male characters, the original tried to contain the threat the eroticization of the female gaze posed to the classical system. Although the eroticization of the female gaze promoted the mass marketing and consumption of films, it encouraged women to position themselves as subjects of desire, which threatened to disrupt the textual practices developed by the film industry to anticipate and standardize the consumption of its products. In this way, I have avoided claiming that Hitchcock remade *The Man Who Knew Too Much* because he did not get it "right" the first time, instead situating the remake in relation to the professionalization of motherhood in the 1950s. I wanted to show that Hitchcock's textual practices were conditioned by concrete historical forces and responded to changes in the social formation. It has been my contention that the differences between the two versions reflect the historicity of Hitchcock's subjectivity, its construction in relation to a historically specific network of discourses that included, but was not limited to, the classical system. Hitchcock's use of sound in the remake differs from his use of sound in the original because he wanted to foreground the acoustic dimension of the bond between mother and child. The remake legitimates the professionalization of motherhood by constructing a fantasy of the maternal voice that recalls the imaginary plenitude and bliss of the spectator's primordial listening experience. In treating Jo's voice as a sonorous envelope that wraps Hank in a blanket of comforting sound, the remake represses the potentially terrifying effects of inhabiting a space organized and defined by the mother's voice and associates it instead with an illusory unity and coherence.

In foregrounding the acoustic dimension of the bond between mother and child, the remake reverses the hierarchy established in the original in which the sound track is subordinate to the image track. Whereas the original subordinates auditory pleasure to visual pleasure in order to maintain the primacy of the image, the remake subordinates visual pleasure to auditory pleasure in order to return the spectator to the imaginary plenitude and bliss of the primordial listening experience.[36] This is not to suggest that Jo in the remake is less bound by the image than is Jill in the original. In both versions of the film, the female voice is subordinated to the female body. As we saw above, Ben forcibly returns Jo's voice to her body in the scene in which he sedates her. In so doing, he interrupts the uncontrolled circulation of her voice as a commodity. Still, her voice is allowed to function independently of her body in the final sequence, because she uses it to reestablish her bond with Hank. The restriction of her voice to the domestic sphere allows for its rehabilitation. In the final sequence, her voice no longer signifies Jo Conway, the famous recording star, but the maternal body, and thus it can function independently of her body without posing a threat to the hierarchical structure of the patriarchal family. She does not use her voice to promote its circulation as a commodity, but to envelope Hank in a blanket of comforting sound. Thus just as Hitchcock developed a system of representation in the original that was specific to the ideological conditions of the 1930s, he developed a system of representation in the remake that was specific **153** to the ideological conditions of the 1950s. In subordinating visual pleasure to auditory pleasure in the remake, he sought to return the spectator to the imaginary plenitude and bliss of the primordial listening experience. He wanted to inscribe the spectator within the discourses of national security, and so he constructed a fantasy of the maternal voice that exploited the auditory traces of the spectator's pre-Oedipal relations with the mother. In so doing, he tried to mobilize the spectator's nostalgia for the illusion of bodily unity and coherence that preceded her/his traumatic entry into language.

"THERE ARE MANY SUCH STORIES"

Vertigo and the Repression of

Historical Knowledge

Bohemianism is not particularly fashionable nowadays, but the image of Bohemia still exerts a powerful fascination—nowhere more so than in the suburbs, who uneasily think of themselves as conformists and of Bohemianism as the heroic road.—Norman Podhoretz, "The Know-Nothing Bohemians"

In *Vertigo* (1958), when Madeleine (Kim Novak) and Scottie (James Stewart) visit a redwood forest on one of their "wanderings," they examine the cross section of a felled tree that has been marked with some of the most important dates in British and U.S. history: the Norman Invasion, the signing of the Magna Carta, the "discovery" of America, and the Declaration of Independence. Madeleine, pretending to be possessed by Carlotta Valdez, her great grandmother who committed suicide in 1857 after being abandoned by her Anglo lover, points to the tree's outer rings and says, "Somewhere here I was born, and there I died. It was only a moment for you, you took no notice." At first sight, Madeleine merely seems to be acknowledging that in comparison to the tree, which was cut down in 1930 when it was more than a thousand years old, Carlotta's life was short and insignificant. Yet in the context of the dates marked on the tree, she also seems to be calling attention to Carlotta's exclusion from the history they narrativize: there is apparently no place in official representations of the nation's past for the story of a Hispanic woman who was seduced and abandoned by her Anglo lover in the nineteenth century. Although the dates on the tree are clearly meant to emphasize the fact that the redwoods are the oldest living things on earth, they also represent American history as a continuous, linear narrative that began in 1066 with the Norman Invasion. In linking the "discovery" of America and the Declaration of Independence to the Norman Invasion and the signing of the Magna Carta, the tree suggests that the founding of the United States represented the fulfillment of British institutions and traditions. Thus, in pointing to the places on the tree that, if marked, would indicate when Carlotta was born and died, Madeleine helps to expose the way in which potentially disruptive stories such as hers have been marginalized and repressed because they contradict official representations of the nation's past. The historical narrative inscribed on the tree acknowledges the nation's Spanish heritage only indirectly in its reference to Columbus's "discovery" of America in 1492. In calling attention to the parts of the nation's past not represented on the tree, however, the film indicates the possibility of constructing a counterhistory of the United States, a history that more accurately represents the experiences of Hispanics in the American West because it includes stories like Carlotta's.

At the same time, however, that the film indicates the possibility of constructing a historical narrative that more accurately represents the nation's past because it does not privilege the nation's British heritage, it also stresses the impossibility of adequately recovering the experiences of Hispanics in the American West. It provides an explanation for the exclusion of Hispanics from official histories of the United States in an earlier scene in which Scottie asks Midge (Barbara Bel Geddes), a woman to whom he was briefly engaged in college, if she knows any authorities on San Francisco history. When she offers to introduce him to a history professor at Berkeley, Scottie replies, "No, no I don't mean that kind of history, I mean the small stuff. You know, people you never heard of." Scottie doubts that a professor at Berkeley who specializes in San Francisco history could tell him about Carlotta Valdez. He wants to find out about a part of San Francisco's past that official historians of the city exclude from their accounts because it supposedly does not constitute "real" history. Midge realizes that by "small stuff," Scottie means "the gay old Bohemian days of gay old San Francisco, juicy stories like who shot who on the Embarcadero in August 1879." Because such stories are to be found in the diaries, private letters, and unpublished memoirs of local families rather than in the official documents housed in the city's archives, she introduces him to Pop Liebl (Konstantin Shayne), the owner of a bookstore familiar with San Francisco lore. In other words, the film suggests that the authority on San Francisco history most qualified to tell Scottie about

Carlotta occupies a similarly marginal position in the city's official culture. A foreigner who speaks with a heavy accent, Pop Liebl sells rather than writes books on San Francisco history, and thus his knowledge of the city's past remains unassimilated by official culture.

Still, as the name of his bookstore, the Argosy, suggests, his familiarity with San Francisco lore constitutes a rich, if underused, alternative historical archive, and in repeating Carlotta's story to Scottie and Midge, he indicates the importance of recovering the history of Hispanics in the American West for constructing a more accurate narrative of the nation's past. For far from unusual, Carlotta's experiences (her seduction and abandonment by an Anglo lover) turn out to have been typical of Hispanic women in "gay old" San Francisco. Pop Liebl informs Scottie and Midge that "there are many such stories" as hers, and he cannot remember her lover's name, which suggests that his exact identity is immaterial because there were so many Anglo men like him in the nineteenth century. For this reason, Carlotta's story hardly constitutes "small stuff," and it definitely deserves a place in official histories of the American West: Carlotta is a representative figure of San Francisco's gay old Bohemian past. The film acknowledges this in its reconstruction of her story, a story that contradicts the official representation of her. She exists in the city's cultural archives primarily as a portrait in the Palace of the Legion of Honor. Although the exhibition of her portrait in the palace officially acknowledges the city's Hispanic heritage, it serves largely to mythologize the city's gay old Bohemian past. Not only does the portrait purify her Hispanic identity by anglicizing her features, but it is known simply as *Portrait of Carlotta*. Because the museum catalogue does not indicate who she was or what happened to her, it contributes to the romanticization of her story, which remains clouded in mystery. The film, then, in reconstructing her story, demythologizes it and by extension San Francisco's gay old Bohemian past in which stories like hers abounded. That is to say, the film calls attention to the discrepancy between the actual experiences of real historical Hispanic men and women in the American West and the representation of those experiences in official histories of the United States.

But despite its recognition that constructing an accurate representation of San Francisco's Bohemian past depends on recovering its Hispanic past, the film too engages in the repression of historical knowledge. For in the late 1950s when it was made, San Francisco had already achieved notoriety as the mecca of the Beat generation.[1] The city's North Beach section became known as the Greenwich Village of the West Coast for the Bohemian writers who gathered in its coffeehouses and jazz clubs to read and discuss their work. Because of their unconventional behavior, these writers quickly became identified as the official spokesmen for a generation in revolt against the stifling conformity of the postwar period. The Beats openly defied middle-class norms of behavior. Rather than settling down in the suburbs and raising families, they experimented sexually and supported themselves by working odd jobs.

To contain this rebellion against middle-class conformity, the media resorted to pathologizing it. Contemporary critics attacked the Beats as immature "perverts" who engaged in homosexual practices. Norman Podhoretz, for example, in *Partisan Review,* claimed that the Beats were incapable of "getting seriously involved with a woman, a job, a cause."[2] Bernard Wolfe put it more bluntly in the *Nation* when he stated that it was "no secret that hip and angry circles are overrun with homosexuals these days."[3] City officials in San Francisco took more direct action to contain the Beats and their rebellion against middle-class conformity. Alarmed by the city's growing notoriety, they ordered the police to clean up North Beach, which, in the wake of the publicity surrounding the Beats, had become one of the city's most popular tourist sights. The police increased their surveillance of the area significantly, searched Beat "pads" for evidence of illegal drug use and illicit sexual activity, and harassed the coffeehouses and jazz clubs where the Beats gathered to read and discuss their work.[4]

Vertigo refers to this aspect of contemporary San Francisco history only indirectly; indeed, it tries to suppress the city's role as the center of a burgeoning counterculture by locating its gay old Bohemian days firmly in the past. In the context of the popular association of San Francisco with the Beat rebellion, contemporary spectators would surely have considered its representation of the city somewhat inaccurate. In shot after shot, we are shown the historic landmarks that made the city famous: the Golden Gate Bridge, Coit Tower, the Palace of the Legion of Honor, and the Mission Dolores. In other words, we are taken on a tour of the city that, by avoiding the parts of it associated with the Beats, corroborates official representations of it. Still, Hitchcock's film does acknowledge San Francisco's role in the burgeoning counterculture; in so doing, it calls attention to the discrepancy between official representations of the city and the more complicated reality those representations tried to suppress. The repeated shots of Coit Tower locate Scottie's apartment in North Beach, the very center of Beat culture. Moreover, the unconventional behavior of Scottie and Gavin Elster (Tom Helmore), Scottie's old acquaintance from college who asks him to investigate the mysterious behavior of his wife, Madeleine, links them to the postwar rebellion against middle-class conformity. Although outwardly they have little in common with the Beats, they also openly reject middle-class values. Scottie, for example, never seriously considers settling down with Midge, despite her declaration that he is the only man for her. Instead he decides after his accident not to return to his job as a detective and to live on his inheritance. Similarly, Elster plots to murder his wife because he resents the responsibilities of the shipbuilding business and longs to relive the "color, excitement, power, freedom" of gay old San Francisco.

In this chapter, I want to examine these indirect references to the part of San Francisco made notorious by the Beats, a part that contradicted official representations of the city. I will show that the film tries to repress San Francisco's role in the burgeoning counterculture because it wants to emphasize the consequences of a lack of historical knowledge. According to the film, the repression of historical knowledge encourages a nostalgic relation to the past in which the part of the past that is the object of nostalgic desire (in this case, gay old Bohemian San Francisco) is removed from its historical context and inserted in a kind of mythic, timeless present; consequently, it can never be properly understood. Because official histories of San Francisco exclude such "small stuff," Carlotta's story can only exist as part of the city's lore, which restricts its availability to those who have access to Pop Liebl's "unofficial" historical archive. The relegation of Carlotta's story to the status of lore because it supposedly does not constitute "real" history allows the film's characters to romanticize it. They treat it as a historical relic; for them, it belongs to the Bohemian days of San Francisco's past. As a result, they seriously misunderstand contemporary social relations. Although Scottie knows there are many such stories as Carlotta's, he fails to see the connection between her experiences and those of the other women in the film. For this reason, he

remains blind not only to the persistence of the city's racist and misogynistic practices and institutions but also to his participation in their
reproduction.

I will try to show that implicit in this emphasis on the consequences of Scottie's lack of historical knowledge is a critique of the
Beats and their rebellion against the stifling conformity of the 1950s.
By referring only indirectly to San Francisco's role in the burgeoning
counterculture, the film makes it possible for the spectator to romanticize Scottie and Madeleine's relationship in the same way that the
characters romanticize Carlotta's relationship with her Anglo lover by
locating it in the city's "gay old Bohemian" past. Unless the spectator
links Scottie and Madeleine's relationship to the rebellion against the
conformity of middle-class life, s/he does not see the way in which it
reproduces the misogynistic structures of middle-class life by reducing
Madeleine to an object of visual pleasure. In this respect, Hitchcock's
film not only thematizes the consequences of the repression of historical knowledge but enacts them as well. In romanticizing Scottie and
Madeleine's relationship, the spectator engages in what amounts to
the construction of an official representation of it, that is to say, a representation that suppresses Madeleine's experience of it.[5] Removed
from its historical context, Scottie and Madeleine's relationship becomes an example of tragic, star-crossed love frozen in a kind of
mythic present rather than a product of the oppressive organization of
gender relations in the 1950s.

Moreover, in stressing the consequences of Scottie's lack of historical knowledge, the film suggests that the rebellion against the conformity of middle-class life does not constitute a rebellion so much as it
does business as usual. Although Pop Liebl informs Scottie and Midge
that Carlotta's lover "threw her away" after taking custody of their
illegitimate daughter because "a man could do that in those days," we
discover that men continue to throw women away when they no
longer want them: Elster quite literally throws his wife away, flinging
her from the bell tower of the mission at San Juan Bautista after
breaking her neck. But because Scottie represses his knowledge of
Carlotta's story, he fails to make the connection between Elster's actions and those of Carlotta's Anglo lover and is easily snared in his
murderous plot. He does not realize that the relation between the
city's past and present is structural and that the city's political and

social institutions continue to oppress women and other historically disenfranchised groups. Nor does he realize that like Carlotta's lover and Elster, he too victimizes women. Granted, he does not actually fling Judy from the mission bell tower at the end of the film, but he rejects her love and drags her up the bell tower stairs where she jumps to her death when a nun suddenly appears on the tower, frightening her. For this reason, his rebellion reinscribes, rather than challenges, middle-class values. In making Judy over and then rejecting her when he discovers that she had been made over once before by Elster, he exercises the "power" over women and "freedom" to abuse them that in the film define middle-class masculinity. Thus, without a proper understanding of the past, he can only repeat it. He does not realize that the very practices and institutions that allowed Carlotta's Anglo lover to seduce and abandon her not only have persisted but also continue to determine the structure of his own relations with women.

The Beats and the Psychopathology
of Rebellion

In order to recover the film's critique of the rebellion against the conformity of the postwar period, it is necessary to examine it in the context of the reaction to the Beats, the writers most associated at the time with the rejection of middle-class values. For although the film follows the example of contemporary critics in pathologizing the resistance to existing social structures, it implies that the "rebellion" for which the Beats had become the spokesmen did not adequately challenge the racist and misogynistic practices of middle-class life. In suggesting that the Beats did not go far enough in rejecting middle-class values, Hitchcock was unusually bold. Even liberal intellectuals were reluctant to call into question values that seemed to ensure the economic prosperity and political stability of the postwar period. As Barbara Ehrenreich has shown, a multiplicity of discursive practices emerged in the 1950s that made men's roles as breadwinners seem natural and inevitable.[6] Although contemporary psychologists could make women's roles as wives and mothers seem natural and inevitable by appealing to biology, they had more difficulty showing that men's responsibilities to their families were biologically determined. For this reason, they constructed a narrative of male development that provided ideological justification for the pressures placed on men to settle down and raise a family in the suburbs; this narrative remained a standard part of high school textbooks on mental "hygiene" well into the 1970s. It stigmatized men who remained single as perverts who suffered from an arrested sexual development. Supposedly fixated on their mothers, such men were considered latently, if not overtly, homosexual. For example, in 1966 the psychoanalyst Hendrick Ruitenbeek remarked that "contemporary America seems to have no room for the mature bachelor. . . . [A] single man over thirty is now regarded as a pervert, a person with severe emotional problems, or a poor creature fettered to a mother."[7]

In stigmatizing single men as perverts who remained fixated on their mothers, the dominant discourse of rebellion had little difficulty containing resistance to middle-class values. Even liberal intellectuals critical of the pressures to conform did not question the official narrative of male development. The novelist and critic Bernard Wolfe, for example, in a review published in the *Nation* in 1958, attacked the Beats for their misogynistic representations of women. Linking them to the Angry Young Men, a similar group of "hip" writers in Great Britain, he complained that the Beats were "professionals in the systematic abuse of women."[8] Because they refused to conform to the norms of middle-class life, they supposedly had "no scruples about roughing up the weaker sex" (318). Consequently, their "rebellion" against the conformity of the postwar period was insufficiently political. Rather than addressing the misogynistic structures of American society, it reproduced them. Indeed, he argued, the Beats did not even seem particularly interested in critiquing postwar American society. Despite their lofty political pronouncements on the atom bomb and the postwar culture of consumption, "the broad world of social structures is not even in their field of vision" (316). When they tried to address pressing contemporary social issues such as the battle between the sexes, they tended to "fall back on the sociological formulas of the thirties" (321). Thus, he claimed, all they had to offer contemporary readers was a "bag full of sociological clichés perfected and worked to death in the thirties" (321).

Although it is true that Wolfe was unusually progressive in attacking the Beats for failing to develop a more totalizing critique of American society, a critique that was not limited to the conformity of the postwar period but included the misogynistic structures of middle-class life, his criticisms of their work nevertheless reinscribed the homophobic categories of the official narrative of male development. He followed the example of contemporary psychologists and argued that the Beats, in rejecting middle-class values, showed signs of emotional and sexual immaturity. Implying that the Beats suffered from an arrested sexual development, he explained that "it is a tricky and technical matter to fix the point at which the wildly misogynistic passes over into the outright homosexual. But our fictional heroes do seem, at the very least, to reel along the borderline" (319). Thus, despite the fact that as part of their rebellion against middle-class life, the Beats actively resisted categorization as either gay or straight (with the exception of Allen Ginsberg, who openly acknowledged his homosexuality in his poetry), Wolfe insisted on labeling them homosexuals. He rejected the distinction between bisexuality and homosexuality to which the Beats appealed when defending their sexual experimentation and stated that "the avoidance of camping mannerisms, and the devotion to the 'male' role in pederasty, do not change the classification so much as refine it" (319). He even suggested that the Beats' misogynistic representations of women were alone sufficient evidence of their homosexuality. The tenacity with which the heroes of their novels clung to women merely indicated that they were "the sort of homosexuals who, afraid to retire outright to a strictly male erotic fraternity, must remain attached parasitically to women in order to batter them over and over" (319). Ironically, by insisting on labeling the Beats homosexuals, Wolfe undermined his own political agenda. Whether intentionally or not, his claim that the Beats were misogynistic ratified the dominant discourse of rebellion because it accepted the official representation of homosexuality as a psychological disorder that supposedly indicated an arrested sexual development.

Wolfe's claim that the Beat rebellion did not adequately challenge existing social structures was typical of the liberal reaction to their work. In general, postwar liberals dismissed the Beats because they did not feel that their rejection of middle-class values was sufficiently political. The Beats' resistance to the conformity of the postwar period supposedly did not reflect a totalizing critique of American society that included the capitalist relations of production. Norman Podhoretz, for

example, in "The Know-Nothing Bohemians," a review of Jack Ker-   **163**
ouac's *On the Road* (1957) published in *Partisan Review* in 1958, complained that the Beats ignored the plight of the working class, the
traditional subject of the social protest novel, and instead sought "the
source of all vitality and virtue in simple rural types and in the dis-
possessed urban groups (Negroes, bums, whores)."[9] Whereas the
writers associated with the Popular Front in the 1930s rejected middle-
class respectability for political reasons, the Beats did so because they
saw it as a sign "not of moral corruption but of spiritual death" (146).
For this reason, their "rebellion" had more in common with the populist tradition in American politics (hence the title's explicit reference to
the Know-Nothings) than with the radicalism of the twenties and
thirties. In marked contrast to the Bohemian writers of the twenties
and thirties, who supposedly "aimed at a state of society in which the
fruits of civilization would be more widely available" (147), the Bohemian writers of the postwar period resented civilization and expressed
nothing but contempt for "coherent, rational discourse which, being a
product of the mind, is in their view a form of death" (147). Her
Podhoretz expressed a kind of nostalgia for the very "sociological
formulas" of the thirties Wolfe argued seriously limited the Beats'
critique of American culture. He felt that the work of the Bohemian
writers of the twenties and thirties remained incomplete: a totalizing
critique of American social structures had yet to emerge. Thus he
criticized the Beats for trying to imitate the "primitive vitality" and
"spontaneity" (147) of jazz in their prose. He also thought they should
abandon their interests in "mystical doctrines" and "irrationalist philosophies" (147) and concentrate instead on continuing the work of
earlier Bohemian writers by making the "fruits" of Western civilization
more widely available. In other words, he wanted them to practice the
kind of "coherent, rational discourse" one encountered in the pages of
Partisan Review.

In attacking the Beats for abandoning what Wolfe disparagingly
referred to as the "sociological formulas" of the social-protest novel,
Podhoretz overlooked the historical specificity of their Bohemianism.
That is to say, he ignored the extent to which their resistance to
middle-class values was rooted in the conditions of the postwar period.[10] He did not acknowledge that the "sociological formulas" developed in the twenties and thirties were no longer applicable to Ameri-

can society and that Bohemian writers needed a new set of formulas for understanding contemporary social relations. Consequently, he seriously misrepresented the importance of the Beat rebellion. In particular, he did not grant the degree to which the Beats' sexual experimentation challenged middle-class values. Although he acknowledged that sexual promiscuity had always been the Bohemian writer's "most dramatic demonstration of his freedom from conventional moral standards, and a defiant denial of the idea that sex was permissible only in marriage and then only for the sake of a family" (148), he denied that it functioned similarly for the Beats. He did not realize that middle-class social conventions had changed considerably since the twenties and thirties. After all, thanks to the popularity of *Playboy*, which began publication in 1953, and other "girlie" magazines aimed at middle-class male consumers, sexual promiscuity was no longer wholly incompatible with middle-class values. Such magazines had not only extended the culture of consumption to sex but legitimated its use as a form of resistance to the suburbanization of middle-class values as well.[11] Because such magazines actively promoted the consumerism of the postwar period, their rejection of middle-class family values was not considered subversive, and the figure of the playboy escaped pathologization as an immature pervert who suffered from an arrested sexual development. Podhoretz, however, seemed oblivious to these changes in middle-class social conventions, or else he chose not to mention them because they complicated his argument. He attacked the Beats because they refused to allow their characters to make love "wantonly or lecherously—no matter how casual the encounter it must always entail sweet feelings toward the girl" (149–50). It did not occur to him that by insisting that their sexual relations entail "sweet feelings," the Beats were perhaps resisting the commodification of sex promoted by *Playboy* and other soft-porn magazines.

Moreover, in attacking the Beats for failing to continue the work of earlier Bohemian writers, Podhoretz underestimated the degree to which liberal cultural critique had become institutionalized in the postwar period. Criticizing American social structures in coherent, rational prose for liberal journals such as *Partisan Review* was no longer Bohemian but had become a perfectly respectable middle-class occupation.[12] The majority of contributors to such journals were embarked on successful academic careers at some of the most prestigious universities in the United States. Consequently, writing for such journals was no longer necessarily oppositional. Indeed, it could be argued that such journals indirectly contributed to the very middle-class conformity the Beats had rejected, because their rigid anti-Stalinism and implacable hostility to popular culture helped to consolidate and maintain the postwar settlement known as the Cold War consensus. Thus, although the Beats had rejected the "deep intellectual seriousness" (147) of earlier Bohemian writers, they had developed a set of oppositional practices specifically adapted to the social conditions of the postwar period. For this reason, their rejection of middle-class values represented more of a challenge to the social order than Podhoretz was willing to acknowledge. The very aspects of their writing that distinguished them from earlier Bohemian writers and that Podhoretz found so objectionable—their celebration of "mystical doctrines" and "irrationalist philosophies" and their spontaneous, improvisational prose that resembled jazz—promised to remain unassimilated by official culture.[13]

But if Podhoretz underestimated the difficulty of engaging in meaningful opposition to existing social arrangements in the postwar period, other liberal intellectuals did not. Indeed, many liberal intellectuals worried that in the postwar period there was nothing to rebel against *except* the pressures to conform. In marked contrast to Podhoretz, for example, Leslie Fiedler in "The Un-Angry Young Men," an essay published in *Encounter* in 1958, complained that younger liberals (by whom he meant the generation of liberals who came of age in the 1950s) were *too* committed to continuing the work of the Bohemian writers of the twenties and thirties. (Like Podhoretz, Fiedler conveniently never identifies these writers.) Rather than experimenting with new forms of political opposition, these liberals supposedly limited their political activity to the sorts of causes that had galvanized his generation of liberals: "Incapable of actual politics, the intellectual young sometimes find it possible to commit themselves to politics-once-removed: a kind of ghostly anti-Fascism, or the rewarmed dream of the New Deal as embodied by Adlai Stevenson."[14] Consequently, they had not adequately distinguished their oppositional practices from those of his generation whose political authority they accepted too readily. He complained that "the young who should be hard at work, fatuously but profitably attacking us, spend a good deal of their time discreetly amending, expanding, analyzing and dissecting—when they are not simply cribbing from us" (391). This was deeply problematic, because the experiences that had determined the forms of rebellion his generation had engaged in (the Depression, World War II), younger liberals had only experienced vicariously through reading history textbooks. As a result, rebellion for them could only be an "empty piece of mimicry, incongruous in a world which has found there is no apocalypse and that contemporary society threatens not exclusion and failure but acceptance and success" (390). In other words, they supposedly lacked the sort of experience that would authorize alternative oppositional practices and were therefore reduced to "mimicking" the liberal revolt of the twenties and thirties, a revolt that, in the context of postwar prosperity, could not possibly disrupt the social order.[15]

To support his claims that postwar prosperity had all but robbed the younger generation of intellectuals of the possibilities of meaningful revolt, Fiedler was forced to suppress the example of the Beats. He restricted his discussion of the Beats to a series of footnotes, thereby minimizing the importance of their opposition to existing social arrangements. But the very fact that he returned to them again and again suggests that, unlike Podhoretz, he recognized the significance of their rebellion; otherwise, he would not have restricted his discussion of them to footnotes. Clearly, their example called into question his claims that meaningful opposition was no longer possible in the 1950s. He did not know where to locate the Beats politically and resorted to claiming that they provided "only another model for the young, essentially that of the twenties—superficially brought up to date" (394). He did not want to believe that they might disrupt the social order, and so he displaced their rejection of middle-class values onto homosexuals, supposedly the "staunchest party of all" (405) in the postwar period. According to him, homosexuality had become "the purest and truest protest of the latest generation, not a burden merely, an affliction to be borne, but a politics to be flaunted" (405). He felt that homosexuals constituted the only group capable of seriously challenging the conformity of the postwar period because their rejection of middle-class values represented "the last possible protest against bourgeois security and the home in the suburbs where adultery is old hat" (406).

But in claiming that homosexuals constituted the "party" most capable of disrupting the social order, Fiedler was not referring to the gays who belonged to the Mattachine Society and who actively challenged the official narrative of male development by calling into question its assumption that the Oedipus complex was natural and inevitable. Rather, he was referring to openly gay writers such as Truman Capote and Tennessee Williams who sought publication in women's magazines because such publication supposedly represented "their passport into an upper bohemia, where good manners are appreciated and high style is savored, a world of chic, eager to read the latest effete exploitation of the Faulknerian scene and the Faulknerian themes of dissolution and infertility" (406). In other words, he meant gays he obviously considered frivolous and immature, gays who were themselves supposedly dissolute and infertile. Thus, despite his complaint that younger liberals had "cribbed" their oppositional practices from his generation, he was more interested in containing than promoting resistance to existing social arrangements. For his analysis of the possibilities of meaningful revolt ultimately corroborated the official narrative of male development. Although he acknowledged that homosexuality represented a potentially powerful oppositional practice, he nevertheless considered it an "affliction" and a "burden."

Despite the tendency among Cold War liberals to dismiss the Beats as apolitical, there were cultural critics in the 1950s who recognized the importance of the Beats and their challenge to the suburbanization of American culture. Norman Mailer, for example, unlike Podhoretz, emphasized the historical specificity of the Beat rebellion. In his controversial essay "The White Negro: Superficial Reflections on the Hipster," published in *Dissent* in 1957, he praised the Beats for developing a set of oppositional practices that were specifically adapted to the political and social conditions of the postwar period. Unlike Podhoretz, Mailer did not feel that a totalizing critique of contemporary social relations was desirable, or even possible. As a result, he thought that the very aspects of the Beat rebellion liberal cultural critics found so objectionable—its spontaneous, improvisational prose, its rejection of "rational, coherent discourse"—represented a significant advance over the established forms of political protest. They supposedly indicated that the Beat rebellion was not based on previously existing knowledge, or outdated "sociological formulas" developed in response to the political and social conditions of the twenties and thirties, but on a knowledge of social relations that was necessarily fragmentary and provisional. Mailer thought that the Beats had learned from the hipster that meaning was determined by context. According to him, they knew that every answer to a social problem immediately posed a new set of questions. Like the hipster, the Beats supposedly had "no interest in viewing human nature, or better, in judging human nature from a set of standards conceived a priori to the experience, standards inherited from the past."[16] The Beats, then, understood that experience constantly gave rise to new knowledge and that they could not always rationally anticipate political and/or social developments. Mailer argued that the Beats abdicated conventional moral responsibility because they had learned from the hipster that "the result of our actions are [sic] unforeseeable, and so we cannot know if we do good or bad" (353). Thus they realized that their theorization of their own experience had to remain provisional.

In attributing to the Beats oppositional practices that seriously challenged existing social structures because they were specific to those structures, Mailer rejected the "sociological formulas" developed in the twenties and thirties to explain the tensions in American society. He realized that historical agency was not located uniquely in the relations of production and that revolutionary struggles would develop only if the necessary political and social conditions were present. For this reason, he replaced the working class with the Beats as the privileged subjects of history. According to him, the Beats were more likely to bring about a revolution because the working class had been reluctant to constitute itself as an agent of historical change. He felt that because the Beat rebellion had emerged directly from the conditions of the postwar period, it constituted a truly popular movement. It did not depend on an intellectual elite or a party vanguard to raise levels of consciousness but rather had an automatic constituency in America's disgruntled youth. He warned that it would be a mistake to underestimate the importance of the Beats because they spoke "a language most adolescents understand instinctively" (343), a language that supposedly matched their experience and desire to rebel. Moreover, Mailer felt that because the Beats demanded absolute sexual freedom, they directly challenged the Cold War consensus, which operated according to the principle that the social order could peacefully accommodate every tendency in American life, however oppositional. Mailer claimed that such a demand rebounded against the "anti-sexual foundation of every organized power in America" (356) and thus could not be absorbed by the social order without significantly altering it. Mailer thought that because the Beat rebellion was so deeply rooted in African-American culture, it threatened "to bring into the air such animosities, antipathies, and new conflicts of interest that the mean empty hypocrisies of mass conformity will no longer work" (356). Such a crisis would necessarily shatter the liberals' faith in consensus politics and the naïve view of human nature on which it rested. Mailer foresaw a time "when every political guide post will be gone, and millions of liberals will be faced with political dilemmas they have so far succeeded in evading, and with a view of human nature they do not wish to accept" (356).

Widely interpreted as an incitement to violence, Mailer's essay drew fire from Cold War liberals who considered it morally irresponsible. Mailer seemed to look forward to the possibility that liberals might discover that they had seriously misjudged human nature or that the Beats might violently overthrow the social order.[17] In "The Know-Nothing Bohemians," for example, Podhoretz remarked that "whenever I hear anyone talking about instinct and being and the secrets of human energy, I get nervous; next thing you know he'll be saying that violence is just fine" (156). Podhoretz was quite right to criticize Mailer's effusions about "instinct" and "the secrets of human energy," for they reflected racist assumptions about a monolithic African-American identity that suppressed the significant differences dividing African Americans along class and gender lines. Mailer seemed oblivious to the existence of an African-American middle class whose values were similar to those of the white middle class or of working-class Blacks who had survived the ghetto without becoming "psychopaths," his term for individuals who engaged in violence solely for the purpose of purging themselves of their violent tendencies.

In "The Black Boy Looks at the White Boy," an essay originally published in *Esquire* in 1961, James Baldwin exposed Mailer's racist assumptions. He pointed out that in trying to exploit white male anxiety about the sexual superiority of Black men, Mailer reinforced the cultural myths about Black masculinity and in so doing ignored the way in which such myths operated so as to insure that Black men internalized the stereotype of "the nigger." Baldwin explained that

Black men could not possibly live up to such myths and thus constantly questioned their masculinity, which never seemed adequate.[18] Alluding to his identity as a gay Black man, Baldwin suggested that, unlike Mailer, he was in a position to know "something about the American masculinity which most men of my generation do not know because they have not been menaced by it in the way that I have been. It is still true, alas, that to be an American Negro male is also to be a kind of walking phallic symbol: which means that one pays, in one's own personality, for the sexual insecurity of others."[19] To substantiate his argument, Baldwin cited his relationship with Mailer, claiming that the myth of the threatening black phallus operated in such a way as to make him feel inferior to him. He explained that Mailer could never accept him because his homosexuality "inevitably connected, not to say collided, with the myth of the sexuality of Negroes which [Mailer], like so many others, refuses to give up" (220).

In addition, it was possible for cultural critics to acknowledge the importance of the Beats without following Mailer's example and abandoning a materialist critique of American society. Paul Goodman, for example, acknowledged the historical specificity of the Beat rebellion but refused to identify the Beats as the privileged subjects of history. Although he too realized that historical agency was not located uniquely in the relations of production, he refused to abandon the "sociological formulas" of the twenties and thirties and tried to adapt them to the conditions of the postwar period. In *Growing Up Absurd* (1960), for example, he argued that precisely because American society had become so affluent in the 1950s, it was "settling for the first time in its history into a rigid class system."[20] He did not deny that the possibilities for social mobility had improved considerably since the Depression but felt that class had become the most crucial determinant of an individual's identity: "One is more definitely in or out, and in a more definite rank" (59). Consequently, he felt that the Beats could not disrupt the social order without extending their critique beyond the conformity of middle-class life to America's economic structures. Indeed, he claimed that in working as farm laborers, dishwashers, and janitors, the Beats did not so much resist the American economic system as capitulate to it. Ironically, at the very moment that they challenged the suburbanization of American culture, they became subservient to the economic system: "Taking such a job, a man loses his freedom, he never stops working. He is used and made a fool of by the system, and this is in itself dishonorable" (69).

Still, Mailer's analysis of the Beats, an analysis that seemed to endorse the violent overthrow of existing social structures, derived from his understanding that the radical transformation of American society would necessarily entail the emergence of new subjectivities. He realized that the liberals, in overseeing the postwar settlement, had gained control over the way in which Americans thought and lived their relations to the world. By limiting the set of narratives available to Americans for making sense of their lived experience, the liberals contained the construction of their subjectivity across a multiplicity of competing discourses. Under the postwar settlement, Americans inhabited a set of discursive structures in which they experienced as subjective relations that were in reality political and social. That is to say, they experienced their lived relations to the world as originating in themselves rather than in specific political and social conditions. Thus Mailer felt that the only way in which Americans would give up their faith in consensus politics was if they experienced a violent shock to their subjectivity, so deeply rooted was that faith in their identities as Americans. He predicted that the discovery that African Americans would not compromise on the issue of civil rights would "tear a profound shift into the psychology, the sexuality, and the imagination of every white alive" (356).

The Power of the Cinematic Spectacle and
the Subjectivization of Experience

In the remainder of this chapter, I want to show that *Vertigo* follows Mailer's example in stressing the historical specificity of the Beat rebellion. As we saw above, postwar psychologists tried to empty the Beat rebellion of its political and social content by pathologizing it. According to the official representation of the Beat rebellion, the resistance to middle-class values had not emerged from the conditions of the postwar period but reflected a disturbance in the Oedipal structures of the middle-class nuclear family. For this reason, its critique of American society supposedly had no validity and was easily dismissed. American society as a whole did not need to be restructured, but individual families unable to adapt to postwar conditions. Hitchcock's film offers an alternative representation of the postwar rebellion. Although at first sight it seems to ratify the official narrative of male development because it pathologizes Scottie's rejection of middle-class values, it nevertheless directly links his "rebellion" to the conditions of the 1950s. It shows that his opposition to middle-class life is firmly rooted in his own personal history, which it represents as the product of his ongoing subjective engagement with the discourses that governed the organization of gender relations in the 1950s. This is not to suggest, however, that like the "white Negro" of Mailer's controversial essay, Scottie consciously engages in opposition to existing social and political structures. On the contrary, because he experiences those structures subjectively, as originating in himself rather than in concrete historical circumstances, his resistance to them is psychologically rather than politically motivated. This does not mean, however, that his resistance to the suburbanization of American culture is not specific to the conditions of the postwar period. Rather, the film suggests that in the 1950s perhaps the only way in which Americans could rebel was psychologically. The repression of historical knowledge, a repression crucial to maintaining the political stability and economic prosperity of the 1950s, virtually guarantees that Scottie will never arrive at an understanding of the historicity of his own subjectivity, its construction in relation to political and social institutions that have a history. For this reason, his opposition to the social order is always already contained. The very practices and institutions whose reach he wants to escape determine the structure of his rebellion. Lacking a knowledge of the past, he subjectivizes his experience, and thus his desire to rebel manifests itself as a psychological trauma that he feels he must repress rather than as a legitimate response to concrete historical forces.

Thus, at the same time that the film acknowledges the historical specificity of the Beat rebellion, it does not share Mailer's claim that the only way in which Americans would abandon their faith in consensus politics was if they experienced a violent shock to their subjectivity. Rather, it shows that most Americans repressed the desire to rebel because it threatened to tear a profound "shift" in their subjectivity. In the famous opening shots of the film, we see Scottie dangling precariously from the gutter of a building. He has lost his footing in leaping from one building to another while in pursuit of a suspect across some rooftops high above San Francisco's skyline. As he looks down, the camera cuts to a shot that simultaneously tracks in and zooms out, thereby indicating the onset of his vertigo. Critics usually interpret his vertigo as an indication that he simultaneously fears and desires death; in so doing, they relate it to his necrophilic desire for the "dead" Madeleine, which supposedly includes a similarly perverse desire for the dead Carlotta, the woman who appears to have taken possession of her.[21] It is the same sort of perverse desire, these critics argue, that later drives him to make Judy over into Madeleine. Although I would agree that the film stresses the perversity of Scottie's desire for the "dead" Madeleine, I would argue that it does so to link it to the postwar rebellion against middle-class conformity. Scottie's sudden loss of perspective in the opening shots of the film is so traumatic because he discovers that what he simultaneously fears and desires is not so much falling to his death as relinquishing his duties as an officer of the law. The dizzying movement of the camera as it simultaneously tracks in and zooms out serves to emphasize the shock of this discovery and the disorienting loss of perspective to which it necessarily leads. Scottie, who we learn from Midge in the next scene was until his accident "the bright young lawyer who wanted to be chief of police," cannot make such a discovery without it tearing a profound "shift" in his subjectivity. The homophobic categories of the dominant discourse of rebellion operate so as to ensure that he will interpret his desire to relinquish his responsibilities for enforcing the law as an indication that he suffers from an arrested sexual development. What I am suggesting is that Scottie's loss of balance in the opening shots of the film is so traumatic because, in discovering that he would rather transgress than enforce the law, he feels feminized. According to the official narrative of male development, he would not experience such a desire unless he were homosexual. Thus he continues to feel haunted by the uniformed policeman who fell to his death while trying to rescue him not so much because he blames himself for the tragic accident but because he has begun to question his own sexuality.

Scottie's desire to transgress rather than enforce the law is already apparent in the opening shots of the film. Scottie's inability to maintain his footing while in pursuit of the suspect may be read as a sudden loss of will, a failure of nerve, in the performance of his duties as an officer of the law. He already seems to be wavering, held in suspension between a desire to apprehend the suspect and a desire to let him go. In losing his footing and almost falling to his death, he does not so much resolve the tension between these two conflicting desires as evade it. Because he feels that his identity as a heterosexual male is directly related to his desire to enforce the law, he can only transgress the law vicariously: it is not he who escapes its reach but the suspect he allows to get away by nearly falling to his death. Moreover, because he has accidentally lost his footing in leaping from one building to another, he does not have to hold himself responsible for the suspect's escape. His desire to transgress the law can remain unconscious because he has not acted on it directly. He does not act on it directly until after his accident when he resigns from the police force. But even then he does not allow the desire to become conscious: he tells Midge that he has decided to resign from the police force because of his vertigo, thereby using his accident as an excuse for officially relinquishing his duties as an officer of the law.

The film, then, exposes the homophobic categories of the official narrative of male development as a mechanism for maintaining the economic prosperity and political stability of the 1950s. Because Scottie experiences his desire to transgress the law as feminizing, it must remain unconscious, which is why he finally agrees to investigate the mysterious behavior of Elster's wife. Although he has no desire to resume work as a detective and at first resists Elster's request, he eventually gives in because following Elster's wife promises to allow him to maintain the fiction that he is enforcing the law when in reality he is breaking it: while investigating Elster's wife, he will participate in Elster's murderous plot. I am trying to suggest that Scottie knows of Elster's plan to murder his wife, but represses the knowledge. In the scene in which Scottie finally gives in to Elster's request, Elster tells him wistfully: "The things that spell San Francisco to me are disappearing fast." He can no longer experience the "color, excitement, power, freedom" of the city's gay old Bohemian past. Pop Liebl later uses the very same words to describe Carlotta's seduction and abandonment by her Anglo lover. As I already indicated, he explains to Scottie and Midge that Carlotta's lover "threw her away" because "men could do that in those days": they had the "power" and the "freedom" to do so. In this way, he explicitly links Elster to Carlotta's lover. But Scottie ignores the evidence against Elster and therefore fails to make the connection between him and Carlotta's lover. In other words, he once again falters in the performance of his duties as an officer of the law. Just as he allows the suspect to escape in the opening shots of the film, so too does he allow Elster's crime to go undetected. Repressing his knowledge of Elster's plot, however, allows him to participate in it without consciously acknowledging that he is doing so. Rather, he can tell himself that he is acting in his official capacity as a detective and thus cannot possibly be a homosexual.

That Scottie does indeed interpret his desire to transgress the law according to the homophobic categories of the official narrative of male development becomes more obvious in the scene immediately following the opening shots of the film. There he appears to have accepted the official representation of his hesitation in the line of duty. He clearly feels insecure about his masculinity. He is wearing a corset as a result of his accident and asks Midge doubtfully, "Do you suppose many men wear corsets?" Moreover, he betrays a lack of sexual experience with women when he asks Midge what she is sketching. She replies, "It's a brassiere. You know about such things, you're a big boy now." Most critics agree with Midge that Scottie is a "big boy." Because he has no desire to settle down with Midge and seems perfectly content to remain "available Ferguson," they consider him sexually and emotionally immature. But in suggesting that he is a "big boy" rather than a grown man, critics reproduce the homophobic categories of the postwar narrative of male development.[22] They construct a reading of Scottie's hesitation in the line of duty that corresponds to the official representation of it, a representation that suppresses Scottie's experience of it. Scottie falters in the performance of his duties not because he suffers from an arrested sexual development, but because he has internalized the dominant discourse on rebellion and fears that he must be a homosexual. This explains more fully why he represses his knowledge of Elster's plan to murder his wife. Because he feels that his hesitation in the performance of his duties has feminized him, he allows Elster to use him as his instrument. He seems to believe that he has forfeited the right to exercise the power and freedom that define masculinity and willingly occupies the same position in relation to

Elster as Judy Barton does. Like Judy, he allows Elster to seduce and abandon him when he no longer needs him to carry out his murderous plot.

Scottie's internalization of the official representation of his hesitation in the line of duty, a representation that contains his desire to transgress the law by positioning him as "the homosexual" of the dominant discourse of rebellion, increasingly determines the structure of his relations with women. Because his subjectivity has been constructed in relation to the official narrative, the only way in which he seems able to desire a woman is through another man. Although Midge tells him that he is the only man for her, he never seriously considers settling down with her because he feels that she is too motherly. When she expresses her disapproval of his resignation from the police force, he says derisively, "Oh, Midge, don't be so motherly." At the same time, however, he clearly encourages her to occupy a motherly position in relation to him. In the scene in which he loses his balance while trying to cure himself of his vertigo, he faints into her arms as though he were a child and rests his head on her shoulder as she repeats, "Oh, Johnny, Johnny." By encouraging her motherliness in this way, he protects himself from her desire for him. He cannot return her love because it would be incestuous for him to do so.

Similarly, he seems to fall in love with Madeleine primarily because she belongs to another man and he can never totally possess her as his own. He reduces her to an object of exchange between him and Elster.[23] He accepts her in return for his silence: he will not reveal his knowledge of Elster's plot to murder his wife if Elster will give him Madeleine. Thus he uses Madeleine to triangulate his desire for Elster: as an object of exchange, Madeleine solidifies his relations with Elster. This use of Madeleine as an object of exchange is especially worth calling attention to because it indicates the extent to which Scottie has internalized the homophobic categories of the official narrative of male development. In the 1950s, the exchange of women was frequently identified as a homosexual practice men engaged in because they could not touch each other directly, and it was used by contemporary critics to identify the Beats as homosexual. Bernard Wolfe, for example, in his review of the Beats published in the *Nation*, did not hesitate to claim that the practice of exchanging women was "a homosexual ritual performed over and through the irrelevant bodies of women"

(320). Thus Madeleine's function as an object of exchange suggests that Scottie positions himself as a homosexual in relation to Elster. He accepts Madeleine in exchange for remaining silent because he and Elster cannot touch each other directly but only over and through Madeleine's "irrelevant" body. Thus the film suggests that the dominant discourse of rebellion contains Scottie's desire to transgress the law by tearing a profound shift in his subjectivity that makes him question his sexual identity. Having internalized the official narrative of male development, Scottie places himself in a position outside the law that the law has determined, and thus he remains firmly within its reach.

That Scottie's desire to transgress the law has indeed forced a shift in his subjectivity becomes clear in the nightmare that precipitates his breakdown. There he confuses his and Madeleine's identities: Madeleine's obsessions with the dead Carlotta become his. Madeleine never actually appears in the dream; rather, Carlotta appears in her place. We first see Carlotta in a shot in which Elster is embracing her in front of one of the windows of the courtroom where the inquest into Madeleine's "death" took place. She slowly turns and looks at Scottie, who is standing beside her. It is as though Scottie and Elster had exchanged her rather than Madeleine. Then the camera cuts to a close-up of her that recalls her portrait in the Palace of the Legion of Honor. Gradually zooming in on her necklace, the shot anticipates the scene at the end of the film in which Scottie discovers the truth about Judy's identity when he realizes that she is wearing the same necklace. In thus conflating Carlotta and Madeleine, the nightmare suggests that Scottie has made the connection between the two women but repressed it. He unconsciously realizes that because of the similarities of their personal histories, they are virtually one and the same woman, both having been seduced and abandoned by men with the power and the freedom to do so.

As several critics have pointed out, Scottie's nightmare as a whole recalls the recurring dream Madeleine recounts to him in the scene in which they kiss passionately by the sea while the waves crash onto the shore. In this dream, Madeleine imagines that she is walking along a dark corridor whose walls are covered with the fragments of a broken mirror. The corridor eventually leads to an open grave that seems to await her. Scottie's nightmare follows a similar narrative trajectory. As in Madeleine's dream, he imagines that he is walking, but rather than in a long corridor, he appears in a dark void, looking ahead inquisitively. Suddenly a rear-screen projection of the Mission Dolores appears in the background, thereby placing him in the cemetery where Carlotta is buried. The camera then tracks forward rapidly toward Carlotta's grave, which is open, and descends into it in a quick, jerking motion that recalls Scottie's traumatic fall in the opening sequence. In so doing, it makes clear that what Scottie finds so disturbing about his hesitation in the line of duty is the way in which it officially identifies him as a homosexual. Because he has internalized the official narrative of male development, his failure to perform his duties makes him question his sexual identity, and thus he cannot desire Madeleine, only identify with her. Scottie's identification with Madeleine culminates when he imagines that it is he, rather than she, who falls from the bell tower of the mission at San Juan Bautista. The spiraling silhouette of Scottie's falling body in this sequence recalls the uniformed policeman who fell to his death in the opening shots of the film while trying to rescue him. For this reason, it suggests that Scottie unconsciously realizes that in identifying with Madeleine, he is policing his own behavior. His internalization of the official narrative of male development leads him to contain his own desire to transgress the law. Thus he identifies not only with Madeleine but also with the uniformed policeman. He seems to have unconsciously assumed the policeman's function in relation to his own desire.

In stressing Scottie's internalization of the official narrative of male development, a narrative that virtually guarantees he will repress his desire to rebel because it positions him as a homosexual, the film provides an alternative representation of the postwar rebellion that refuses to reduce the resistance to the suburbanization of American culture to a psychological disorder. The film appears to suggest that the narratives available for understanding the postwar rebellion prevent Americans from acting on their desire to rebel by forcing them to subjectivize their experience of social reality. Americans experience the desire to rebel as originating in themselves rather than in concrete historical circumstances. As a result, their rejection of middle-class values can never seriously disrupt the social order. It remains wholly personal, grounded in their subjective experience of social reality. As I noted above, Scottie experiences his desire to transgress the law as a

psychological trauma that he must repress. Because he interprets it **179**
according to the homophobic categories of the official narrative of male
development, for him to act on it consciously, he would have to
occupy the position of "the homosexual" openly. For this reason, he
does not realize that his desire to transgress the law reflects his ongoing subjective engagement with the set of discourses that regulated
the construction of gendered identity in the 1950s.

In this respect, the film diverges significantly from Mailer's analysis of the Beat rebellion in his controversial essay "The White Negro."
As we saw above, Mailer refused to empty the Beat rebellion of its
political and social content by reducing it to a psychological disorder
that could be cured through therapy. Rather, he identified the revolt
against conformity as a form of psychopathic violence directly related
to the deterioration of middle-class values; in so doing, he implied that
it could not be contained. He claimed that unlike the neurotic who
could eventually be made through therapy to adjust to middle-class
life, the psychopath "knows instinctively that to express a forbidden
impulse actively is far more beneficial to him [sic] than merely to
confess the desire in the safety of a doctor's room" (346). Consequently, the psychopath's rejection of middle-class values truly threatened to disrupt the social order. Although the psychopath's resistance
to the conformity of the postwar period may have resulted from her/
his inability to resolve the Oedipus complex, it nevertheless could not
be cured through therapy. Hitchcock's film offers a different interpretation of the Beat rebellion. It suggests that the Beats did not
adequately challenge the social order because in limiting their critique
to the conformity of middle-class life, they ignored the structural
inequalities between the sexes in American society. The film tries to
show that the only way in which Scottie's resistance to the suburbanization of American culture could be meaningfully oppositional is if it
derived from an understanding of his own historicity, that is, the
construction of his subjectivity in relation to practices, discourses, and
institutions that have a history. Because Scottie's desire to transgress
the law remains wholly personal, he does not realize that the very
practices he wants to disrupt have determined the form his rebellion
has taken.

The film relates Scottie's subjectivization of his experience of social
reality directly to his repression of historical knowledge. Despite his

knowledge of San Francisco's gay old Bohemian past, a knowledge that should help him to recognize the historical production of his own subjectivity, he represses it, substituting a psychological for a historical understanding of social reality. For example, when Elster first tells him about his wife's mysterious behavior, which he explains supernaturally as an indication that the dead Carlotta has entered and taken possession of her soul, Scottie tells him that he should take her to "the nearest psychiatrist, or psychologist, or neurologist, or psychoanalyst, or maybe just the plain family doctor, and I'd have him check on you, too!" He refuses to believe that her behavior can be explained in any other way except psychologically. He insists that her recurring dream derives from a traumatic experience that she has repressed, and he believes that he can cure her of it by taking her to the mission at San Juan Bautista and making her relive it. The film stresses the consequences of this repression of historical knowledge by calling attention to the inadequacy of official representations of social reality that psychologize it. At the inquest into Madeleine's death, for example, the judge never questions Elster's claims that Madeleine committed suicide, and he blames her death on Scottie's "unfortunate condition," a medically resonant phrase that corroborates the official representation of Scottie as an emotionally immature man who suffers from an arrested sexual development. Consequently, the judge allows Elster's crime to go undetected. Moreover, the psychiatrist's description of Scottie's breakdown—he tells Midge that Scottie is suffering from "acute melancholia together with a guilt complex"—does not accurately represent the psychological trauma Scottie has experienced. Rather than relating it to the organization of gender relations in the postwar period, such a description wholly personalizes Scottie's breakdown. Scottie, however, needs to subjectivize his experience of social reality. For if he does not subjectivize it, he will have to acknowledge the structural relation between the city's gay old Bohemian past and its supposedly more law-abiding present, which will mean that he can no longer deny his participation in the reproduction of the misogynistic practices of American society.

In making Scottie question his sexual identity, the official narrative of male development ensures his participation in the reproduction of the structural inequalities between the sexes. According to the film, participating in the reproduction of the practices and institutions that victimized women and other historically disenfranchised groups was a prime component of the official construction of masculinity in the 1950s. Because Scottie wants to recover the power and freedom that define masculinity and that he feels he forfeited when he hesitated in the performance of his duties, he ignores Judy's remonstrances and relentlessly tries to make her over. It is not so much that he wants to regain Madeleine as that he wants to reclaim his masculinity. Thus whereas he did not hesitate to identify with Madeleine because he had internalized the official narrative of male development, he refuses to identify with Judy for precisely the same reason. This explains why he is so traumatized when he discovers the truth about Judy's identity. He learns not only that Judy has already been made over by Elster and therefore can never wholly belong to him, but also that Elster did a better job of making her over than he did. In the scene in which he drags her up the stairs of the bell tower of the mission at San Juan Bautista, back to the scene of the crime, he says angrily, "You played the wife very well, Judy. He made you over didn't he? He made you over just like I made you over. Only better." Still, in refusing to identify with her, he shows that he deserves the right to exercise the power and freedom that continued to define masculinity in the 1950s. He treats her in the same way Elster did, discarding her when she no longer serves his purposes.

Scottie's participation in the reproduction of the misogynistic practices that helped to maintain the stability of postwar American society is not limited to his refusal to identify with Judy but also includes his treatment of Midge. The final shot of Midge in the film is of her walking along the corridor of the sanitarium where she has been visiting Scottie, visibly dejected. When she reaches the end of the corridor, she turns slowly toward the camera, and the scene gradually fades around her. Because it recalls Madeleine's description of her recurring dream, this sequence suggests that Midge has experienced a kind of death at Scottie's hands. She never appears again in the film, because Scottie's continuing indifference to her has killed her off. In linking Midge explicitly to Carlotta, the film tries to reverse the repression of historical knowledge that was crucial to maintaining the social and economic stability of the postwar period. It stresses the structural relation between the past and the present by suggesting that Midge is a victim of practices that have a history and that are *not* specific to the postwar period, although the forms they take are. Like Carlotta, Midge has been discarded by a man who has the power and the freedom to do so. Thus the film makes clear that a rebellion that does not extend to the misogynistic practices of American society, practices that are not specific to the postwar period but are deeply rooted in the nation's history, can never seriously disrupt the social order.

The film reinforces this critique of the postwar rebellion against middle-class conformity by abruptly shifting the spectator's point of view from Scottie to Judy, with Judy's flashback in the second part of the film. Because the first part of the film is shot almost entirely from Scottie's point of view, the spectator tends to identify with him. The second part of the film, however, discourages the spectator from identifying with him by reconstructing the first part from Judy's point of view. With the flashback, the spectator gains a knowledge of Judy's involvement in Elster's murderous plot that Scottie lacks, and thus the spectator begins to identify with her rather than Scottie. During the flashback, the spectator learns that Judy has fallen in love with Scottie and that she wants to try to make him love her for herself and not because she resembles the "dead" Madeleine. For this reason, the spectator identifies with her increasingly futile attempts to resist Scottie's desire to regain Madeleine. It would be difficult to exaggerate the importance of this shift in identification for the film's critique of the rebellion against the conformity of middle-class life. It forces the spectator to experience Judy's victimization and, by extension, that of Carlotta and Midge. The spectator can no longer ignore the persistence of the structural inequalities between the sexes in American society. Judy's experiences are too similar to Carlotta's, and thus they cannot be dismissed as an isolated occurrence reflecting her own personal circumstances but should be seen as directly related to her position as a woman. In this way, the film encourages the spectator to acknowledge the historicity of female subjectivity, its construction in relation to misogynistic practices and institutions that have not changed significantly since the nineteenth century.

At the same time, however, that the film exposes the persistence of the structural inequalities between the sexes, it also tries to decenter the spectator's subjectivity by making her/him simultaneously occupy contradictory subject positions. For the spectator continues to identify with Scottie, despite his relentless attempts to make Judy over. The film continues to be shot almost wholly from his point of view and thus tends to decenter the spectator's subjectivity. The spectator's continuing identification with Scottie conflicts with her/his identification with Judy and places her/him in a kind of double bind. The spectator cannot identify with Judy's victimization without resenting Scottie's desire to regain Madeleine; nor can s/he identify with Scottie's desire to regain Madeleine without overlooking his victimization of Judy. In this way, the film helps to destabilize the spectator's understanding of social reality, which remains unfixed. One of the effects of the film's constant shift in point of view is that it tears a shift in the spectator's subjectivity that encourages her/him to question her/his understanding of social reality. Simultaneously occupying contradictory subject positions, the spectator experiences a kind of vertigo, or disorienting loss of perspective, in which s/he becomes conscious of the constructedness of social reality, its mediation by representation. That is to say, the spectator discovers through this disorienting loss of perspective that social reality is not only an effect of representation but also its excess, or what remains uncontained by representation and thus can destabilize or rupture it. According to the film, this excess makes possible the construction of alternative representations of social reality.

But the film does more than try to make the spectator conscious of the constructedness of social reality by decentering her/his subjectivity; it also renders explicit its own complicity with the dominant construction of social reality in the postwar period. In following Madeleine in his car from one historical landmark to another, Scottie becomes a kind of cinematic spectator, absorbed in the diegesis as it unfolds on the screen before him. Like a cinematic spectator, he is immobilized and must limit his activity to looking through the windshield of his car, which functions as a kind of screen and which yields him a surplus of visual pleasure by providing him with glimpses of both Madeleine and San Francisco.[24] In this way, the film implicates its own system of representation in the repression of historical knowledge. It calls attention to the way in which film in general psychologizes social reality. In reducing Madeleine to a kind of cinematic spectacle, Scottie's relation to her encourages him to repress his knowledge of San Francisco's gay old Bohemian past. He derives more pleasure from psychologizing the link between her and Carlotta than he would from historicizing it. For him to acknowledge Madeleine's victimization as a woman, he would have to see her as a subject constituted in history rather than as an object of visual pleasure. As a result, he remains blind not only to the misogynistic structures of American society but also to his participation in their reproduction.

In emphasizing its participation in the dominant construction of social reality in the 1950s, the film suggests that the cinematic apparatus has itself hindered the emergence of a critique of American society that adequately addresses the structural inequalities between the sexes. Its economy of pleasure guarantees that the spectator subjectivizes her/his experience of social reality. Because of the spectator's libidinal investment in the filmic text, s/he does not question its construction of social reality. Thus Hitchcock's film helps to show that the power of the cinematic apparatus resides in its ability to repress the spectator's knowledge of her/his participation in the reproduction of existing social relations. The spectator's absorption in the diegesis through the process of identification ensures that her/his participation in the reproduction of existing social relations remains pleasurable. Not only does the spectator not realize that in reducing Madeleine to an object of visual pleasure, s/he is contributing to the perpetuation of the very practices that victimize her, but s/he derives pleasure from doing so because s/he has been absorbed in the diegesis. Thus the film's decentering of the spectator's subjectivity helps to make her/him conscious of the possibility of an alternative construction of social reality, a construction that does not psychologize it. In identifying with Judy rather than Scottie, the spectator understands that her/his libidinal investment in the film depends on a regime of pleasure specific to the postwar period, a regime that, in reducing women to objects of visual pleasure, denies their subjectivity. It is a regime of pleasure that discourages the spectator from challenging the misogynistic practices and institutions that helped to ensure the stability of postwar society because participating in their reproduction yields her/him a surplus of pleasure.

HITCHCOCK
THROUGH THE LOOKING GLASS
Psycho and the Breakdown of the Social

Waving the flag with one hand, and picking pockets with the other—that's your patriotism!—Alicia Huberman, *Notorious*

A son is a poor substitute for a lover.—Norman Bates, *Psycho*

At the conclusion of *Psycho* (1960), a psychiatrist tries to explain Norman Bates's (Anthony Perkins) dangerously disturbed behavior by tracing it to his troubled relationship with his mother. Barely concealing his disgust, the psychiatrist tells the other characters assembled in the police chief's office that Norman's mother was a "clinging, demanding woman." Since her husband's death, she had lived with Norman as if "there was no one else in the world," and so when she fell in love with another man, Norman felt betrayed and killed her and her lover. But because "matricide is the most unbearable of crimes, most unbearable to the son who commits it," Norman could not live with his guilt and tried to erase what he had done. He retrieved his mother's body and tried to preserve it by treating it with chemicals. He still did not feel satisfied, however. Although he had preserved his mother's body, he had not brought her back to life, and so he "began to think and speak for her, give her half his life, so to speak." According to the psychiatrist, this led to a split in Norman's personality, which explains his motives for murdering Marion Crane (Janet Leigh). Because Norman assumed that his mother was as jealous of him as he was of her, when he met Marion and felt attracted to her, the "mother half" of his personality took over and killed Marion in a jealous rage. Concluding his explanation of Norman's behavior, the psychiatrist states rather sententiously that "when the mind houses two person-alities, there's always a conflict, a battle. In Norman's case, the battle is over and the dominant personality has won."

Although *Psycho* is often cited as an exemplary instance of classical Hollywood cinema because of its narrative structure, critics tend to agree that the psychiatrist's protracted explanation of Norman's behavior raises more questions than it answers and fails to provide the film with narrative closure.[1] Leo Braudy, for example, dismisses the psychiatrist as an explicit agent of containment and denial who resorts to scientific jargon to "explain" Norman and in so doing tries to repress the continuum established in the film between the normal and the abnormal.[2] Braudy is quite right to suggest that the psychiatrist's explanation fails to provide the film with narrative closure. The psychiatrist does indeed seem more interested in containing than in resolving the questions raised by the film. He reconstructs Norman's psychological history from an overly schematic and reductive psychoanalytic perspective and makes Norman's actions seem more meaningful and coherent than they actually are. While the psychiatrist's claim that Norman murdered Marion because his desire for her conflicted with his desire for his mother seems relatively plausible, the spectator experiences Marion's murder as an utterly random and meaningless act. Because the first part of the film is shot almost entirely from Marion's point of view, the spectator tends to identify with her, which makes her violent and abrupt disappearance from the film seem arbitrary. Moreover, Norman murders her shortly after she has decided to return to Phoenix and replace the money she has stolen, or, in other words, when the spectator most identifies with her. Thus, despite the psychiatrist's explanation, the most crucial questions raised by the film's narrative structure remain unanswered. Why, for example, does Norman suddenly replace Marion as the spectator's main point of identification? What is the connection, if any, between Marion's and Norman's stories, and why does the one so abruptly and irrevocably eclipse the other?

But to claim, with Braudy, that the psychiatrist's explanation fails to resolve the questions raised by the film is not to suggest that the film lacks narrative closure or is seriously flawed. Braudy's criticisms only make sense if the psychiatrist's reconstruction of Norman's psychological history is meant to provide the film with narrative closure. Because Braudy fails to distinguish the psychiatrist's point of view from that of the film, he mistakenly assumes that we are meant to accept the psychiatrist's reductive explanation as definitive. Consequently, he overlooks the possibility that Hitchcock intended the scene to foreground the inadequacy of the psychiatrist's explanation, or to call attention to the difficulty of adequately explaining Norman's behavior in purely psychoanalytic terms. What is perhaps most striking about the scene is the way in which the police constantly defer to the psychiatrist, thereby conceding to him their own authority to interpret Norman's behavior and to solve Marion's murder. The scene opens, for example, with Sheriff Chambers (John McIntire) reassuring Sam (John Gavin) and Lila (Vera Miles) that "if any one gets any answers, it'll be the psychiatrist." Despite the fact that Sheriff Chambers has known Norman since he was a little boy, Norman refuses to talk to him, and thus the sheriff must rely on the psychiatrist to solve the case.

Moreover, the scene constantly emphasizes the police's lack of expertise, or specialized knowledge, and thereby indirectly calls into question their ability to solve Marion's murder. When the police chief infers from the psychiatrist's explanation that Norman likes to dress in his mother's clothing because he is a transvestite, the psychiatrist corrects him, explaining somewhat pedantically that "a man who dresses in women's clothing in order to achieve a sexual change or satisfaction is a transvestite. But in Norman's case, he was simply doing everything possible to keep alive the illusion of his mother being alive." Indeed, despite the psychiatrist's reconstruction of Norman's psychological history, a reconstruction that despite its inadequacy attests to the ability of psychoanalytic discourse to provide a series of random and meaningless acts with the structure and coherence of a linear narrative, the police continue to think of Marion's murder in conventional terms. When the psychiatrist finally concludes his explanation, the police chief asks him what Norman did with the money stolen by Marion. The police chief still does not understand that Norman's motives were psychological rather than material, and thus the psychiatrist must reformulate his explanation in the police chief's own terms. He tells the police chief that "these were crimes of passion, not profit."

In this respect, the film seems less interested in providing an adequate and convincing psychoanalytic explanation of Norman's behavior than in calling attention to the rise of the expert in postwar

188   American culture and its impact on the organization of social relations. Postwar Americans relied heavily on trained professionals to tell them how to organize and manage their everyday life.[3] They increasingly sought advice from doctors, psychiatrists, family counselors, and social workers about how to raise their children, structure their leisure activities, and conduct their marriages; as a result, the expertise of trained professionals gradually replaced more popular and traditional forms of knowledge. Historians of postwar American society usually relate this development to the dramatic changes in the structure and organization of middle-class family life that accompanied the rapid growth of the suburbs in the 1950s.[4] Postwar Americans who settle in the suburbs tended to forsake traditional family and ethnic ties and to establish communities around the shared experiences of homeownership, child rearing, and consumerism. Consequently, they tended to have more freedom and independence than those Americans who continued to live in the closely knit, traditionally structured ethnic communities of cities and rural areas. At the same time, however, they were also cut off from the collective wisdom and shared experience that bound those communities together. The middle-class suburban housewife separated from her female relatives in the city or on the farm could no longer benefit from their knowledge of child rearing and had to rely on the expert advice of male "specialists" such as Dr. Spock, whose 1946 book, *The Common Sense Book of Baby and Child Care*, remained a best seller throughout the 1950s.

In stressing the extent to which the police must rely on the psychiatrist to interpret Norman's behavior and solve Marion's murder, the scene in the police chief's office foregrounds this development and calls attention to its impact on the operations of power in postwar American society. The psychiatrist's use of his specialized knowledge to reconstruct Norman's psychological history points to the dispersal of power in postwar America, a dispersal directly related to the rise of the expert. Because of the growing authority of trained professionals, power was no longer confined to the ideological and state apparatuses that had traditionally organized and regulated the social field but had become mobile and could be exercised from a multiplicity of social sites. The police in *Psycho* constantly defer to the psychiatrist because he has assumed their responsibility for maintaining law and order; in the era of the expert, the police had become obsolete and the psychiatrist had superseded them. But rather than undermining the authority of the state and its apparatuses, the increasing mobility of power, its dispersal across the social field, actually reinforced it. The psychiatrist and the other trained professionals to whom the state increasingly delegated its own responsibility for maintaining law and order did not compete with the police for jurisdiction over the social field so much as work with them. For the rise of such professionals all but guaranteed that the postwar subject internalized the law and consented freely and spontaneously to the terms of the postwar settlement. The increasing reliance of postwar Americans on psychiatry and other scientific discourses legitimated and consolidated the institutionalization of specialized knowledge; indeed, for many Americans in the 1950s, such knowledge acquired the status of the law. Because of his professional expertise, the psychiatrist in *Psycho* has the authority not only to enforce the law but also to define it. His reconstruction of the case suggests that the real criminal is not Norman but his "clinging, demanding" mother whose "unnatural" relations with her son supposedly resulted in his psychotic behavior. In other words, the crime the police should be investigating is not Marion's murder but Mrs. Bates's violation of the "laws" regulating the eroticized space of the middle-class nuclear family.

At the same time, however, that the film shows that the state's authority increased significantly in the postwar period because of the decentralization of its power, it also foregrounds the impossibility of containing the social, of fixing or stabilizing its meaning in a closed system of differences. The fact that the psychiatrist's explanation of Norman's behavior does not seem wholly plausible calls into question the ability of psychoanalytic discourse to give random and meaningless acts the structure and coherence of a linear narrative. Indeed, the psychiatrist's reductive use of Freudian categories seems to multiply rather than fix the potential meanings of Norman's behavior. On the one hand, the final shots of Norman sitting in a jail cell wrapped in a blanket soliloquizing in his mother's voice seems to confirm the psychiatrist's reconstruction of the case. The "mother half" of Norman's personality does indeed seem to have won the battle for control of him. On the other hand, the mother's voice-over suggests that the psychiatrist's use of Freudian categories does not adequately explain Norman's motives for murdering Marion, which remain unclear. Although the psychiatrist claims that Norman thought that his mother murdered Marion and "like a dutiful son" covered up all traces of the crime, the mother's voice-over insists that Norman killed Marion and then tried to blame the murder on her. Thus we never know which half of Norman's personality committed the murder and why. In this way, the film suggests that the dispersal of power in the postwar period led to a proliferation of points of resistance. With the rise of the expert, individuals, groups, and classes became mobile, assuming variable positions in the social field from which they simultaneously exercised and resisted power. That is to say, in postwar American society, relations of power were not fixed, but mobile. Constantly forming and dissolving, they made possible the exercise of power from below. Because Norman's behavior cannot be adequately explained in psychoanalytic terms, it calls attention to the inability of psychoanalytic discourse to construct a satisfying and coherent narrative that gives order and meaning to the world and in so doing regulates and controls the way in which the subject internalizes and makes sense of it.

Psycho, then, focuses on a surplus of meaning uncontained by the social and the semiotic and discursive practices that organize and define the individual's lived relations to the world. Although it shows that the specialized knowledge of trained professionals had acquired that status of law in postwar America, it also emphasizes the limited ability of the state and its representatives to organize and regulate the social field. Norman and his mother are not the only characters in the film who refuse to abide by the "laws" that regulated Oedipal desire in the 1950s. Marion, too, resists the authority of the state and its representatives to legislate psychosexual norms. As I noted above, Marion is our main point of entry into the film's narrative, the character in whom we have the strongest investment. Although she steals Cassidy's (Frank Albertson) money, we continue to identify with her because she is tired of meeting Sam secretly in cheap hotels and wants to live with him openly and respectably as his wife. Moreover, she genuinely regrets the theft and decides to return to Phoenix and replace the money. Still, her motives are more complicated than this implies. When she flees Phoenix in her car and imagines Cassidy's reaction to the theft, she smiles mysteriously. She seems to derive pleasure from the thought that he will make her replace the money with her "fine, soft flesh." Indeed, it is as though she wanted to be punished by him. Thus she, too, threatens to disrupt the signifying practices that organized and defined individual and collective identities. Like Norman, she is divided by conflicting desires and seems to lack a fixed, stable identity. Although she wants to "normalize" her relationship with Sam by marrying him, she also derives pleasure from occupying a position outside the law. For this reason, her identity remains virtually unintelligible to the spectator. It cannot be understood or interpreted within the horizon of meanings and knowledges available in the 1950s for explaining the construction of female subjectivity.

Psycho's emphasis on the breakdown of the practices and discourses that anchored and guaranteed the construction of gendered identity in the 1950s is surprising, for it exactly reverses the focus of *North by Northwest* (1959), the film Hitchcock made immediately before it. In *North by Northwest*, Hitchcock showed that the discourses of national security virtually guaranteed that gender and nationality functioned as mutually reinforcing categories of identity. At the beginning of the film, the hero, Roger Thornhill (Cary Grant), displays many of the same characteristics as Norman Bates. Like Norman, he is overly dependent on his mother and seems to lack a fixed, stable identity. He is simultaneously a Madison Avenue advertising executive, a notorious playboy, a falsely accused fugitive from justice, a jealous lover, a devoted son, and an unofficial agent for the American government. His career as a Madison Avenue advertising executive only reinforces the construction of his subjectivity across a multiplicity of competing discourses. As he himself remarks at one point in the film, "In the world of advertising, there is no such thing as a lie, there is only the expedient exaggeration." Yet when he is mistaken for George Kaplan, a wholly fictitious agent created by the American government as a decoy to entrap Vandamm (James Mason), a Communist agent who has stolen some classified documents, he begins to occupy a more stable and unitary subject position. He rescues Eve Kandall (Eva Marie Saint) when Vandamm discovers that she is an agent for the American government and thus shows that he has overcome his dependence on his mother and has internalized the Law of the Father. In this way, the film suggests that his entry into full masculinity as signified in the Symbolic order and his willingness to perform his patriotic duty are mutually reinforcing. Thus whereas *Psycho* emphasizes the proliferation of points of resistance to which the dispersal of power across the social field had led in the 1950s, *North by Northwest* shows that the construction of gender and national identity anchored and guaranteed each other in postwar America. Whereas in *Psycho* the operations of power that constantly threatened to disrupt the hegemonic articulation of identity occupy center stage, in *North by Northwest* they remain safely in the background.

Why in *Psycho* would Hitchcock reverse the focus of *North by Northwest*? Why in *Psycho* would he stress the limited ability of the state to contain the construction of the individual's subjectivity across a multiplicity of competing discourses when in *North by Northwest* he showed that the discourses of national security linked the construction of gender and national identity? In the following pages, I want to try to answer these questions. I will stress the inverted relation between the two films and suggest that *Psycho* constitutes a mirror image of *North by Northwest* in which Hitchcock reversed the focus of the earlier film in order to revise significantly its representation of the operations of power in postwar America. In foregrounding the discursive practices that reinforced the construction of the individual's subjectivity across a plurality of contending discourses, *Psycho* called attention to the mobility, or lack of fixity, of power relations in postwar American society and suggested that such relations were potentially reversible. Whereas Thornhill internalizes the discourses that linked the construction of gender and national identity in the 1950s, Norman Bates resists them. Thus *Psycho* stresses the limited ability of the state to determine the individual's subjective engagement with the signifying practices that regulate and control the production of meaning at a given historical moment. In so doing, it points to a surplus of meaning that remained uncontained by the dominant construction of social reality in the postwar period and therefore made possible the emergence of alternative constructions. It was this surplus that Hitchcock tried to suppress in *North by Northwest*, because it threatened to undermine his representational practices and their ability to give meaning to the events of the world.

Psycho's opening titles, designed by Saul Bass, immediately call attention to the film's inverted relation to *North by Northwest*. Whereas *North by Northwest*'s opening titles, also designed by Bass, provide a kind of map of the social meant to locate or orient the spectator, those of *Psycho*, which closely resemble them, try to disorient her/him. As *North by Northwest* opens, a series of intersecting lines, clearly intended to invoke a map or graph, traverse a blank screen placed at an angle to the camera.[5] They eventually dissolve into a shot of an office building whose glass and steel facade reflects the moving traffic on the busy street below. By beginning in this way, the film demonstrates its ability to conjure reality, to construct a representation of the world that the spectator does not question but assumes accurately reflects contemporary society because of its perceptual intensity or so-called impression of reality. The mirrorlike surface of the facade that emerges from the intersecting lines functions as a screen on which the images of the busy street below are not so much reflected as projected. Consequently, the opening titles seem to suggest that as a semiotic practice, the film has the ability to organize and define reality, to construct a map of it that fixes its meaning for the spectator. The intersecting lines that traverse the screen and eventually dissolve into the building's facade form a kind of definitional grid that organizes the images of moving traffic projected onto the building from the street below. In this way, the opening titles call attention to the artificiality or constructedness of the film's representation of reality. The film actively constructs, rather than passively reflects, reality. It provides the spectator with the coordinates that enable her/him to locate and define her/his position in the world and thereby make sense of it.

In marked contrast, *Psycho*'s opening titles seem meant to disavow film's ability to organize and give meaning to the events of the world. They suggest that despite its ability to conjure reality, film reinforces, rather than limits, the construction of the individual's subjectivity across variable axes of difference. Unlike the lines that traverse the screen at the beginning of *North by Northwest*, those at the beginning of *Psycho* do not intersect to form a grid. Rather, sets of horizontal and vertical lines appear alternately on the screen, cutting across and fragmenting the credits. Eventually, vertical lines of varying lengths appear and then dissolve into a shot of a city skyline dotted with skyscrapers. The way in which the credits fragment and vanish immediately after they appear on the screen suggests that the film's ability to provide a map of the social that organizes and defines it is limited. Because the spectator participates in a plurality of contending social formations, the film is unable to suture her/his identity. The spectator's inscription within filmic discourse can never wholly exhaust her/his subjectivity. Indeed, the spectator's inscription within filmic discourse threatens to multiply and disperse her/his identity rather than fix or stabilize it. As the camera pans the city skyline after the opening titles have faded, the name of a city (Phoenix) appears on the screen, followed by a date and a time, the significance of which remains unclear. The camera then tracks forward and descends toward a building, hesitates, chooses a window, then enters the window, after again hesitating. In this way, the opening sequence seems to suggest that the film cannot organize and define reality, only record it. It can identify the place, date, and time of the events we are about to see but it cannot explain why they have been chosen or what they mean. Indeed, the identification of the film's setting only emphasizes the arbitrary and random way in which it has been chosen. Identifying the film's setting should contribute to the meaning of the events we are about to see but does not.

North by Northwest similarly begins by emphasizing the impossibility of fixing the social in a closed network of meanings. In the opening sequence, we are shown shot after shot of the chaotic bustle and seemingly aimless movement of New York's crowded pavements during rush hour. When the camera finally focuses on Roger Thornhill, whom it picks out of the crowd almost randomly, it shows him emerging from an elevator jammed with office workers. The camera almost loses sight of him as it follows him through the crowded lobby onto the street where his erratic behavior and disjointed conversation with his secretary only add to the confusion. For example, when he sees a taxi pull up to the sidewalk, he rushes for it, pushing aside the man who has hailed it. Once inside he glances at a newspaper, interrupts his secretary, who is repeating his dictation, and asks her if he has put on weight. As the taxi drops him off at the hotel where he is supposed to meet some clients for drinks, he tells his secretary to call his mother and remind her of their theater engagement later that evening. But when the taxi pulls away, he suddenly remembers that his mother is playing bridge with some friends and cannot be reached by telephone. In this way, the opening sequence suggests that he is a typical product of New York's crowded pavements and bustling traffic. Like the crowds of workers who come and go in the opening shots, he seems to lack direction. His life is disorganized and chaotic and seems to be made up of purely random events that bear no relation to one another. Indeed, purely by accident, he is kidnapped shortly after he arrives at the hotel by two of Vandamm's men, who mistake him for the fictitious American agent George Kaplan.

But Thornhill's kidnapping is not as random and arbitrary as it appears; rather, it is directly related to his lack of a fixed, stable identity. His erratic behavior and disjointed conversation in the opening sequence link him to Norman Bates in *Psycho* and suggest that, like him, he occupies a position outside the law. He too has failed to internalize the "laws" that regulate Oedipal desire. Not only does he drink too much, but he has been married twice and remains emotionally dependent on his mother. Moreover, he occupies a series of constantly shifting subject positions that threaten to multiply and disperse his identity. As I noted above, he is simultaneously a devoted son, a womanizer, a jealous lover, a successful advertising executive, a falsely accused fugitive from justice, and an agent for the CIA. Thus it is hardly surprising that he is mistaken for another man; his identity is not clearly defined. Following the example of contemporary psychoanalytic discourse, the film traces his lack of a clearly defined identity to his continuing dependence on his mother. Although unlike Mrs. Bates in *Psycho* Thornhill's mother is not a "clinging, demanding woman," Thornhill is overly devoted to her. Indeed, his devotion to her is indirectly responsible for his kidnapping, for it is when he tries to send her a telegram reminding her of their theater engagement that he is mistaken for Kaplan. Thus his kidnapping is not random and arbitrary but serves as punishment for his continuing dependence. Because he has failed to internalize the Law of the Father, his identity remains unsutured and he is susceptible to manipulation by Communist agents like Vandamm.

Nor are the other events that befall Thornhill random and arbi-

196   trary; on the contrary, they are part of the American government's
carefully orchestrated plan to entrap Vandamm by having Eve infil-
trate his organization and retrieve the classified documents he has
stolen. The American government remains fully in control of Thornhill's experiences, guaranteeing their unity and coherence and determining their significance. Although the Professor (Leo G. Carroll)
does not anticipate Thornhill's kidnapping, he refuses to allow it to
interfere with Eve's counterespionage activities. In the scene in the
conference room at the intelligence agency, he coldly consigns Thornhill to his fate when he learns that Thornhill has been mistaken for
Kaplan. He announces to his advisers that Thornhill's survival is "his
problem." Even when Thornhill shows a determination to discover
Kaplan's identity and threatens to expose Eve as a double agent, the
American government remains in control of the events that befall him.
The Professor gains Thornhill's cooperation by revealing Eve's identity to him and persuades him to continue impersonating Kaplan until
the stolen classified documents have been retrieved. In this respect,
Thornhill's kidnapping shows the extent to which the American government continued to regulate and control the production of the postwar subject, despite the increasing mobility of power relations and the
proliferation of points of resistance to which it led. By exploiting the
anti-Communist hysteria of the postwar period, the discourses of
national security all but guaranteed the production of forms of subjectivity that were unequivocally social. That is to say, although the
construction of the individual's subjectivity reflected her/his personal
history, it conformed to the nation's security interests. Thornhill's
kidnapping is not a punishment so much as it is an intervention. It
involves him directly in the crisis over national security and enables
the government to intervene in the construction of his subjectivity.
The organization of his everyday life is increasingly determined by
questions of national security.

In following the example of contemporary psychiatric discourse
and tracing Thornhill's lack of a sutured identity to his continuing
dependence on his mother, *North by Northwest* participated in the
network of diverse but congruent discourses that in the 1950s linked
communism and homosexuality in the nation's political imaginary.
Such discourses constantly warned against the potentially pernicious
effects of motherhood and point to a reaction against the emergence of

the so-called feminine mystique of the 1950s.[6] On the one hand, post-war American culture experienced a proliferation of glorified representations of motherhood designed to lure women back into the home following the demobilization of American troops. On the other hand, many Americans resented the glorification of motherhood because it supposedly gave women too much power over the domestic sphere. For example, Philip Wylie, who coined the term *momism* in his best-selling book *Generation of Vipers* (1942), argued that American society was rapidly becoming a matriarchy in which domineering and overly protective mothers disrupted the Oedipal structure of the middle-class nuclear family by smothering their sons with "unnatural" affection. As Michael Rogin has shown, with the outbreak of the Cold War, momism became linked to the spread of communism in the nation's political imaginary and led to the creation of a demonology of motherhood.[7] Suddenly, mothers who disregarded the professional advice of Dr. Spock and other "experts" on child rearing risked not only disrupting the Oedipal structure of the middle-class nuclear family but also making their sons susceptible to Communist propaganda. Indeed, to emphasize the American government's vulnerability to Communist infiltration, the discourses of national security tended to treat communism as a form of momism. Like the demonized mothers of Wylie's *Generation of Vipers*, Communists allegedly gained control over unsuspecting Americans by exploiting their political naïveté and seducing them with Marxist propaganda.

Rogin tries to explain the reaction against the feminine mystique by suggesting that it constituted the "demonic version" of the discourses and ideologies mobilized by the American government to lure women back into the home.[8] He locates the source of the discourses of momism in the child's pre-Oedipal relations with the mother in which the child simultaneously fears and desires invasion and incorporation by the mother. Drawing on object-relations theory, he claims that Wylie's demonization of motherhood inscribes "the buried anxieties over boundary invasion, loss of autonomy, and maternal power generated by domesticity."[9] Although in return for accepting their political and economic subordination, women were empowered in the domestic sphere, the emergence of the feminine mystique brought to the surface misogynistic fears that were deeply rooted in the American psyche and that worked to limit their authority as mothers. But in trying to explain the emergence of a national demonology of mother-hood in purely psychoanalytic terms, Rogin overlooks the way in which the discourses of momism legitimated and consolidated the institutionalization of specialized knowledge and reinforced the link between the construction of gender and national identity. In vilifying domineering mothers, Wylie helped to lay the foundation for the identification of homosexuality and lesbianism as threats to national security. Although he did not explicitly link momism to homosexuality and lesbianism, Wylie identified communism as a form of political deviance directly related to incompetent mothering; in so doing, he reinforced the association in the nation's political imaginary between communism and same-sex eroticism. After all, contemporary psychiatric discourse had located the source of homosexuality and lesbianism in incompetent mothering. Thus the discourses of momism limited women's empowerment in the domestic sphere and ensured that their child-rearing practices conformed to the nation's security interests. For if women disregarded the expert advice of psychiatrists and other trained professionals, they risked producing children who were Communists as well as homosexuals.

In *North by Northwest*, this aspect of the demonization of mother-hood, a demonization that was not limited to the discourses of momism but was also apparent in the identification of homosexuality and lesbianism as threats to national security, is most obvious in Thornhill's relationship with his mother. Although Mrs. Thornhill has little in common with the domineering, overly protective mothers vilified by Wylie and his followers, Thornhill's relationship with her constitutes a form of momism. His devotion to her is indirectly responsible for his kidnapping, which propels him into the Communist underworld, an underworld marked by sexual as well as political deviance. In conformity with the discourses of national security, the film associates communism with same-sex eroticism. The typical Hitchcockian villain, Vandamm's secretary, Leonard (Martin Landau), is coded as homosexual, and the film sexualizes his relationship with Vandamm.[10] As Lesley Brill has pointed out, Hitchcock uses the sound track to suggest that the two men are lovers.[11] In the scene in which Thornhill, disguised as a redcap, carries Eve's bags into the Chicago train station, the sound track plays the musical theme it has associated with the couple's lovemaking as they are shown descending the train and

walking rapidly toward the station. It continues to play the theme as
the camera cuts from a close-up of Eve's face to a shot of Vandamm and
Leonard, who are following closely behind. It suggests that like Eve
and Thornhill, the two men form a couple. The homoeroticism of the
relationship between the two men becomes even more apparent in the
scenes at the house in Rapid City at the end of the film. While they are
waiting for the plane to arrive, Leonard tells Vandamm that his "woman's intuition" has made him suspect Eve of being a double agent.
Although Vandamm does not believe him, he tells Leonard that he is
"touched" by his jealousy.[12]

In helping to underwrite and consolidate the link between communism and homosexuality in the discourses of national security, the
film suggests that Thornhill's involvement in the Communist underworld is not purely coincidental but is indirectly related to his devotion
to his mother. The film tries to show that because he has failed to
internalize the Law of the Father and remains emotionally dependent
on his mother, there is a sense in which his irresponsible behavior is
complicit with the Communist infiltration of the American government. According to the film, the world of political and sexual deviance
is not so different from the world of advertising. As a Madison Avenue
advertising executive, Thornhill is a master of the "expedient exaggeration." Like Vandamm, who constantly playacts and falsifies his
identity, Thornhill does not hesitate to misrepresent his motives and to
deceive others. As Eve puts it when they are making love on the train,
"You're very clever with words, can probably make them do anything
for you, sell people things they don't need, make women who don't
know you fall in love with you." This is not to exaggerate the similarities between Thornhill and Vandamm; nor is it to suggest that
Thornhill is coded as homosexual. My point is simply that even before
Thornhill is kidnapped, his behavior has a direct bearing on the nation's security, which is why the government intervenes in it. The film
calls attention to the resemblance between Thornhill and Vandamm
because Thornhill's sexual immaturity is incompatible with the nation's security interests. In the postwar period, the nation's political
stability and economic prosperity were thought to depend upon the
production of subjects who had internalized the rules and regulations
governing Oedipal desire. Thus Thornhill is not so different from the
film's Communists and homosexuals, who are conspiring to over-

throw the government, because he has resisted inscription within the discourses of national security.

Critics tend to dismiss Thornhill's activities as an American agent as the film's MacGuffin, or pretext for addressing larger, supposedly more important issues.[13] According to them, Thornhill's quest for a stable identity and a proper mate cannot possibly be related to or contingent upon his activities as an American agent. Moreover, they see little difference between Vandamm and the Professor and claim that both men are equally corrupt, Vandamm because he deals in stolen classified documents, the Professor because he is prepared to sacrifice Eve in the name of national security. Thus they suppress the film's participation in the network of discourses that linked the construction of gender and national identity in the postwar period. We are supposedly meant to agree with Thornhill when he tells the Professor angrily, "Perhaps we'd better start learning to lose a few cold wars" because such wars threaten to politicize the domestic sphere. It is important to point out that Hitchcock encouraged this reading of the film, a reading that depoliticizes its representation of the construction of gendered identity by suppressing its relation to the discourses of national security. When Truffaut interviewed Hitchcock and asked him to define the MacGuffin, Hitchcock explained that it was "the term that we use to cover all that sort of thing: to steal plans or documents, or discover a secret, it doesn't matter what it is. And the logicians are wrong in trying to figure out the truth of a MacGuffin, since it's beside the point. The only thing that really matters is that in the picture the plans, documents, or secrets must seem to be of vital importance to the characters. To me, the narrator, they're of no importance whatever."[14] In this way, Hitchcock discouraged critics from politicizing his films by situating them historically. He wanted to ensure their canonization as great works of art. Though a subject constituted in history and continuously engaged in the discourses and ideologies that organized and defined the individual's lived relation to the world in the 1950s, he supposedly did not have a vested interest in underwriting and legitimating the practices that linked the construction of gender and national identity. Rather, he tried to address more timeless and universal issues.

But critics who do not question Hitchcock's definition of the MacGuffin and who dismiss the stolen microfilm in *North by Northwest* as a pretext for addressing "larger" issues overlook the way in which Thornhill's activities as an American agent anchor and guarantee his construction as a subject who consents freely and spontaneously to the terms of the postwar settlement. For it is only when Thornhill agrees to impersonate Kaplan that he demonstrates his maturity as an American citizen; only then does it become clear that he has overcome his dependence on his mother and internalized the "laws" regulating Oedipal desire. Admittedly, when he discovers that the Professor has lied to him and that Eve will be defecting with Vandamm, he refuses to continue cooperating with the American government: he disregards the Professor's instructions and tries to rescue Eve. But in disregarding the Professor's instructions, he indirectly promotes the nation's security interests. His inscription within the discourses of national security first becomes apparent in the scene in which the Professor stages his "murder" at the Visitor's Center at Mount Rushmore. When Eve shoots Thornhill with blank bullets, she "kills" Kaplan, the man Thornhill has been impersonating, and enables Thornhill to return to being himself. Because Thornhill has shown that he is willing to perform his patriotic duty, he no longer needs to assume Kaplan's identity and can act independently without the Professor's supervision. That is to say, the American government no longer needs to intervene directly in the organization of his everyday life. He has been sexually rehabilitated through Eve and can now safely return to the private sphere. Thus it is more important for him at this point in the film to rescue Eve from Vandamm than to follow the Professor's instructions. The point is not that he should continue to act as an official agent for the American government, but that he should return to the private sphere where he can assume the role of breadwinner, a role that was considered crucial to maintaining the stability of postwar American society and that he has resisted throughout the film.

Thornhill's consent to the terms of the postwar settlement, terms that require him to assume the role of breadwinner freely and spontaneously, becomes obvious when he disregards the Professor's instructions and rescues Eve. For in rescuing Eve, he not only returns her to the private sphere, but shows that he is more capable of judging the nation's security interests than the Professor. According to the terms of the postwar settlement, Eve is sexually immature before she becomes an agent for the American government. When Thornhill asks her how she first became involved with Vandamm, she tells him, "I had nothing to do that weekend, so I decided to fall in love." Although her activities as an American agent partially redeem her by showing her willingness to perform her patriotic duty, she nevertheless continues to occupy a position outside the law. She explains to Thornhill that she originally agreed to spy on Vandamm because it "was the first time anyone asked me to do anything worthwhile." Yet the only way in which she can perform her patriotic duty is by violating the rules and regulations that governed female sexuality in the 1950s. Thus she remains only partially rehabilitated as a citizen. This becomes apparent when Thornhill refers to her as a "treacherous little tramp" and accuses her of using sex "like a fly swatter." Despite the fact that her counterespionage activities constantly place her in danger, she remains a "marked" woman. Consequently, when Thornhill rescues her from Vandamm, he enables her to do something genuinely worthwhile for the nation. Her counterespionage activities allow him to reclaim her for the private sphere; they show that she is ready to become a "proper" wife and mother. Whereas the Professor constantly places Eve in compromising positions that force her to violate the terms of the postwar settlement, Thornhill enables her to perform her true patriotic duty by returning her to the private sphere.

To clarify the way in which Thornhill's activities as an American agent ensure his inscription within the discourses of national security, I want to turn to *Notorious* (1946), a film that also explores the link between gender and national identity in postwar America. But whereas *North by Northwest* focuses on the construction of *male* heterosexual subjectivity in relation to the discourses of national security, *Notorious* focuses on the construction of *female* heterosexual subjectivity. Despite the differences between the two films, *Notorious* can help to clarify Thornhill's construction as a subject who consents freely and spontaneously to the terms of the postwar settlement because it addresses the link between gender and national identity more explicitly than *North by Northwest*. In *Notorious*, the espionage activities of the hero and heroine, Devlin (Cary Grant) and Alicia Huberman (Ingrid Bergman) cannot be reduced to the status of a MacGuffin. Although their formation as a couple seems to displace the discovery of the source of the uranium ore as the object of their assignment, the two activities are directly related and must be undertaken simultaneously. That is to say, the American government virtually guarantees Devlin and Alicia's inscription within the discourses of national security by mobilizing their desire for each other. Because their formation as a couple depends upon their discovering the source of the uranium ore, they remain libidinally invested in their espionage activities. Thus their desire for each other cannot be separated from their espionage activities, for it is at once a product of those activities and productive of them.

Tania Modleski has recently complained that *Notorious* collapses the distinction between the public and private spheres and thereby displaces the political onto the personal.[15] Although critics have tended to celebrate the way in which the film supposedly reduces the discovery of the uranium ore to the status of a MacGuffin, Modleski argues that feminists should feel troubled by this aspect of the film, because it denies that the personal is political.[16] Modleski is quite right to suggest that the film collapses the distinction between the public and private spheres and displaces the political onto the personal. As I noted above, Devlin and Alicia's formation as a couple is contingent upon their discovering the source of the uranium ore. But it seems to me that she is wrong to suggest that feminists should feel troubled by this aspect of the film. For, far from denying that the personal is political, the film exposes the extent to which the personal had become the political in the postwar period. Devlin and Alicia's inscription within the discourses of national security enables the American government to regulate and control the most personal aspects of the construction of their subjectivity, including the organization of their sexuality. Moreover, by displacing the political onto the personal, the film appears to maintain the distinction between the public and private spheres when in fact it collapses it. Although Devlin and Alicia eventually complete their assignment and discover the source of the uranium ore, their espionage activities seem to be motivated by their desire for each other rather than by politics. Thus, despite the fact that the film helps to legitimate the government's control over the production of the postwar subject, it seems to suggest that the personal should remain separate from the political; indeed, it tries to show that the political threatens to disrupt the personal.

Whereas Devlin and Alicia seem to maintain the distinction between the public and private spheres despite their activities as agents for the American government, the Nazis in the film collapse it and in so doing violate the rules and regulations that governed the eroticized space of the middle-class nuclear family in the postwar period. The Nazis in the film disrupt the Oedipal structure of the middle-class nuclear family by politicizing it. For example, Sebastian's (Claude Rains) commitment to the Nazi cause is directly related to his erotically charged relations with his mother (Leopoldine Konstantin), which constitute a form of momism.[17] Mrs. Sebastian exemplifies the overly protective, domineering mothers vilified by Wylie in *Generation of Vipers* for sexualizing their relationships with their sons. She has perverted Sebastian politically and sexually by making her love for him contingent upon his commitment to the Nazi cause, and he is unable to detach himself from her. Even when he marries Alicia, he remains politically and sexually dependent on her. Indeed, marrying Alicia only reinforces his dependence on his mother. He is powerless to prevent Alicia from betraying him and the other Nazis and must rely on his mother to protect him from her. A castrated male whose very name, Alex (A-lex), indicates his problematic relation to the law, he has been denied entry into the Symbolic order.[18] Rather than controlling women, he is controlled by them. As he himself remarks when he discovers that Alicia is an agent for the American government, "I must have been insane, mad, behaved like an idiot, to believe in her with her clinging kisses." Thus the only way in which he can defend himself against Alicia is by renewing his dependence on his mother, who is as controlling as Alicia. His mother persuades him to poison Alicia in order to prevent the other Nazis from finding out about her identity.

Politics similarly perverts Alicia's relationship with her father. According to psychoanalytic theory, seduction fantasies in which the subject submits passively to the father function as myths of origin that enable the subject to understand the emergence and upsurge of her/ his sexuality.[19] Such fantasies operate in such a way as to reorganize the pre-Oedipal sexual field through an alignment of a set of identifications and object attachments that assign a meaning to the position occupied by the subject in relation to desire. Masculinity and femininity become terms that correspond respectively to the active and passive aims of the subject's libido.[20] Moreover, the subject's access to the father as an object of desire now depends upon a feminine identification with the mother, which entails a loss of phallic activity. In *Noto-*

rious, the reorganization of Alicia's sexuality according to this pattern **205**
of development has been hindered by her relationship with her father,
which her father has politicized by making his love for her contingent
upon her willingness to spy for the Nazis. Disregarding his function in
relation to the law, her father tries to seduce her politically by offering
her direct access to him rather than through a feminine identification
with her mother. Indeed, he tries to persuade her to relinquish her
identification with her mother in return for continuing her phallic
activity. Her refusal to spy for the Nazis is directly related to her
identification with her mother. When her father tries to recruit her
for the Nazi cause, she tells him, "My mother was born here. We
have American citizenship." But he thinks that her obligations to him
should outweigh her allegiance to her mother, and he responds, "The
blood in your veins is German." In other words, he tries to create a
political seduction scenario in which her access to him depends not on
a feminine identification with her mother but on a masculine identification with him; in so doing, he violates the "laws" that governed
Oedipal desire in the postwar period. Rather than forbidding her
phallic activity, he urges her to continue it for political purposes.

This helps to clarify the connection between Alicia's activities as an
American agent and her inscription within the discourses of national
security. Critics often remark that when we first see Devlin, he is
seated in the left foreground with his back to the camera, silently
observing Alicia as she interacts with the other guests at the party.[21]
For this reason, he could be another spectator seated a few rows ahead
of us whose rapt attention stages our own voyeuristic relation to the
exhibitionistic display of Alicia's body. Yet this overlooks the way in
which the shots of him recall those of Alicia's father at the beginning of
the film: standing with his back to the camera, silent and immobile
before the judge. The similarities between these two sequences suggest that we are meant to see a certain resemblance between Devlin
and Alicia's father. For, like Alicia's father, Devlin tries to seduce Alicia
politically by mobilizing her desire. But whereas her father expects her
to relinquish her feminine identification with her mother in return for
continuing her phallic activity, Devlin creates a political seduction
scenario in which she occupies a position in relation to desire that is
based on a feminine identification with her mother. In the scene in
which he tries to persuade her to undertake the assignment, he tells

her that cooperating with the American government will enable her to make up for her "daddy's peculiarities." Thus her activities as an American agent promise to allow her to renounce her identification with her father and align herself with her mother. That is to say, they promise to create a seduction scenario that operates in such a way as to reorganize her sexuality according to a set of identifications and object attachments that is more compatible with national security because it places her in a passive, rather than an active, position in relation to desire.

The American government, then, ensures Alicia's inscription within the discourses of national security by creating a kind of fantasy scenario that provides a setting for her desire that orients and grounds it. According to psychoanalytic theory, fantasy is not the object of the individual's desire but its setting, or mise-en-scène.[22] Fantasy does not so much fix or stabilize the individual's desire as limit its potentially endless dispersal and displacement; that is to say, it regulates and organizes the individual's desire by grounding it. Moreover, despite the diversity of its forms of elaboration, fantasy is limited in its thematic scope and remains structurally constant. It is characterized by a fixity of terms as well as a variability of narrative content.[23] Thus, in creating a fantasy scenario in which Alicia's access to her father depends upon a feminine identification with her mother that entails a loss of phallic activity, the American government limits the potentially endless dispersal and displacement of her desire. Her supposedly aberrant sexuality is directly related to her father's lack of fidelity to the law and failure to perform his paternal function. On the plane to Rio, she tells Devlin that when she found out about her father's activities for the Nazis, "Everything went to pot. I didn't care what happened to me." But in creating a fantasy scenario that reinforces her feminine identification with her mother, her activities for the American government provide a setting for her desire that orients and grounds it. She begins to occupy a position in relation to desire that is more in keeping with the terms of the postwar settlement. Marriage and domesticity become increasingly desirable to her. In the scene in which she cooks dinner for Devlin, she rhapsodizes, "Marriage must be wonderful with this kind of thing going on every day." Thus her espionage activities guarantee that her identity as a woman and her identity as an American citizen are mutually reinforcing. Because her patriotism is rooted in a feminine identification with her mother, it reinforces and solidifies her passivity as a desiring subject.

Devlin's activities as an American agent similarly ensure his inscription within the discourses of national security by creating a fantasy scenario that mobilizes and orients his desire for Alicia. In his paper "A Special Type of Object Choice Made by Men," Freud describes the rescue fantasies of a type of man whose pattern of behavior closely resembles Devlin's. Freud claims that a specific set of conditions determines the choice of love object made by this type of man. The first of these conditions is that the love object must already be attached to another man. This enables the type of man described by Freud to gratify his hatred of the other man by depriving him of his love object. The second condition is that the love object must have a reputation for being promiscuous. The only way in which the type of man described by Freud can sustain his desire for the love object is by feeling jealous of other men because it increases the love object's value in his eyes. Freud explains that when this set of conditions obtains, the man invariably feels moved to rescue the love object. The man is convinced that the love object "has need of him, that without him she would lose all hold on respectability and rapidly sink to a deplorable level."[24] Freud locates the source of the man's rescue fantasies in his pre-Oedipal attachment to his mother, which they restage. Like the man's mother, the love object is not only sexually knowledgeable but also attached to another with whom he must compete for her love. In other words, the man's rescue fantasies stage an Oedipal scenario in which he possesses his mother and takes revenge against his father.

The similarities between Devlin in *Notorious* and the type of man described by Freud suggest that Devlin remains libidinally invested in his activities for the American government because they create a fantasy scenario that restages his pre-Oedipal attachment to his mother. Devlin's pattern of behavior can be plotted almost point by point onto Freud's paper. Like the type of man discussed by Freud, Devlin desires a woman who is not only sexually knowledgeable but also attached to another man. Moreover, the woman is constantly in danger and must be rescued before she sinks to a deplorable level. Devlin's desire for Alicia is grounded in a rescue fantasy that stages an Oedipal scenario, guaranteeing that he will internalize the Law of the Father and assume his rightful place in the Symbolic order. According to the

Oedipal logic of his fantasy, in rescuing Alicia from Sebastian, he supplants his father. From the very beginning of the film, Devlin simultaneously fears and desires Alicia, who seems to threaten his masculinity. When they are having drinks at a café in Rio, he tells her, "I've always been scared of women." Apparently, she is no exception. Before they go for a drive in Miami, he ties a scarf around her bare midriff, as though her desirability threatens rather than arouses him, and when she tries to push him out of the car, the only way in which he can gain control of her is by knocking her out. But by creating a fantasy scenario in which Alicia becomes a kind of mother surrogate who must be rescued from a hated rival, the American government increases her desirability considerably and in so doing gains Devlin's free and spontaneous consent to the terms of the postwar settlement. His and Alicia's formation as a couple becomes as important to him as discovering the source of the uranium ore, and when he rescues her from Sebastian, he achieves both objectives at once. After all, Alicia could not reveal the source of the uranium ore if he did not rescue her.

Thus, far from a MacGuffin, the discovery of the source of the uranium ore enables the American government to retain control over Devlin's and Alicia's construction as desiring subjects. According to psychoanalytic theory, the role of fantasy in the construction of subjectivity and sexual identity is originary, which suggests that by creating fantasy scenarios that contain the potentially endless dispersal and displacement of their desire, Devlin and Alicia's espionage activities guarantee that their identities as American citizens and the organization of their sexuality are mutually reinforcing. Devlin and Alicia's activities for the American government create fantasy scenarios that operate in such a way as to reorganize their sexuality. Through their activities as American agents, Devlin and Alicia come to occupy positions in relation to desire that are more in keeping with their gender. Alicia's desire for Devlin is rooted in a feminine identification with her mother; Devlin's desire for Alicia restages his pre-Oedipal attachment to his mother. At the same time, the unconscious fantasies engendered by their espionage activities enable the American government to suture their identities as citizens. Devlin and Alicia remain libidinally invested in their assignment because it provides a setting for their desire that limits its potentially endless dispersal. The discovery of the source of the uranium ore stages an Oedipal scenario that reinforces their desire for each other. In this way, the government reorganizes their sexuality according to a set of identifications and object attachments that is more compatible with the nation's security interests. Alicia renounces her phallic activity, and Devlin overcomes his fear of castration; in so doing, they demonstrate their patriotism. The reorganization of their sexuality makes possible their formation as a couple.

To return to *North by Northwest,* this analysis of the relation between gender and nationality in *Notorious* suggests that Thornhill's activities as an American agent guarantee his consent to the postwar settlement by creating a fantasy scenario that reorganizes his sexuality. Thornhill's choice of Eve as a love object seems to depend on the same set of conditions described by Freud in the paper discussed above. Like Devlin in *Notorious,* Thornhill desires a woman who is both sexually knowledgeable and already attached to another man. Moreover, he is convinced that she needs his protection and that he must rescue her before she loses all hold on respectability. In other words, his activities as an American agent create a fantasy scenario that puts an end to his womanizing by limiting the potentially endless dispersal and displacement of his desire. Like Alicia in *Notorious,* Eve becomes a kind of mother surrogate who must be rescued from a hated rival. In this way, the recovery of the stolen microfilm reclaims Thornhill's sexuality for the private sphere. By engendering an unconscious rescue fantasy in which he supplants his father, Thornhill's espionage activities guarantee his inscription within the discourses of national security. The organization of his sexuality no longer poses a threat to national security but corresponds to the set of identifications and object attachments upon which the nation's political stability and economic prosperity were thought to depend. Thornhill's unconscious rescue fantasy increases his desire for marriage and domesticity considerably. The domestic sphere becomes a kind of fantasmatic space that not only provides a refuge from the government, which has recklessly endangered his and Eve's lives, but also constantly restages his pre-Oedipal attachment to his mother. Thus his espionage activities ensure that the organization of sexuality and his identity as a citizen are mutually reinforcing. In recovering the stolen microfilm, he overcomes his resistance to his role as a breadwinner.

**The Hard Work of Respectability: *Psycho* and
the Dispersal of Desire**

In *North by Northwest*, then, Hitchcock stresses the ability of the American government to regulate and control the construction of the individual's subjectivity. According to the discourses of national security, Thornhill's resistance to his role as breadwinner is un-American, and his activities as an American agent create a fantasy scenario that reorganizes his sexuality according to a supposedly more patriotic set of identifications and object attachments. The recovery of the stolen microfilm engenders an unconscious rescue fantasy that, in restaging his pre-Oedipal attachment to his mother, ensures that he will return to the private sphere and become a breadwinner. In *Psycho*, however, Hitchcock complicates this representation of the operations of power in postwar American society. There Hitchcock foregrounds the proliferation of points of resistance to which the dispersal of power across the social field had led and in so doing stresses the *in*ability of the American government to regulate and control the construction of the individual's subjectivity, which remains decentered. Indeed, he tries to show that relations of power in the postwar period were potentially reversible. Whereas in *North by Northwest* the discourses of national security engender an unconscious rescue fantasy that orients and grounds Thornhill's desire, in *Psycho* the discourses of national security create fantasy scenarios that encourage the potentially endless dispersal and displacement of the characters' desire. *Psycho* suggests that in prohibiting certain sexual practices because they were supposedly incompatible with security interests, the discourses of national security only encouraged their proliferation and multiplication. The characters in *Psycho* derive pleasure from occupying a position outside the law because it enables them to prevent the American government from determining the organization of their sexuality. They engage in the very sexual practices prohibited by the discourses of national security precisely because they have been prohibited. In *Psycho*, then, the discourses of national security engender unconscious fantasies that encourage resistance to the terms of the postwar settlement.

This emphasis on the production and dispersal of forms of fantasy and desire that actually discourage inscription within the discourses of national security becomes apparent in the film's opening scene. Whereas in *North by Northwest* Thornhill's activities for the American government put an end to his womanizing, in *Psycho* the prohibitions against certain "un-American" sexual practices incite rather than re-press Sam's desire for Marion. Sam's desire is clearly contingent upon meeting Marion secretly in cheap hotels in violation of the "laws" that governed American middle-class sexuality in the 1950s. For example, when Marion tells him that she is tired of meeting him secretly and proposes that they get married, he says, "I've heard of married cou-ples who deliberately spend an occasional night in a cheap hotel." Moreover, when she accuses him of making respectability sound "dis-respectful," he replies, "Oh, no, I'm all for it. It requires patience, temperance, a lot of sweating out. Otherwise, though, it's just hard work." Thus his reasons for not wanting to get married are only partially related to his precarious financial situation. For him, respect-ability is "hard work," and if he and Marion got married, he would no longer desire her so intensely. This is not to suggest that he does not genuinely love Marion. After all, he assures her, "Whenever it's possi-ble, I want to see you, and under any circumstances, even respectabil-ity." My point is simply that engaging in pre-marital sex with Marion intensifies his desire for her because it defies the government's author-ity to determine the organization of his sexuality. That is to say, the discourses of national security organize his sexuality according to a set of identifications and object attachments that are incompatible with the nation's security interests. They create a fantasy scenario in which he transgresses the prohibitions against certain supposedly un-American sexual practices by carrying on a secret affair with Marion.

Despite her desire for respectability, Marion similarly derives plea-sure from resisting inscription within the discourses of national se-curity. I have already suggested that her motives for stealing Cassidy's money are more complicated than they appear. Although critics usu-ally assume that Marion steals the money so that she and Sam can get married, this overlooks her desire to occupy a position outside the law. She clearly wants to disrupt Cassidy's plan to use the money to buy a house for his daughter who is getting married. Cassidy proudly shows Marion a picture of his daughter and brags that she is only "eighteen years old, and she hasn't had an unhappy day in any one of those years"; in so doing, he calls attention to the differences between her and Marion, whose desire for the American dream has been frustrated by Sam's unwillingness to get married. Unlike Marion, Cassidy's daughter promises to become the kind of wife and mother glorified by Dr. Spock and other "experts" on child rearing. Thus, in stealing the money, Marion tries to prevent Cassidy's daughter from having the kind of life she wants but cannot have. But she also steals the money because she wants to retaliate against Cassidy for propositioning her. Cassidy seems to feel that because unlike his daughter Marion must work for a living, she is not respectable and will sleep with him. Engaging in a kind of phallic display clearly meant to seduce her, he flashes the money in front of her. But she gets the money without having to sleep with him by stealing it. Marion wants Cassidy to think that she intended to steal the money and deliberately deceived him so that he will feel used. While driving from Phoenix to Fairvale, she smiles when she imagines how he will react when he discovers that she has stolen the money: "Hot creepers! She sat there while I dumped it out. Hardly even looked at it. Plannin' and even flirtin' with me!" Thus stealing the money enables Marion to solidify her position outside the law. She wants to occupy a position outside the law so that she can act as a subject rather than as an object of desire.

In focusing on the production and dispersal of what we might call counterfantasies, or fantasies that encourage rather than discourage the set of identifications and object attachments that were considered incompatible with the nation's security interests, *Psycho* calls into question the ability of the American government to regulate and control the production of the postwar subject, an ability *North by Northwest* simply took for granted. Whereas in *North by Northwest* the domestic sphere functions as a kind of fantasmatic space that provides Thornhill with a refuge from the American government, in *Psycho* it is wholly aligned with the American government and functions as one of its apparatuses. As we saw above, the discourses of national security enabled the American government to determine the organization of family life in the 1950s. The discourses of momism located the sources of communism and homosexuality in incompetent mothering and in so doing ensured that women's child-rearing practices contributed to the reproduction of the national security state. *Psycho* calls attention to this aspect of the structure of the middle-class nuclear family by making Sheriff Chambers and his wife the only couple in the film whose desire corresponds to the law. Sheriff Chambers and his wife seem wholly inscribed within the discourses of national security. They attend church regularly and urge Sam and Lila to file a missing person's report, claiming that they are trying to circumvent the law by searching for Marion on their own. In this way, the film shows that the family had become a crucial site for the reproduction of the national security state. After all, Sheriff Chambers is a representative of the law, and thus his relationship with his wife serves to underscore the way in which the middle-class nuclear family had become the normative family structure in the postwar period. At the same time, however, the film also stresses the inability of the American government to determine the organization of family life. It suggests that the American government constantly had to intervene in the family to maintain its structure. Caroline (Patricia Hitchcock), for example, so dislikes married life that she must constantly sedate herself in order to remain content. At one point, when Marion complains about having a headache, Caroline offers her a tranquilizer, explaining that a doctor prescribed tranquilizers for her on her wedding day and that she has been taking them ever since. Moreover, the film shows that the eroticized space of the family engenders forms of fantasy and desire that cannot be repressed or contained by the American government. To cite the most obvious example, the discourses of momism do not prevent Norman from overidentifying with his mother and fantasizing about assuming her identity.

This representation of the eroticized space of the family as a site for the production of counterfantasies that threaten to disrupt the reproduction of the national security state calls into question the ability of the American government to determine the construction of the individual's subjectivity. Whereas in *North by Northwest* the American government is able to suture Thornhill's identity by creating a fantasy scenario that organizes his sexuality in such a way that it conforms to the nation's security interests, in *Psycho* the eroticized space of the family splits or fragments the characters' identities by encouraging the dispersal and displacement of their desire. In *Psycho*, the discourses of national security lack the ability to suture or contain the dislocating operations of the psyche, which constantly undermine the unity and coherence of the characters' identities. The sexuality of the characters

214   remains polymorphously perverse because their subjectivity is constructed across a multiplicity of conflicting discourses and cannot be exhausted by their inscription within a single or unitary subject position. In shot after shot, we see the characters reflected in mirrors. As the film opens, we see Marion's back reflected in a mirror. Later, when she is preparing to leave Phoenix with the money, she interrupts her packing and looks at herself in another mirror. Later still, when she is in the washroom at the car dealer, we again see her in a mirror. Similarly, the other characters appear repeatedly in mirror reflections. Lila, for example, is startled when she suddenly sees herself in a pair of mirrors while searching Mrs. Bates's bedroom. This constant reflection of the characters suggests the multiplication and dispersal of their identities as well as their desires, reflecting the fact that they have not been organized and contained by other discourses, e.g. the discourses of national security. The pursuit of respectability by characters like Marion reflects middle-class fantasies about domestic life, but the prohibitions against certain sexual practices supposedly incompatible with the nation's security interests incite rather than repress her desire. In other words, the American government is unable to contain the construction of the characters' subjectivity, and thus their identities are fractured and incoherent.

These fragmented identities call attention to a surplus of meaning that remains uncontained by the dominant system of representation and that threatens to destabilize or rupture it. Because the characters cannot be understood or interpreted within the horizon of meanings accepted in postwar American society as constituting and defining individual and collective identities, they remain virtually unintelligible to the spectator. I have already suggested that in tracing Norman's psychotic behavior to his troubled relationship with his mother, the film participated in the network of diverse but congruent discourses that in the 1950s demonized motherhood. Yet the existence of a kind of demonology of motherhood in the nation's political imaginary does not adequately explain Norman's psychological development. As we saw above, the police chief is wrong to infer from the psychiatrist's explanation that Norman is a transvestite. Although Mrs. Bates is a "clinging, demanding woman" who resembles the domineering, overly protective mothers vilified by Wylie for contributing to the crisis over national security, Norman is coded as neither a Communist nor a homosexual. He dresses in his mother's clothing because he overidentifies with her, not because it excites him sexually. But Norman is not the only character in the film whose behavior cannot be adequately explained by the available postwar discourses of identity. Similarly the discourses of national security are unable to inscribe Sam within a fixed, stable subject position that the spectator can easily interpret. He and Norman function as mirror images of each other. Marion's encounter with Norman at the hotel reverses her encounter with Sam in the film's opening scene. Whereas Norman offers her food instead of sex, Sam offers her sex instead of food. The first words we hear him utter are, "You never did eat your lunch, did you?" while we are shown a shot of a half-eaten sandwich. Moreover, the film stresses the close physical resemblance between the two men. As Robin Wood has pointed out, in the scene in which the two men face each other over the office counter while Lila searches the house, they are so similar in appearance that they are virtually interchangeable.[25] In this way, the film suggests indirectly that Sam's treatment of Marion is not so different from Norman's. Sam's unwillingness to marry Marion prevents her from achieving the American dream and thus constitutes a kind of murder.

In this respect, the film stresses the production of forms of subjectivity that are irreducibly personal rather than unequivocally social. Although it acknowledges the materiality of subjectivity, its embeddedness in a concrete, historically specific fantasmatic regime, it suggests that it is an ongoing construction rooted in the individual's personal history and cannot be sutured. Marion's identity similarly cannot be understood or interpreted according to the postwar discourses and knowledges explaining the construction of female subjectivity. On the one hand, her pursuit of respectability points to her inscription within the discourses of national security. She fantasizes about becoming a dutiful wife and mother whose sexuality corresponds to the nation's security interests. In the opening scene, she tells Sam that she would willingly live with him in a spare room at the back of his hardware store; indeed, she would even "lick the stamps" of his alimony payments to his ex-wife. On the other hand, it is clear that her fantasies—whose source is ultimately the discourses of national security—cannot contain the dispersal and displacement of her desire. Her treatment of Norman in the scenes at the motel points to a similarity between her and Mrs. Bates. Like Mrs. Bates, she seems to enjoy dominating Norman and making him feel insufficiently masculine. When, showing her the cabin, he cannot bring himself to say the word "bathroom," she is amused by his prudishness and says it for him. Moreover, she seems to want to test his manhood and behaves provocatively. When he returns to the house to make her a sandwich, she overhears Mrs. Bates taunt him for not being more manly: "Go tell her she'll not be appeasing her ugly appetites with my food, or my son. Or do I have to tell her 'cause you don't have the guts? Huh, boy? You have the guts, boy?" When he returns to the cabin with the sandwich, Marion seems to want to find out if he does indeed have the "guts." She leans against the door of the cabin suggestively, as though inviting him in, and then smiles when he becomes uncomfortable and proposes that they eat in the office instead. In this way, the film indicates that she has the potential to become a clinging, demanding woman who resembles Mrs. Bates rather than the dutiful, self-sacrificing mother glorified by the discourses and ideologies designed to lure women back into the home. Despite her willingness to lick Sam's stamps, it does not seem likely that living in a spare room at the back of his hardware store would satisfy her.

I have been stressing *Psycho*'s inverted relation to *North by Northwest* in order to show that it complicates the earlier film's representation of the operations of power in postwar American society. We have seen that in *North by Northwest* the American government guarantees Thornhill's free and spontaneous consent to the terms of the postwar settlement by creating a fantasy scenario that orients and grounds his desire. The unconscious rescue fantasy engendered by his espionage activities reorganizes his sexuality and thereby ensures that he will return to the private sphere and become a breadwinner. We have also seen, however, that *Psycho* reverses this focus and stresses the points of resistance to which the dispersal of power across the social field had led in the 1950s. In *Psycho*, the discourses of national security engender counterfantasies. Sam and Marion derive pleasure from engaging in pre-marital sex because it has been defined as un-American. In other words, the production and dispersal of forms of fantasy and desire through the prohibition of homosexuality and other supposedly perverted sexual practices make it possible for the characters to derive pleasure from resisting inscription within the discourses of national security. In foregrounding this aspect of the construction of male and female subjectivity in the postwar period, *Psycho* calls attention to the inability of the American government to suture individual and collective identities through the invocation of the nation's security interests. *Psycho*'s emphasis on the dislocating operations of the psyche suggests that inscription within the discourses of national security cannot exhaust the individual's subjectivity. In *Psycho*, subjectivity is an ongoing construction, grounded in the individual's personal history; consequently, it is constantly shifting.

This is not to suggest that in *Psycho* Hitchcock rejects his earlier representation of the operations of power in postwar American society. *Psycho* represents a kind of paranoid fantasy in which the discourses of national security not only fail to guarantee the individual's consent to the postwar settlement but actually encourage her/his resistance to them. Whereas *North by Northwest* stresses the way in which gender and nationality functioned as mutually reinforcing categories of identity in postwar America, *Psycho* focuses on a surplus of meaning that remained uncontained by the dominant construction of social reality under the postwar settlement and therefore threatened to rupture it. Still, in providing a more complicated representation of the operations of power that refused to totalize the ability of the American government to regulate and control the production of the postwar subject, *Psycho* indicated the possibility of constructing an alternative representation of social reality. Unlike *North by Northwest*, *Psycho* conceives of the social field as heterogeneous and made up of multiple, overlapping, and intersecting discourses that are historically produced and reproduced through the practices of everyday life and that implicate the individual in contradictory ways. In *Psycho*, the American government fails to delimit the construction of the characters' subjectivity. At the same time that characters like Marion long for the American dream and fantasize about raising a family in the suburbs, they also derive pleasure from occupying a position outside the law and disrupting the reproduction of the national security state. For this reason, their inscription within the discourses of national security can never exhaust their subjectivity. Whereas in *North by Northwest* Hitchcock shows how the discourses of national security operate so as to contain resistance to the postwar settlement, in *Psycho* he shows how they must constantly compete with other discourses in order to maintain their hegemony. In so doing, he suggests that the discourses of national security cannot exhaust all social experience and that their ability to regulate and control the construction of male and female subjectivity is necessarily limited because it is based on exclusions and repressions. It is these exclusions and repressions that open up a space in the social field for the emergence of alternative social formations.

CONCLUSION

In an interview with François Truffaut shortly before the premiere of *Frenzy* at the Cannes Film Festival in 1972, Hitchcock speculated about the impact of the collapse of the Cold War consensus on the American film industry. When Truffaut asked him to comment on the pressures the studios were placing on directors to produce films full of nudity and violence and that had a social and/or political message, Hitchcock suggested that the changes in the American film industry reflected "the moral climate and the way of life that prevail today in the United States, as well as being a result of national events that have had an impact on the film-makers and on the public. Still, American cinema dealt with social and political themes long ago, without attracting crowds to the box office."[1] Hitchcock did not limit his comments about the nation's deteriorating "moral climate" to the growing interest in films that had a social and/or political message. He also used the collapse of the Cold War consensus to explain the declining popularity of his own films. His response to Truffaut's question echoed a letter he had written to Truffaut in 1970 in which he described his frustration in trying to find new and interesting projects and complained that "a film must contain some anti-establishment elements" in order to attract a large audience.[2] Hitchcock's willingness to acknowledge the historical forces that conditioned his practices as a director was unusual. As we have seen, he tried to promote his reputation as an auteur by encouraging a teleological understanding of his work that stressed its thematic unity and coherence and that installed him as the stable point of textual origin. Still, we should not be misled by Hitchcock's willingness to acknowledge that his practices as a director were historically conditioned. For in attributing the declining popularity of his films to the collapse of the Cold War consensus, he continued to position himself as an auteur. He wanted to project the image of the misunderstood genius who had been forced by Hollywood to compromise his standards by pandering to a vulgar public.

In concluding this book with a discussion of *Psycho* and its inverted relation to *North by Northwest*, I have tried not only to call attention to the link between Hitchcock's practices as a director and the continuing hegemony of Cold War liberals, a link that problematizes Hitchcock's attempts to position himself as a misunderstood genius, but also to show that his films contributed to the very crisis in the American film industry that he claimed was responsible for the declining popularity of his work. I have stressed *Psycho's* inverted relation to *North by Northwest* in order to suggest that it constituted a paranoid fantasy in which the discourses of national security encouraged rather than discouraged resistance to the terms of the postwar settlement. As I demonstrated, in *North by Northwest*, Thornhill's activities as an American agent engender an unconscious rescue fantasy that, in limiting the dispersal of his desire, guarantees his inscription within the discourses of national security. Thornhill assumes the identity of George Kaplan, a fictitious agent created by the American government, and in so doing freely and spontaneously inserts himself into a relatively fixed subject position. In *Psycho*, on the other hand, the discourses of national security encourage the dispersal of the characters' desire by engendering counterfantasies, or fantasies that organize their sexuality according to a set of identifications and object attachments that conflict with the nation's security interests. In this way, *Psycho* inadvertently called into question the ability of the American government to regulate and control the production of the postwar subject. In foregrounding the rise of the expert in postwar America and the dispersal of power across the social field to which it had led, *Psycho* indicated the possibility of constructing an alternative representation of social reality, a representation that was more inclusive than the one that had become hegemonic under the postwar settlement.

But I have not limited my discussion of the ways in which Hitchcock's practices as a director contributed to the collapse of the Cold War consensus to *Psycho* and its representation of the potential reversibility of power relations in postwar America. On the contrary, throughout this book I have stressed how Hitchcock's films simultaneously contributed to and undermined the consolidation of the Cold War consensus. By calling attention to a surplus of meaning that remained uncontained by the dominant system of representation, the films made possible the emergence of an alternative construction of social reality. In using Hitchcock's films to clarify the political construction of gender and sexual identity in postwar America, I have placed as much emphasis on the contradictions and inconsistencies of the liberal construction of social reality as on its unity and coherence. On the one hand, I have tried to show that Cold War liberals were able to produce a relatively united cultural front that combined a multiplicity of dispersed wills with heterogeneous and contradictory aims into a single collective will based on a shared interpretation of reality by shifting attention from the material world to the individual's subjective experience of it. The cultural criticism of anti-Stalinist intellectuals tended to focus on those aspects of postwar American society that Marxist theory could not adequately explain or that did not readily lend themselves to a Marxist critique because it lacked a fully developed theory of subjectivity. I have also tried to show that the liberal construction of social reality was not a given, but faced constant competition from alternative constructions and that Cold War liberals had to renew its hegemony continuously. The discourses of national security could not exhaust all social experience because their ability to regulate and define the social field was based on exclusions and repressions.

I have wanted to claim that the attempts of Cold War liberals to link questions of gender and sexual identity to questions of national security eventually precipitated a crisis of transformism in which Cold War liberals were no longer able to articulate alternative conceptions of the world in a way that contained or neutralized their potential antagonism.[3] I have tried to show that America in the 1950s experienced the emergence of an increasingly heterogeneous social field in which various conceptions of the world competed for dominance. On the one hand, the American government tried to justify the expulsion of an indeterminate group of gays and lesbians who "passed" as straight by appealing to a medical model of same-sex eroticism. On the other hand, gays and lesbians began to organize politically and to challenge the medicalization of homosexuality and lesbianism. Appropriating the rhetoric of the civil rights movement, they argued that homosexuality and lesbianism should be considered categories of identity similar to other categories of identity (such as race and ethnicity). I have tried to show that the way in which Cold War liberals prevented this and other potentially oppositional constructions of social reality from becoming openly antagonistic and precipitating a crisis of transform-ism was by exploiting the anti-Communist hysteria unleashed by the McCarthy hearings. The construction of "the homosexual" and "the lesbian" as national-security risks all but guaranteed that gender and nationality functioned as mutually reinforcing categories of identity. Homosexuality and lesbianism became inextricably linked to commu-nism in the nation's political imaginary, thanks to a network of diverse but congruent discourses that located the source of all three in incom-petent mothering.

In stressing the way in which the films examined in this study contributed to the consolidation of the postwar settlement, I wanted to call attention to their function as an articulatory practice, or nodal point, that helped to fix the excess meaning of the social in a relatively closed system of differences by containing the construction of the spectator's subjectivity across variable axes of difference. I have ar-gued that the spectator of the films Hitchcock made in the 1950s no longer participated in a plurality of contending social formations but became part of a united cultural front that not only incorporated the interests of women and other historically disenfranchised groups but also organized them into a popular and seemingly unified collective will dedicated to containing communism. Hitchcock's films tried to blackmail the spectator into occupying a relatively stable subject posi-tion by invoking the homophobic categories of Cold War political discourse. They positioned the spectator who refused to occupy the Oedipalized subject position they made available as "the homosexual" or "the lesbian" of the discourses of national security. At the same time, however, I have also stressed that Hitchcock's ability to manage and contain the construction of the spectator's subjectivity was neces-sarily limited. The spectator's insertion into a fixed, stable subject position contradicted her/his lived experience and therefore remained unstable and incomplete. Indeed, Hitchcock's attempts to suture the spectator's identity inadvertently acknowledged that the social field was made up of a plurality of competing discourses that were histor-ically produced and reproduced through the practices of everyday life and that implicated her/him in contradictory ways.

In the course of writing this book, using Hitchcock's films to reconstruct the link between the discourses of national security and the organization of gender relations in the 1950s has struck me as an increasingly urgent task. To begin with, many of the Cold War liberals we have encountered in these pages continue to influence public policy by appealing to a "vital center" of American culture, despite the end of the Cold War. Nathan Glazer and Arthur Schlesinger, for example, in their capacity as members of the New York State Social Studies Review and Development Committee, have recently intervened in the debates on multiculturalism and political correctness. Upholding a consensual model of American history, Glazer has accused the multicultural curriculum proposed by the committee of "hypostatizing" racial and ethnic identities and of trying to suppress the history of assimilation that has characterized racial and ethnic minorities in the United States.[4] Schlesinger has criticized the proposed curriculum for similar reasons, claiming that it places too much emphasis on the "pluribus" and not enough on the "unum" of American society.[5] My reconstruction of the project undertaken by Cold War liberals in the 1950s to define reality in such a way that it did not lend itself readily to a Marxist analysis suggests that there is a disturbing consistency in Glazer's and Schlesinger's attacks on multiculturalism and the reemergence of a conflictual model of American history. Glazer and Schlesinger continue to oppose any challenge to the hegemonic construction of "America" as a racial and ethnic melting pot. They are against the introduction of multicultural curricula and cultural studies programs because they raise important questions about the relation between the individual's identity as a social being and the construction of her/his subjectivity.

This is not to deny that the hypostatization of minority identities is a very real danger of multicultural curricula and cultural studies programs, as Glazer pointed out when he dissented from the report prepared by the Social Studies Review and Development Committee. To avoid reducing an individual's ethnic or racial identity to an inherent or ineluctable part of her/his subjectivity, multicultural curricula and cultural studies programs must approach the historical production of minority identities as a hegemonic process that necessarily involves the marginalization and repression of competing constructions of the same identities. As we have seen, the struggle in postwar America to define homosexuals and lesbians as members of an oppressed minority with its own history and traditions was an exclusionary process that marginalized and repressed forms of gay and lesbian subjectivity (gay male camp, butch-femme role playing) that were considered controversial and threatened to undermine the homophile movement. Moreover, multicultural curricula and cultural studies programs must acknowledge, as well as constantly interrogate, the impact of their own interventions on the historical production and hegemonic articulation of minority identities (which constructions of the identities they are privileging and why). My point in linking Glazer's and Schlesinger's interventions in the debates over multiculturalism and political correctness to the attempts of Cold War liberals in the 1950s to invalidate Marxist categories by focusing on the individual's subjective experience of the material world is to show that their objections to the committee's report are politically motivated, despite their claims to the contrary. On the one hand, they accuse the proponents of multiculturalism and cultural studies programs of politicizing the production of knowledge. On the other hand, they claim that their adherence to a consensual model of American history is not political but historically justified.

But there is an even more compelling reason for using the films discussed in this study to clarify the political construction of gender and sexual identity in postwar America. As I was completing this manuscript and preparing it for submission, the Republican party had launched one of the most viciously homophobic and misogynistic presidential campaigns of the postwar period. In a speech delivered on the opening night of the Republican National Convention, Patrick Buchanan set the tone of the campaign by declaring that "there is a religious war going on in this country for the soul of America."[6] Although he carefully distinguished this "religious war" from the Cold War, he explained that it would be "as critical to the kind of nation we shall be as the Cold War itself," as it too was a war "for the soul of America."[7] To be sure, Buchanan never specifically stated that homosexuals, lesbians, and working mothers were the primary targets of this war, but he had no need to, claiming that homosexuals, lesbians, and working mothers as part of a "cultural elite" were committed to undermining the traditional family. In his words to the assembled delegates, "we must take back our cities, and take back our culture and take back our country."[8] Following the convention, most political commentators accepted Buchanan's distinction between the war to defend "family values" and the Cold War, and speculated that homosexuals, lesbians, and working mothers would become the Willie Horton of the 1992 presidential campaign.[9] According to these commentators, just as in 1988 the Bush campaign used the example of Willie Horton, a convicted murderer who raped a white woman while participating in a furlough program supported by Governor Dukakis, to suggest that Governor Dukakis was "soft" on crime, in 1992 the Bush campaign would use the example of Clinton's support of gay and lesbian rights to suggest that he was "soft" on "family values."

My use of the films Hitchcock made in the 1950s to clarify the political construction of gender and sexual identity in postwar America indicates that more is involved in Buchanan's declaration of war than an attempt to depict Clinton as "soft" on "family values." By claiming that homosexuals, lesbians, and working mothers were responsible for the decline of the traditional family, Buchanan was, in effect, prolonging the Cold War. Indeed, he was, in effect, vowing to continue it on the domestic front. Although the collapse of the Soviet Union prevented him from explicitly linking the decline of the traditional family to questions of national security, he followed a well-established pattern, which I have tried to describe in this book, of identifying homosexuals, lesbians, and working mothers as the "enemy within." Ernesto Laclau has recently argued that one of the necessary conditions for the emergence of populist movements is a crisis of transformism in which the various factions of the power bloc try to establish their hegemony through the use of populist discourse.[10] According to him, populist discourse is a particularly effective tool for mobilizing mass support because it has no fixed class content but interpellates individuals simply as "the people." Applying Laclau's analysis to Buchanan's declaration of war suggests that it should be seen as an attempt by the American Right to renew its hegemony by reviving the homophobic categories of Cold War political discourse. Buchanan's defense of "family values" implied that they are not specific to a particular group or class (white heterosexual suburbanites) but belong to the American people as a whole (excluding, of course, homosexuals, lesbians, and working mothers, who apparently are not a part of the American polity). In other words, in trying to identify homosexuals, lesbians, and working mothers as the "enemy within," Buchanan was adopting the very strategies Cold War liberals used in the 1950s to achieve and retain hegemony over American culture. It is

226   my hope that *In the Name of National Security* will contribute to the understanding of this latest attempt to link the construction of gender and national identity through the deployment of homophobia by calling attention to the disturbing similarities between Buchanan's demonization of homosexuals, lesbians, and working mothers and the attempts of Cold War liberals in the 1950s to regulate and control the production of the postwar subject.

NOTES

Introduction

1. Arthur Schlesinger, Jr., *The Vital Center: The Politics of Freedom* (Boston: Houghton Mifflin, 1949), ix.

2. Ibid.

3. Lionel Trilling, *The Liberal Imagination: Essays on Literature and Society* (New York: Viking, 1950), xv.

4. Leslie Fiedler, "Hiss, Chambers, and the End of Innocence" in *The Collected Essays of Leslie Fiedler* (New York: Stein and Day, 1971), 1:24.

5. On the role of anti-Stalinist intellectuals in the establishment and consolidation of the postwar settlement, see in particular Andrew Ross, *No Respect: Intellectuals and Popular Culture* (New York: Routledge, 1989), 42–64. See also Thomas Hill Schaub, *American Fiction in the Cold War* (Madison: University of Wisconsin Press, 1991), 3–24. Although both of these studies make important contributions to our understanding of American culture in the era of the Cold War, they overlook the homophobia of anti-Stalinist intellectuals and its role in the management and containment of opposition to the postwar settlement.

6. I remain unconvinced by the argument that the United States won the Cold War or that the recent collapse of the Soviet Union vindicates the narrative of containment underpinning U.S. foreign policy since World War II. For an example of this argument, see Arthur Schlesinger, "The Radical," *New York Review of Books* 11 February 1993, 3–8. Schlesinger's essay is a review of George Kennan's recently published book, *Around the Cragged Hill: A Personal and Political Philosophy,* and his description of Kennan as a radical indicates the continuing distortion of his perception of the Cold War. Schlesinger remains unwilling to acknowledge that geopolitical concerns were used to justify the stifling of dissent in the United States. Because I do not believe that the United States can legitimately claim that it won the Cold War, I have limited the focus of this book to the domestic politics of Cold War liberals. My assumption is that the geopolitical concerns they expressed in their writings were primarily a cover for their anxieties about the emergence of competing constructions of social reality.

7. Even those critics who have avoided adopting a strictly psychoanalytic approach to Hitchcock's films have shown little or no interest in situating them

historically. For two such recent examples, see Lesley Brill, *The Hitchcock Romance: Love and Irony in Hitchcock's Films* (Princeton: Princeton University Press, 1988) and Robin Wood, *Hitchcock's Films Revisited* (New York: Columbia University Press, 1989). Both Brill and Wood adopt an auteurist approach to the films that borders on intentionalist, and they overlook the extent to which the cluster of narrative structures, recurrent themes, and images they attribute to a coherent and unified subject, "Hitchcock," was historically determined.

8. Mulvey's essay was originally published in *Screen* 16, no. 3 (Autumn 1975): 6–18. It has since been reprinted in *Feminism and Film Theory*, ed. Constance Penley (New York: Routledge, 1988), 57–66. Mulvey has since revised her position somewhat. See Laura Mulvey, "Afterthoughts on 'Visual Pleasure and Narrative Cinema' Inspired by *Duel in the Sun*" also reprinted in *Feminism and Film Theory*, 69–79.

9. Mulvey's tendency to elide the differences among and within male spectators is typical of Lacanian film theory and constitutes one of its most serious limitations. It certainly limits its application to a study of the politics of spectatorship in postwar America. As I try to show, the politicization of same-sex eroticism in the postwar period called into question the stability of male heterosexual identities and precipitated a crisis in the dominant system of representation. The publication in 1948 of the Kinsey report on male sexual behavior made postwar Americans only too conscious of the differences among and within male spectators.

10. See Raymond Bellour, "Le blocage symbolique," *Communications* 23 (1975): 235–50. Bellour's textual analyses of Hitchcock's films have been extremely influential in Lacanian film studies. For his discussion of *Marnie* (1964), see Raymond Bellour, "Hitchcock, the Enunciator," *Camera Obscura* 2 (1977): 66–87. For his discussion of *Psycho* (1960), see Raymond Bellour, "Psychosis, Neurosis, Perversion," *Camera Obscura* 3–4 (1979): 66–103.

11. Teresa de Lauretis discusses the multiply affiliated subject in *Technologies of Gender: Essays on Theory, Film, and Fiction* (Bloomington: Indiana University Press, 1987), 1–30. See also her theorization of experience in *Alice Doesn't: Feminism, Semiotics, Cinema* (Bloomington: Indiana University Press, 1984), 158–86. De Lauretis's theorization of the subject differs significantly from that of other poststructuralists. She argues that the subject is not so much split or divided as it is multiple and contradicted. I will argue that it is the tensions resulting from this contradictedness that allows for the hegemonic articulation of identities.

12. Although it has been influenced by film studies, my use of the term *suture* is not limited to the spectator's perceptual placement within the diegesis but includes the subject's inscription within political and cultural discourse. For an excellent discussion of the cinematic suturing of spectators through

the use of interlocking shots, see Kaja Silverman, *The Subject of Semiotics* **229**
(Oxford: Oxford University Press, 1983), 201–36. See also Stephen Heath, "On
Suture," in *Questions of Cinema* (Bloomington: Indiana University Press, 1981),
76–112.

13. Laclau and Mouffe's emphasis on the "impossibility of society" is part of
their project to reformulate the Gramscian concept of hegemony in the light of
the social fragmentation of late capitalism. See in particular Ernesto Laclau and
Chantal Mouffe, *Hegemony and Socialist Strategy: Towards a Democratic Politics*
(London: Verso, 1985), 93–148. See also Ernesto Laclau, "The Impossibility of
Society," in *New Reflections on the Revolution of Our Time* (London: Verso, 1990),
89–92. In an interesting reading of ideology that uses the Lacanian conceptual
apparatus, Slavoj Žižek has noted the similarity between Laclau and Mouffe's
theory of the impossibility of society and the Lacanian Real, a hard, impenetra-
ble "kernel" that resists symbolization but is nevertheless constitutive of the
Symbolic as defined by Lacan. See Slavoj Žižek, *The Sublime Object of Ideology*
(London: Verso, 1989). I want to be quite clear, however, that when I refer to
the impossibility of fixing the social in a sutured totality, I have in mind the
subject's construction across a multiplicity of contradictory discourses, and
not the Lacanian Real.

14. Laclau and Mouffe have recently been criticized for characterizing their
work as "post-Marxist." See, for example, Neil Lazarus, "Doubting the New
World Order: Marxism, Realism, and the Claims of Postmodernist Social
Theory," *differences* 3, no. 3 (1991): 94–138. I find Lazarus's critique of Laclau
and Mouffe for the most part convincing (except for his attempt to reinstall
class as *the* crucial determinant of social identity), and I want to be quite clear
that in emphasizing the impossibility of fixing the social in a sutured totality, I
am not trying to position myself as a post-Marxist.

15. I have found Laclau and Mouffe's concept of "nodal points" especially
useful because it can refer to subcultural identity formations (such as gay,
lesbian, African American) as well as to hegemonic identity formations. I will
argue that the emergence in the 1950s of subcultural constructions of gay and
lesbian identities that openly challenged the hegemonic constructions of those
same identities made possible the establishment of the postwar settlement
because it led to a proliferation of antagonisms, one of the necessary conditions for the emergence of hegemonic social formations.

16. This is Kaja Silverman's argument in *The Acoustic Mirror: The Female Voice
in Psychoanalysis and Cinema* (Bloomington: Indiana University Press, 1988),
42–71. Although Silverman's use of Lacanian psychoanalysis is less reductive
than that of Mulvey and Bellour in that it conceives of male subjectivity as
continually at risk rather than as monolithically phallic, it ignores the extent to
which the cinematic apparatus functions as a social technology that implants

desire in the spectator. For another example of this tendency to minimize the function of the cinematic apparatus as a social technology, see Slavoj Žižek, *Looking Awry: An Introduction to Jacques Lacan through Popular Culture* (Cambridge: MIT Press, 1990). Žižek's use of Hitchcock to explicate different aspects of Lacanian theory, although interesting, overlooks the way in which Hitchcock's films are constitutive of as well as constituted by the Symbolic order.

17. For a detailed discussion of this aspect of fantasy, see Jean Laplanche and Jean-Bertrand Pontalis, "Fantasy and the origins of sexuality," in *Formations of Fantasy*, ed. Victor Burgin, James Donald, and Cora Kaplan (London: Routledge, 1986), 5–34. See also their discussion of fantasy in *The Language of Psychoanalysis*, trans. Donald Nicholson-Smith (New York: Norton, 1973), 314–19 and Žižek, *The Sublime Object of Desire*, 118.

18. In arguing that fantasy constructs a frame that enables the subject to desire, I do not mean to suggest that the subject's desire is reducible to her/his fantasies. Teresa de Lauretis has argued persuasively that the subject's desire is always in excess of her/his fantasies. See Teresa de Lauretis, "Film and the Visible," in *How Do I Look? Queer Film and Video*, ed. Bad Object-Choices (Seattle: Bay Press, 1991), 223–64. De Lauretis's analysis of butch-femme fantasies has important implications for the recent masculinization of the gay subculture. The gay macho style has usually been seen as encouraging an erotic investment in, and an identification with, the very forms of masculinity that oppress gay men. See, for example, Leo Bersani, "Is the Rectum a Grave," in *AIDS: Cultural Analysis, Cultural Activism*, ed. Douglas Crimp (Cambridge: MIT Press, 1988), 197–222. See also Kaja Silverman, *Male Subjectivity at the Margins* (New York: Routledge, 1992), 340–47. Applying de Lauretis's argument to gay male subjectivity suggests, however, that the gay macho style may function as the mise-en-scène of gay male desire rather than as its object.

19. Given the emphasis of *In the Name of National Security* on the politicization of same-sex eroticism in postwar America, it is extremely significant that the founders of the Mattachine Society, Henry Hay, Bob Hull, and Chuck Rowland, were former members of the Communist party who used the Marxist notion of false consciousness to theorize gay and lesbian oppression. They embodied the link in Cold War political discourse between same-sex eroticism and communism, which no doubt accounts for their eventual expulsion from the Mattachine Society by members who were concerned that the homophile organization might appear subversive.

20. For a discussion of the marginalization and suppression of this aspect of the lesbian subculture of the 1950s by the Daughters of Bilitis, see Sue-Ellen Case, "Towards a Butch-Femme Aesthetic," *Discourse* 11, no. 1 (1988–89): 56–75.

21. This aspect of the anti-Communist hysteria unleashed by the McCarthy hearings has been all but suppressed by the standard political histories of the period. See, for example, David Caute, *The Great Fear: The Anti-Communist Purge Under Truman and Eisenhower* (New York: Simon and Schuster, 1978). The impact of the politicization of same-sex eroticism on postwar American culture has also been suppressed by cultural historians. See, for example, John Patrick Diggins, *The Proud Decades: America in War and Peace 1941–1960* (New York: Norton, 1988). For a useful corrective, see John D'Emilio, *Sexual Politics, Sexual Communities: The Making of a Homosexual Minority in the United States, 1940–1970* (Chicago: University of Chicago Press, 1983), 1–53. See also Elaine Tyler May, *Homeward Bound: American Families in the Cold War Era* (New York: Basic Books, 1988), 114–36. Film scholars interested in the organization of gender relations in postwar America have also tended to overlook the politicization of same-sex eroticism and its relation to the construction of gender and sexual identity in the 1950s. See, for example, Jackie Byars, *All That Hollywood Allows: Re-Reading Gender in 1950s Melodrama* (Chapel Hill: University of North Carolina Press, 1991).

22. There are some exceptions to the argument that voyeurism and other forms of desire preexist the cinematic apparatus and are not constituted by it. See, for example, Linda Williams, *Hard Core: Power, Pleasure and "The Frenzy of the Visible"* (Berkeley and Los Angeles: University of California Press, 1989). Williams argues that the emergence of the film industry "normalized" voyeurism and scopophilia by making it possible for male spectators to engage in them legitimately. See also Miriam Hansen, *Babel and Babylon: Spectatorship in American Silent Film* (Cambridge: Harvard University Press, 1991). Hansen argues that the advertising and film industries in the 1920s institutionalized specifically female forms of voyeurism and scopophilia.

23. Significantly, Wyler later explained that *The Best Years of Our Lives* "came out of its period, and was the result of the social forces at work when the war ended." He also claimed that the film had been "written by [historical] events." It was no doubt this aspect of the film that made Warshow and other Cold War liberals so critical of it. See William Wyler, "No Magic Wand," in *Hollywood Directors 1941–1976*, ed. Richard Koszarski (New York: Oxford University Press, 1977), 104.

24. I have borrowed the term *political pre-conscious* from Donald E. Pease. Pease distinguishes the political pre-conscious from the political unconscious as defined by Fredric Jameson. See Donald E. Pease, "Leslie Fiedler, The Rosenberg Trial, and the Formulation of an American Canon," *boundary 2* 17, no. 2 (1990): 155–98. For Jameson's definition of the political unconscious, see Fredric Jameson, *The Political Unconscious: Narrative as a Socially Symbolic Act* (Ithaca: Cornell University Press, 1981).

1. Arthur Schlesinger, Jr., *The Vital Center: The Politics of Freedom* (Boston: Houghton Mifflin, 1949), 126. Hereafter all citations refer to this edition.

2. Schlesinger's homophobia was not limited to his description of the Communist party and the "techniques" members supposedly used to identify one another. He compared the political intrigue inside the Kremlin to the "situational" homosexuality one supposedly encountered at all-male boarding schools. He explained that totalitarian regimes did not wholly abolish political dissent but "perverted" it into "something secret, sweaty and furtive like nothing so much, in the phrase of one wise observer of modern Russia, as homosexuality in a boy's school: many practicing it, but all those caught to be caned by the headmaster" (151). He also tried to discredit Popular Front intellectuals by describing their glorification of the "people" in terms that recalled the standard psychoanalytic explanation of homosexuality: they had not fully resolved their Oedipus complexes and were overly dependent on their mothers. He reduced their populism to a "somewhat feminine fascination with the rude and masculine power of the proletariat, partly in [their] desire to compensate for [their] own sense of alienation by immersing [themselves] in the broad maternal expanse of the masses" (46). Needless to say, it did not occur to Schlesinger that many Popular Front intellectuals were women.

3. For an excellent history of the Popular Front and the Communist fellow traveling of liberal intellectuals, see Richard H. Pells, *Radical Visions and American Dreams: Culture and Social Thought in the Depression Years* (Middletown, CT: Wesleyan University Press, 1984).

4. For a discussion of the impact of Arendt's *Origins of Totalitarianism* on Cold War liberals, see Richard H. Pells, *The Liberal Mind in a Conservative Age: American Intellectuals in the 1940s and 1950s* (Middletown, CT: Wesleyan University Press, 1989), 85–96. See also Neil Jumonville, *Critical Crossings: The New York Intellectuals in Postwar America* (Berkeley and Los Angeles: University of California Press, 1991), 65–66.

5. Hannah Arendt, *The Origins of Totalitarianism* (New York: Harcourt Brace Jovanovich, 1975), 460. Hereafter all citations refer to this edition.

6. It is worth noting that many contemporary Marxists also tried to show that the category of class could not adequately explain the emergence of totalitarianism and sought an explanation for the appeal of totalitarian propaganda in mass psychology. Still, the category of class remained an important element in these analyses of the totalitarian state, and Arendt would have been familiar with them. See, for example, Max Horkheimer and Theodor Adorno, *Dialectic of Enlightenment*, trans. John Cumming (New York: Continuum, 1991).

7. Lionel Trilling, *The Liberal Imagination: Essays on Literature and Society* (New York: Viking, 1950), xiii. Hereafter all citations refer to this edition.

8. For a discussion of the relation between Parrington's cultural criticism and the historiography of the Progressive Era, see Pells, *The Liberal Mind in a Conservative Age*, 147–62.

9. Jonathan Arac, "F. O. Matthiessen: Authorizing an American Renaissance," in *The American Renaissance Reconsidered*, ed. Walter Been Michaels and Donald E. Pease (Baltimore: Johns Hopkins University Press, 1985), 90–112. For a related discussion, see Geraldine Murphy, "Romancing the Center: Cold War Politics and Classic American Literature," *Poetics Today* 9, no. 4 (1988): 737–47. For a different reading of Matthiessen's ideological project as a literary historian, see David Bergman, *Gaiety Transfigured: Gay Self-Representation in American Literature* (Madison: University of Wisconsin Press, 1991), 85–102. Whereas Arac argues that Matthiessen had to repress his homosexuality in order to authorize the American Renaissance, Bergman argues persuasively that his sexual identity influenced his reconstruction of American literary history in important ways.

10. It is, of course, not quite accurate to claim that Marxism lacked a fully developed theory of subjectivity. The Frankfurt school had been addressing issues of subjectivity since the 1930s. This work tried to combine the insights of both Marxism and psychoanalysis and was widely available in English. It included Theodor Adorno's *Authoritarian Personality* (1950) and Herbert Marcuse's *Eros and Civilization* (1955). Moreover, with its emphasis on the rise of the culture industry and the increasing atomization of postwar society, this work had much in common with the cultural criticism we have been examining. Still, Cold War liberals would not have considered this work adequately nuanced because it sought to theorize the construction of subjectivity in relation to concrete historical circumstances (in this particular instance, the emergence of the bureaucratic or totally administered society).

11. Both Schlesinger and Trilling clearly identified with Hawthorne and used his work to establish their authority as cultural critics. They tried to suggest that their criticisms of the Popular Front were the postwar equivalent of Hawthorne's criticisms of the utopian reformers who settled at Brook Farm. In other words, they could legitimately position themselves as the guardians of the liberal tradition because, like Hawthorne, they had the courage to dissent from the orthodoxies of dissent.

12. Baldwin's criticisms of Wright's novel led to a particularly vicious backlash against him. Ironically, in the 1960s Black nationalist intellectuals tried to undermine Baldwin's cultural authority by attacking him as a homosexual. They reduced his criticisms of Wright to an Oedipal struggle in which Baldwin sought to replace the best-selling novelist as the spokesman for the African-

American community. Thus just as Cold War liberals tried to discredit Popular Front intellectuals by representing their cultural politics as a kind of repressed or latent homosexuality, Black nationalists tried to discredit Baldwin by suggesting that he suffered from an arrested sexual development and was incapable of understanding the experience of "real" Black men. For a discussion of the backlash against Baldwin, see Morris Dickstein, *The Gates of Eden: American Culture in the Sixties* (New York: Basic Books, 1977), 154–82. Although Dickstein quite rightly attacks the homophobia of Black nationalist intellectuals, he too reduces Baldwin's criticisms of Wright to an Oedipal struggle in which Baldwin was unable to replace Wright as the greatest authority on African-American experience; consequently, he inadvertently reinscribes the homophobic categories of Black nationalist intellectuals. For a more balanced discussion, see Andrew Ross, *No Respect: Intellectuals and Popular Culture* (New York: Routledge, 1989), 88–89.

13. James Baldwin, *Notes of a Native Son* (Boston: Beacon, 1984), 19. Hereafter all citations refer to this edition.

14. It is important to point out that Trilling was not wholly critical of the report. Trilling used his critique of the report as the occasion to attack the instrumentalization of the social sciences by the capitalist state. Anticipating Herbert Marcuse's analysis of the totally administered society in *One-Dimensional Man* (1964), Trilling complained that "the social sciences in general no longer pretend that they can merely describe what people do; they now have the clear consciousness of their power to manipulate and adjust. First for industry and then for government, sociology has shown its instrumental nature" (226). Trilling welcomed the publication of the report because it promised to reverse this situation. He explained that the publication of the report made "sociology a little less the study of many men [sic] by a few men and a little more man's study of himself. There is something right in turning loose the Report on the American public—it turns the American public loose on the Report" (227).

15. Certainly many gays and lesbians interpreted Kinsey's statistics as evidence that homosexuality and lesbianism were as "normal" as heterosexuality. For a discussion of the reception of the Kinsey report in the gay and lesbian communities and its impact on the homophile movement, see John D'Emilio, *Sexual Politics, Sexual Communities: The Making of a Homosexual Minority in the United States, 1940–1970* (Chicago: University of Chicago Press, 1983), 33–39.

16. Trilling's use of psychoanalysis to counter the report's findings on homosexuality seems based less on a careful reading of Freud than on a knowledge of the way in which Freud had been interpreted in the United States, especially by psychoanalysts influenced by ego psychology. He cer-

tainly does not seem to have been familiar with Freud's arguments concerning homosexuality in *Three Essays on the Theory of Sexuality*. Trilling objected in particular to the idea that "homosexuality is to be accepted as a form of sexuality like another and that it is as 'natural' as heterosexuality" (240) and charged that Kinsey and his colleagues had not read Freud carefully. Yet in *Three Essays on the Theory of Sexuality* Freud used homosexuality to problematize that understanding of heterosexuality and to show precisely that it was not "natural" but socially constructed. See Sigmund Freud, *Three Essays on the Theory of Sexuality*, trans. James Strachey (New York: Basic Books, 1962), 1–38.

17. For a discussion of the controversy surrounding the publication of the Kinsey report and its impact on postwar attitudes toward sexuality, see in particular John D'Emilio and Estelle Freedman, *Intimate Matters: A History of Sexuality in America* (New York: Harper, 1988), 268–71 and 285–87. See also John Patrick Diggins, *The Proud Decades: America in War and Peace, 1941–1960* (New York: Norton, 1988), 205–6.

18. Although, as I show in chapter 2, the expulsion of homosexuals and lesbians from the federal government on a wide scale did not begin until 1950 following congressional hearings, charges by Republicans that the Truman administration was as "soft" on homosexuals and lesbians as it was on Communists first surfaced in the late 1940s and were widely covered by the media. For a discussion of this controversy and its relation to the growing crisis over national security, see, D'Emilio, *Sexual Politics, Sexual Communities*, 40–53.

19. Robert Warshow, *The Immediate Experience: Movies, Comics, Theatre and Other Aspects of Popular Culture* (New York: Doubleday, 1962), xxv. Hereafter all citations refer to this edition.

20. Interestingly, in his grant application to the Guggenheim Foundation, which was eventually used as the preface to *The Immediate Experience*, Warshow mentions Siegfried Kracauer's *From Caligari to Hitler: A Psychological History of The German Film* (1947) as an example of the kind of film criticism he did not want to write because it was supposedly too theoretical and ignored the subjective experience of watching films. He considered Kracauer a representative critic who approached film from a rigid theoretical perspective. He claimed that Kracauer limited his focus "to those elements which he believes to be affecting or expressing 'the audience' rather than with what he himself responds to" (xxv). Yet Warshow's approach to film did not differ significantly from Kracauer's. Although Warshow scrupulously avoided indulging in totalizing claims about film as a social text, like Kracauer, he tended to treat film as an unmediated reflection of mass psychology. Indeed, just as Kracauer used the films of the Weimar period to examine the mass psychology that gave rise to nazism, Warshow used the films of the postwar period to examine the mass psychology that led to the Stalinization of American society. Neither Kracauer

nor Warshow conceived of filmic discourse as at once constituted by and constitutive of historically specific forms of subjectivity. For a reappraisal of Kracauer's film criticism that tries to defend it against the charge that it relied on a naïve notion of realism, see Miriam Hansen, "Decentric Perspectives: Kracauer's Early Writings on Film and Mass Culture," *New German Critique* 54 (Fall 1991): 47–76. See also in the same volume Patrice Petro, "Kracauer's Epistemological Shift," 127–38.

21. Scholars have often noted the similarity between Warshow's critique of American popular culture and the Frankfurt school critique of the culture industry. See in particular Jumonville, *Critical Crossings*, 65–66. See also Pells, *The Liberal Mind in a Conservative Age*, 217. Certainly, Warshow's cultural criticism had much in common with the work of the Frankfurt school in that it related the emergence of the mass subject in postwar America to the rise of the culture industry. But, unlike the Frankfurt school theorists, Warshow was not interested in developing a theory of subjectivity that situated the emergence of the mass subject in relation to concrete historical circumstances. On the contrary, he tried to show that the individual's subjective experience of the material world was not conditioned by concrete historical forces and could not be reduced to the category of class.

22. Warshow's analysis of McCarey's use of a "fixed" system of representation, in particular his use of the conventions of the gangster film, to demonize the Communist party in many respects anticipates Michael Rogin's analysis of Cold War films in *Ronald Reagan, The Movie and Other Episodes in Political Demonology* (Berkeley and Los Angeles: University of California Press, 1988), 236–71.

23. Odets defended himself against the anti-Communist hysteria sweeping the nation, perhaps more effectively, by naming names—six, to be precise. For an account of Odets's appearances before the House Un-American Activities Committee, first in 1941 and then in 1953, see Larry Ceplair and Steven Englund, *The Inquisition in Hollywood: Politics in the Film Community, 1930–1960* (Berkeley and Los Angeles: University of California Press, 1983), 155–67 and 372–79.

24. Kaja Silverman has recently used Warshow's insights into the sexual politics of *The Best Years of Our Lives* to substantiate her claims that the postwar period was marked by a crisis in male heterosexual subjectivity. See her *Male Subjectivity at the Margins* (New York: Routledge, 1992), 71–73, 89–90.

25. See André Bazin, "In Defense of Mixed Cinema," in *What is Cinema?* vol. 1, trans. Hugh Gray (Berkeley and Los Angeles: University of California Press, 1967), 53–75.

26. For a discussion of the reception of Miller's work by Cold War liberals

and their reaction to his testimony before the House Un-American Activities Committee, see Pells, *The Liberal Mind in a Conservative Age*, 324–28.

2 Reconstructing Homosexuality

1. Alain Marty, "*L'inconnu du Nord-Express* et le Maccarthisme," *Son et Image* 2 (1980): 117. My translation. All further references will be cited in the text.

2. For Bellour's analysis of *North by Northwest*, see "Le blocage symbolique," *Communications* 23 (1975): 235–50. For his analysis of *Marnie*, see "Hitchcock, the Enunciator," *Camera Obscura* 2 (1977): 66–87. For his analysis of *Psycho*, see "Psychosis, Neurosis, Perversion," *Camera Obscura* 3–4 (1979): 66–103.

3. For quite specific feminists critiques of Bellour, see Jacqueline Rose, "Paranoia and the Film System," *Feminism and Film Theory*, ed. Constance Penley (New York: Routledge, 1988), 57–68, and Susan Lurie, "The Construction of the Castrated Woman in Psychoanalysis and Cinema," *Discourse* 4 (1981–82): 52–74. See also Janet Bergstrom, "Enunciation and Sexual Difference," *Feminism and Film Theory*, 159–88.

4. Mary Ann Doane, *The Desire to Desire: The Woman's Film of the 1940s* (Bloomington: Indiana University Press, 1987), 16. See also Laura Mulvey, "Visual Pleasure and Narrative Cinema," *Feminism and Film Theory*, 57–68 and her "Afterthoughts on 'Visual Pleasure and Narrative Cinema' Inspired by *Duel in the Sun*" in the same volume, 69–79.

5. Teresa de Lauretis, *Alice Doesn't: Feminism, Semiotics, Cinema* (Bloomington: Indiana University Press, 1984), 103–57.

6. Tania Modleski, *The Woman Who Knew Too Much: Hitchcock and Feminist Theory* (New York: Methuen, 1988), 1–15.

7. There are some exceptions. For theories of male spectatorship that stress male masochism, see D. N. Rodowick, "The Difficulty of Difference," *Wide Angle* 5 (1982): 4–15, and Janet Bergstrom, "Sexuality at a Loss: The Films of F. W. Murnau," *Poetics Today* 6 (1985): 185–203. See also Gaylyn Studlar, *In the Realm of Pleasure* (Urbana: Illinois University Press, 1988) and Kaja Silverman, "Masochism and Male Subjectivity," *Camera Obscura* 17 (1988): 31–66. For a forceful feminist critique of these theories, see Modleski, *The Woman Who Knew Too Much*, 9–13. The problem with these theories, including Modleski's critique of them, is that they restrict the bisexuality of the male spectator to his masochistic attachment to the mother during the pre-Oedipal phase, and they ignore his pre-Oedipal attachment to the father with its fantasies of replacing the mother. As a result, they repress the homoerotics of male spectatorial pleasure. As I will show, an alternative reading of psychoanalytic theory

suggests that the male spectator's identification with the hero involves the repression of a homosexual object cathexis that recalls his pre-Oedipal attachment to the father.

8. Insofar as the filmic text engages the male spectator libidinally, it can be said to function as a machinery for ideological investment that makes the spectator's insertion into the sex-gender system not only desirable but pleasurable. For a discussion of this aspect of textual practice in general, see Fredric Jameson, *The Political Unconscious: Narrative as a Socially Symbolic Act* (Ithaca: Cornell University Press, 1981), 17–102. For a discussion of it as it relates specifically to classical Hollywood cinema, see Kaja Silverman, *Male Subjectivity at the Margins* (New York: Routledge, 1992), 52–121.

9. Sigmund Freud, *The Ego and the Id*, trans. Joan Riviere (New York: Norton, 1960), 20.

10. For more detailed chronologies of these events, see John D'Emilio, *Sexual Politics, Sexual Communities: The Making of a Homosexual Minority in the United States 1940–1970* (Chicago: University of Chicago Press, 1983), 40–53, John D'Emilio and Estelle Freedman, *Intimate Matters: A History of Sexuality in America* (New York: Harper, 1988), 288–95, and Allan Bérubé, *Coming Out Under Fire: The History of Gay Men and Women in World War Two* (New York: Free Press, 1990), 255–70.

11. *The Employment of Homosexuals and Other Sex Perverts in Government* (Washington: Government Printing Office, 1950), 2. Hereafter all citations refer to this edition.

12. See D'Emilio and Freedman, *Intimate Matters*, 275–300.

13. Alfred Kinsey et al., *Sexual Behavior in the Human Male* (Philadelphia: Saunders, 1948), 627. Hereafter all citations refer to this edition.

14. Quoted in D'Emilio, *Sexual Politics, Sexual Communities*, 33.

15. Quoted in ibid., 81.

16. See ibid., 75–91. See also Toby Marotta, *The Politics of Homosexuality: How Lesbians and Gay Men Have Made Themselves a Political and Social Force in Modern America* (Boston: Houghton Mifflin, 1981), 1–68.

17. For a discussion of the impact of this social and sexual upheaval on cinematic representation, see Silverman, *Male Subjectivity at the Margins*, 52–121, and Dana Polan, *Power and Paranoia: History, Narrative, and the American Cinema, 1940–50* (New York: Columbia University Press, 1986), 251–308.

18. See D'Emilio, *Sexual Politics, Sexual Communities*, 9–53. See also Bérubé, *Coming Out Under Fire*, 175–201.

19. Patricia Highsmith, *Strangers on a Train* (London: Penguin, 1988), 27. Hereafter all citations refer to this edition.

20. Although critics of *Strangers on a Train* have neglected its relation to the "homosexual menace," they have long noted its homosexual subplot. See in

particular Vito Russo, *The Celluloid Closet: Homosexuality in the Movies* (New
York: Harper, 1987), 94–95, 99. Russo cites evidence that Robert Walker deliberately played Bruno Anthony as a homosexual. See also Donald Spoto, *The
Art of Alfred Hitchcock* (New York: Doubleday, 1979), 209–17, and Marty, *"L'inconnu du Nord-Express,"* 120.

21. Insofar as Bruno's relationship with his mother constitutes a form of
"momism," Hitchcock's film indicates another possible dimension to the representations of momism in Cold War movies discussed by Michael Rogin in
Ronald Reagan, The Movie, and Other Episodes in Political Demonology (Berkeley
and Los Angeles: University of California Press, 1987), 236–71. The demonization of the mother in Cold War movies may also encode anxieties over the
"homosexual menace."

22. For a discussion of the triangulation of male desire that sees it as
normative, see Réné Girard, *Deceit, Desire and the Novel: Self and Other in
Literary Structure*, trans. Yvonne Freccero (Baltimore: Johns Hopkins University Press, 1965). For an important feminist revision and application of Girard's
mimetic theory of desire, see Eve Kosofsky Sedgwick, *Between Men: English
Literature and Male Homosocial Desire* (New York: Columbia University Press,
1985), 21–27. See also Toril Moi, "The Missing Mother: The Oedipal Rivalries
of Réné Girard," *Diacritics* 12 (1982): 21–31.

23. Mary Ann Doane, "Film and Masquerade—Theorizing the Female
Spectator," *Screen* 23 (1982): 72–87.

24. When I presented an earlier version of this chapter at Dartmouth
College, a member of the audience informed me that the term "merry-go-
round" was used in the 1950s to refer to the gay subculture. If this is so, then
the merry-go-round in the final scene provides another indication that Bruno
is meant to represent "the homosexual" of contemporary juridical discourse.

25. In this respect, Bruno is merely one of a long line of psychopathic gay
men and women who die violently in Hollywood films. For a "necrology" of
gay men and women who meet violent deaths in Hollywood films, see Russo,
The Celluloid Closet, 347–49. Russo compares the psychopathic gay and lesbian
killers who populated Hollywood films in the postwar period to the stereotypical Black characters played by Butterfly McQueen, Hattie McDaniel, and
Stepin Fetchit in the 1930s and 1940s. But clearly more is involved here than
the perpetuation of homophobic stereotypes. Films such as Hitchcock's *Strangers on a Train* in which the gay or lesbian killer is more charismatic than the
other characters are perhaps best understood as heterosexual paranoid fantasies about the instability of the sex-gender system.

26. Contributing to this potentially destabilizing aspect of identification
was the disparity between Robert Walker's and Farley Granger's screen images. Granger was perhaps best known for his role in an earlier Hitchcock

film, *Rope* (1948), in which he played David Kentley, Shaw Brandon's homosexual lover, and it seems likely that contemporary spectators would have seen a parallel between his role as Kentley and his role as Guy. Moreover, he seemed passive and ineffectual in comparison to the more charismatic Robert Walker, whose performance won praise from critics. Hitchcock was apparently concerned about this. In his interviews with François Truffaut, he commented: "I must say that I . . . wasn't too pleased with Farley Granger; he's a good actor, but I would have liked to see William Holden in the part because he's stronger. In this kind of story the stronger the hero, the more effective the situation." See François Truffaut, *Hitchcock: The Definitive Study of Alfred Hitchcock by François Truffaut*, rev. ed. (New York: Simon, 1983), 199.

3 Resisting History

1. Leslie A. Fiedler, *The Collected Essays of Leslie Fiedler* (New York: Stein and Day, 1971), 1:xxii. Hereafter cited in my text by volume and page number only.

2. For a good discussion of the role of liberal intellectuals in shaping the postwar settlement, see Richard H. Pells, *The Liberal Mind in a Conservative Age: American Intellectuals in the 1940s and 1950s* (Middletown, CT: Wesleyan University Press, 1989). See also Andrew Ross, *No Respect: Intellectuals and Popular Culture* (New York: Routledge, 1989), 1–64. For an interesting discussion of the way in which the Cold War consensus shaped the study of American literature in the 1950s, see Geraldine Murphy, "Romancing the Center: Cold War Politics and Classic American Literature," *Poetics Today* 9, no. 4 (1988): 737–47. Murphy relates the idea, common to American studies, that the characteristically American literary form is the romance rather than the novel to what she calls the "vital-center liberalism" of the Cold War.

3. For the most authoritative discussion of this aspect of hegemony, see Antonio Gramsci, *Prison Notebooks: Selections*, trans. Quintin Hoare and Geoffrey N. Smith (New York: International Publishers, 1971). See also Stuart Hall, "The Toad in the Garden: Thatcherism among the Theorists" in *Marxism and the Interpretation of Culture*, ed. Cary Nelson and Lawrence Grossberg (Chicago: University of Illinois Press, 1988), 35–57. The most comprehensive and useful discussion of Gramsci's theory of hegemony is to be found in Anne Showstack Sassoon's *Gramsci's Politics* (Minneapolis: University of Minnesota Press, 1987).

4. These acts were: the Smith Act (1940), the Taft-Hartley Act (1947), the McCarran Internal Security Act (1950), the McCarran-Walter Act (1952), and the Communist Control Act (1954). For a detailed discussion of these acts and their impact on leftist politics in general, see David Caute, *The Great Fear: The*

Anti-Communist Purge under Truman and Eisenhower (New York: Simon and Schuster, 1978). For a history of leftist politics in Hollywood and the impact of McCarthyism on the film industry, see Larry Ceplair and Steven Englund, *The Inquisition in Hollywood: Politics in the Film Community, 1930–1960* (Berkeley and Los Angeles: University of California Press, 1979).

5. I have chosen to discuss this particular collection of essays because it includes contributors from a broad spectrum of academic disciplines (history, sociology, political science, linguistics) and because its critique of postwar American culture is representative of the vital-center liberalism discussed by Murphy in "Romancing the Center." Other examples of critiques of postwar American culture that were inspired by vital-center liberalism and that would serve my argument equally well include, but are not limited to, Arthur M. Schlesinger, Jr., *The Vital Center: The Politics of Freedom* (Boston: Houghton Mifflin, 1949) and Lionel Trilling, *The Liberal Imagination* (New York: Viking, 1950), both of which I discussed in some detail in chapter 1.

6. Richard Hofstadter, "The Pseudo-Conservative Revolt" in *The New American Right*, ed. Daniel Bell (New York: Criterion, 1955): 52. Hereafter all citations refer to this edition.

7. For a discussion of television that sees the spectacle form of American politics as in crisis, see Paolo Carpignano, Robin Anderson, Stanley Aronowitz, and William Difazio, "Chatter in the Age of Electronic Reproduction: Talk Television and the 'Public Mind,' " *Social Text* 25/26 (1990): 33–55. See also John Fiske, *Television Culture* (London: Routledge, 1988). Fiske persuasively refutes the liberal critique of television that sees television as constructing a passive spectatorial subject who substitutes television viewing for meaningful political action.

8. Even the contributors to Bell's collection of essays were aware of the spectatorial aspect of American politics. See Bell's discussion of the "cider election" of 1840, which he identifies as a turning point in American politics, in "Interpretations of American Politics" in *The New American Right*: 22–23.

9. Michael Rogin persuasively refutes this interpretation of McCarthyism in *The Intellectuals and McCarthy* (Cambridge: MIT Press, 1967). He shows that the most active supporters of McCarthyism were not populists, but rank-and-file members of the Republican party who thought that an anti-Communist platform would undermine Democratic control of the House and Senate.

10. Andrew Ross discusses this essay and its relation to the postwar debate over high-brow, middle-brow, and low-brow culture in *No Respect*, 15–41. For a reading of *An End to Innocence* that is more sensitive to the subtleties of Fiedler's critical project, see Donald E. Pease, "Leslie Fiedler, the Rosenberg Trial, and the Formulation of an American Canon," *boundary 2* 17 (1990): 155–98.

11. See in particular Jean Douchet, "Hitch et son public," *Cahiers du Cinema* 113 (November 1960): 7–15. See also Donald Spoto, *The Art of Alfred Hitchcock* (New York: Doubleday, 1979), 237–49, and Laura Mulvey, "Visual Pleasure and Narrative Cinema" in *Feminism and Film Theory*, ed. Constance Penley (New York: Routledge, 1968), 57–68. For a persuasive feminist critique of these readings of Hitchcock's film, see Tania Modleski, *The Woman Who Knew Too Much: Hitchcock and Feminist Theory* (New York: Methuen, 1988), 73–85.

12. For an excellent discussion of the emergence of narrative cinema as the dominant form and its dependence on identification as its primary mode of address, see David Bordwell, Janet Staiger, and Kristin Thompson, *The Classic Hollywood Cinema* (New York: Columbia University Press, 1985). For a discussion of "primitive" cinema and the radically different way in which it positions the spectator, see Miriam Hansen, *Babel and Babylon: Spectatorship and American Silent Film* (Boston: Harvard University Press, 1991). See also Tom Gunning, "The Cinema of Attractions: Early Film, its Spectator and the Avant-Garde" in *Early Cinema: Space, Frame, Narrative*, ed. Thomas Elsaesser (London: British Film Institute, 1990), 56–62.

13. Feminist film theorists have recently begun to challenge this masculinist conception of spectatorial pleasure. See in particular Mary Ann Doane, *The Desire to Desire: The Woman's Film of the 1940s* (Bloomington: Indiana University Press, 1987). See also Teresa de Lauretis, *Alice Doesn't: Feminism, Semiotics, Cinema* (Bloomington: Indiana University Press, 1984) and Modleski, *The Woman Who Knew Too Much.* The problem with these feminist challenges to Lacanian theories of the cinematic apparatus is that they themselves rely on a psychoanalytic understanding of female subjectivity and therefore do not adequately address the historicity of filmic pleasure, its discursive construction in a specific historical context and in relation to hegemonic social and political structures.

14. For a discussion of this aspect of the cinematic apparatus, see Jean-Louis Baudry, "The Apparatus," *Camera Obscura* 1 (1977): 104–28. See also Christian Metz, *The Imaginary Signifier*, trans. Celia Britton, Annwyl Williams, Ben Brewster, and Alfred Guzzetti (Bloomington: Indiana University Press, 1982), 1–87.

15. Michael Rogin discusses these films in detail in *Ronald Reagan, The Movie, and Other Episodes in Political Demonology* (Berkeley and Los Angeles: University of California Press, 1987), 236–71.

16. Modleski makes a similar point in *The Woman Who Knew Too Much*, 80–81, but she tries to claim that Lisa's empathy for Miss Lonely Heart and Miss Torso represents an alternative way of looking that is not voyeuristic. The implication of her argument is that it would be politically incorrect for the feminist-identified woman to derive pleasure from looking at others.

17. Mulvey, "Visual Pleasure and Narrative Cinema," 65–66.

18. This attempt on the part of the film to make available to the spectator a liberal interpretation of reality to which she or he will consent spontaneously leads me to question Ina Rae Hark's recent analysis of Hitchcock's so-called political films. Hark claims that Hitchcock's political films (which of Hitchcock's films are not political?, one might legitimately ask) "challenge citizens to break suture and disrupt those performances designed to lull them into complacent reliance upon authority." See "Keeping Your Amateur Standing: Audience Participation and Good Citizenship in Hitchcock's Political Films," *Cinema Journal* 29, no. 2 (1990): 14. Although I would agree with Hark that Hitchcock's films (and not just those she identifies as political?) try to position the spectator as a "good" citizen, I would argue that what constitutes good citizenship for Hitchcock varies from historical moment to historical moment. I would also argue that Hitchcock's films, rather than challenging the spectator to break suture, work actively to absorb her or him into the diegesis. The abhorrence of totalitarianism Hark attributes to Hitchcock clearly did not extend to his own authoritarian performances.

4   The Fantasy of the Maternal Voice

1. The best example of a critic who considers Hitchcock's system of representation typical of the classical system as a whole is Raymond Bellour. See, for example, his highly influential reading of *Psycho* (1960), "Psychosis, Neurosis, Perversion," *Camera Obscura* 3–4 (1979): 66–103. Bellour sees this most idiosyncratic of classical Hollywood texts as exemplary of the classical system. He argues that it follows the typical narrative trajectory of the classical Hollywood film in that its ending responds to its beginning. Using psychoanalytic theory, he explains away the rupture in the film's narrative trajectory when Marion (Janet Leigh) is brutally killed and Norman (Anthony Perkins) abruptly replaces her as the spectator's main point of entry into the narrative and claims that Norman's psychosis is the male counterpart of Marion's neurosis.

2. William Rothman, *Hitchcock: The Murderous Gaze* (Cambridge: Harvard University Press, 1982), 111. Rothman exemplifies the tendency I discuss below of auteurist critics who attribute to Hitchcock an unproblematic authorial agency. He contends that Hitchcock is one of the few Hollywood directors who successfully conveys to the spectator that his films have been "authored." See Rothman, *The Murderous Gaze*, 106. For an important feminist critique of Rothman's auteurist approach to Hitchcock's corpus and its misogynistic implications, see Tania Modleski, *The Woman Who Knew Too Much: Hitchcock and Feminist Theory* (New York: Methuen, 1988), 118–20.

3. Ibid., 112.

4. Ina Rae Hark, "Revalidating Patriarchy: Why Hitchcock Remade *The Man Who Knew Too Much*," in *Hitchcock's Rereleased Films: From Rope to Vertigo*, ed. Walter Raubicheck and Walter Srebnick (Detroit: Wayne State University Press, 1991), 209–20. For a slightly different but no less auteurist reading of the original version of the film, see also her "Keeping Your Amateur Standing: Audience Participation and Good Citizenship in Hitchcock's Political Films," *Cinema Journal* 29, no. 2 (1990): 8–22.

5. Hark, "Keeping Your Amateur Standing," 211.

6. Ibid., 211.

7. François Truffaut, *Hitchcock: The Definitive Study of Alfred Hitchcock by François Truffaut*, rev. ed. (New York: Simon and Schuster, 1983), 64.

8. In addition to Rothman's *The Murderous Gaze*, I also have in mind here Lesley Brill's *The Hitchcock Romance: Love and Irony in Hitchcock's Films* (Princeton: Princeton University Press, 1988) and Robin Wood's *Hitchcock's Films Revisited* (New York: Columbia University Press, 1989). Wood's *Hitchcock's Films Revisited* contains a reading of the two versions of *The Man Who Knew Too Much* that also argues that Hitchcock remade the film because he did not get it "right" the first time, although, in marked contrast to Hark, he sees both films as feminist in their implications. See Wood, *Hitchcock's Films Revisited*, 358–70.

9. For the most thorough examination of the problems surrounding discussions of authorship in film studies, see the collection of essays edited by John Caughie, *Theories of Authorship: A Reader* (London: Routledge, 1981).

10. The standard discussion of the emergence of the classical system and the institutionalization of classical codes remains David Bordwell, Janet Staiger, and Kristen Thompson, *The Classical Hollywood Cinema: Film Style and Mode of Production to 1960* (New York: Columbia University Press, 1985). Rick Altman has recently criticized this account for exaggerating the homogeneity and uniformity of classical norms and for repressing the roots of classical Hollywood cinema in nineteenth-century melodrama and other forms of popular entertainment. See Rick Altman, "Dickens, Griffith and Film Theory Today," *South Atlantic Quarterly* 88 (Spring 1989): 321–59.

11. The other ways in which Hitchcock left his signature on his films include the trailers he made to market his films, such as those for *The Birds* (1967) and *Frenzy* (1972). These trailers differ significantly from the ones traditionally used to market Hollywood films. Exploiting his reputation as a master of suspense, Hitchcock appears in them to announce the release of his latest film. In other words, these trailers market the films as Hitchcock productions.

12. Eric Rohmer and Claude Chabrol, for example, published the first full-length study of Hitchcock's corpus in 1957. It has since been translated into English as *Hitchcock: The First Forty-Four Films*, trans. Stanley Hochman (New

York: Ungar, 1979) and stresses Hitchcock's supposedly Catholic sensibilities. In addition to François Truffaut, Jean Douchet also wrote extensively about Hitchcock's films. See, for example, Jean Douchet, "Hitch et son public," *Cahiers du Cinema* 113 (November 1960): 7–15.

13. For an especially useful discussion of the incorporation of sound technology and the strategies the film industry developed for maintaining the primacy of the image, see Bordwell, Staiger, and Thompson, *The Classical Hollywood Cinema*, 298–308.

14. For a discussion of this particular aspect of sound technology, see Tom Levin, "The Acoustic Dimension: Notes on Cinema Sound," *Screen* 25, no. 3 (May–June 1984): 55–68. See also Rick Altman, "Moving Lips: Cinema as Ventriloquism," *Yale French Studies* 60 (1980): 67–79.

15. For a thorough discussion of the strategies the film industry developed for anticipating and standardizing the consumption of its products, see Bordwell, Staiger, and Thompson, *Classical Hollywood Cinema*, 155–240.

16. For an especially good discussion of Hollywood's attempts to develop textual strategies that would minimize the racial, ethnic, class, and gender differences dividing early film audiences, see Miriam Hansen, *Babel and Babylon: Spectatorship in American Silent Film* (Cambridge: Harvard University Press, 1991), 23–89. See also Douglas Gomery, *Shared Pleasures: History of Movie Presentation in the United States* (Madison: University of Wisconsin Press, 1992), 18–56.

17. On this particular aspect of the synchronization of voice and image in early sound films, see Mary Ann Doane, "The Voice in the Cinema: The Articulation of Body and Space" in *Theory and Practice of Film Sound*, ed. Elizabeth Weis and John Belton (New York: Columbia University Press, 1985), 162–76. See also Amy Lawrence, *Echo and Narcissus: Women's Voices in Classical Hollywood Cinema* (Berkeley and Los Angeles: University of California Press, 1991), 1–32.

18. The term *cinema of attractions* refers to the direct mode of address of so-called primitive cinema and was originally coined by Tom Gunning. Gunning argues persuasively that "primitive" cinema was frankly exhibitionistic and relied on a method of soliciting the spectator's gaze that had more in common with county fairs, variety shows, and vaudeville than with the continuity editing and invisible narration of the classical system. See Tom Gunning, "The Cinema of Attractions: Early Film, its Spectator and the Avant-Garde," in *Early Cinema: Space, Frame, Narrative*, ed. Thomas Elsaesser (London: British Film Institute, 1990), 56–62.

19. My discussion of the female voice in classical Hollywood cinema draws extensively on Kaja Silverman, *The Acoustic Mirror: The Female Voice in Psychoanalysis and Cinema* (Bloomington: Indiana University Press, 1988), 42–71. It also draws on Lawrence, *Echo and Narcissus*, 1–32.

20. Silverman, *The Acoustic Mirror*, 48–49.

21. Ibid., 61.

22. Ibid., 42–71.

23. On the emergence of the New Woman, see Estelle B. Freedman, "The New Woman: Changing Views of Women in the 1920s," *Journal of American History* 56, no. 2 (September 1974): 372–93. See also Esther Newton, "The Mythic Mannish Lesbian: Radclyffe Hall and the New Woman," in *Hidden From History: Reclaiming the Gay and Lesbian Past*, ed. Martin Duberman, Martha Vicinus, and George Chauncy, Jr. (New York: New American Library, 1989), 281–93. For a detailed discussion of the erosion of the Victorian double standard and the reorganization of gender relations in American society following World War I, see John D'Emilio and Estelle B. Freedman, *Intimate Matters: A History of Sexuality in America* (New York: Harper and Row, 1988), 171–300.

24. For an excellent discussion of the role of the film industry in integrating women into the consumer culture of the 1920s, see Hansen, *Babel and Babylon*, 245–94. See also Gomery, *Shared Pleasures*, 18–56.

25. For a different reading of the implications of Hitchcock's decision to dub Alice's voice, see Lawrence, *Echo and Narcissus*, 116–25. See also Modleski, *The Woman Who Knew Too Much*, 17–30. Both Lawrence and Modleski stress Hitchcock's focus on the problem of the speaking woman, but neither of them tries to historicize that focus.

26. The classic discussion of the star system and its mobilization of more sustained structures of identification is Richard Dyer, *Stars* (London: British Film Institute, 1979). See also Richard deCordova, "The emergence of the star system in America," in *Stardom: Industry of Desire*, ed. Christine Gledhill (London: Routledge, 1991), 17–29.

27. On the use of the voice-off in classical Hollywood cinema, see Doane, "The Voice in the Cinema." See also Silverman, *The Acoustic Mirror*, 130–33, 136–40.

28. Andrew Sarris, "Notes on the Auteur Theory in 1962," in *Perspectives on the Study of Film*, ed. John Stuart Katz (Boston: Little, Brown, 1971), 137. Hereafter all citations refer to this edition.

29. John Caughie, "Introduction," in *Theories of Authorship*, 10. See also Edward Bushcombe, "Ideas of Authorship," in Caughie, *Theories of Authorship*, 22–34.

30. On the professionalization of motherhood in postwar American society, see Elaine Tyler May, *Homeward Bound: American Families in The Cold War Era* (New York: Basic Books, 1988), 135–61.

31. Dr. Benjamin Spock, *The Common Sense Book of Baby and Child Care* (New York: Duell, Sloan and Pearce, 1957), 3. Hereafter all citations refer to this edition.

32. For a particularly good discussion of the developmental psychology of the postwar period, see Barbara Ehrenreich, *The Hearts of Men: American Dreams and the Flight From Commitment* (New York: Doubleday, 1983), 14–28.

33. On the importance of the mother's voice in the child's perceptual development, see Silverman, *The Acoustic Mirror*, 101–41.

34. The locus classicus of this particular fantasy of inhabiting a space organized and defined by the maternal voice is Guy Rosolato, "La voix: entre corps et langage," *Revue française de psychanalyse* 37, no. 1 (1974): 79–87. For a powerful feminist critique of Rosolato's theory as itself a fantasy, see Silverman, *The Acoustic Mirror*, 79–80, 84–85.

35. The locus classicus of this particular fantasy of inhabiting a space organized and defined by the maternal voice is Michael Chion, *La Voix au cinema* (Paris: Éditions de l'Etoile, 1982). For a critique of Chion's misogynistic formulation of this particular fantasy, see Silverman, *The Acoustic Mirror*, 74–79.

36. Hitchcock's choice of Doris Day to star as Jo no doubt contributed to the subordination of the spectator's visual pleasure to her/his auditory pleasure. Day was the least glamorous of Hitchcock's leading ladies in the postwar period. These included Ingrid Bergman, Marlene Dietrich, Grace Kelly, Kim Novak, and Tippi Hedren. Day was certainly less glamorous than Edna Best, the actress who played Jill in the original version of the film, and had made her career playing the part of the all-American, girl-next-door type. Nevertheless, her voice has a rich, sonorous quality that Hitchcock exploits in several scenes, such as the one at the end of the film in which we hear her singing "We'll Love Again" in the background. (There are also several scenes at the beginning of the film in which he uses the voice-off to indicate her presence in the diegesis.) In these scenes, the spectator is clearly meant to derive more pleasure from listening to her than from looking at her.

5 "There Are Many Such Stories"

1. For a history of the Beat rebellion, see Bruce Cook, *The Beat Generation* (New York: Scribner, 1971). For an excellent discussion of the Beats that locates them culturally, see Barbara Ehrenreich, *The Hearts of Men: American Dreams and the Flight From Commitment* (New York: Doubleday, 1983), 52–67. See also John Patrick Diggins, *The Proud Decades: America in War and Peace, 1941–1960* (New York: Norton, 1988), 167–71. For a good but brief discussion of San Francisco's history as a center of Bohemian culture, see John D'Emilio, *Sexual Politics, Sexual Communities: The Making of a Homosexual Minority in the United States* (Chicago: University of Chicago Press, 1983), 176–199.

2. Norman Podhoretz, *Doings and Undoings: The Fifties and After in American Writing* (New York: Farrar, Straus, 1964), 157.

3. Bernard Wolfe, "Angry at What?" *The Nation*, 1 November 1958, 319.

4. For a more detailed discussion of San Francisco's attempt to "clean up" North Beach and discourage tourists from visiting it, see D'Emilio, *Sexual Politics, Sexual Communities*, 179.

5. It seems to me that this is precisely what most critics of the film have done. See, for example, Robin Wood's analysis of *Vertigo* in his *Hitchcock's Films Revisited* (New York: Columbia University Press, 1989), 108–30. Wood seems primarily interested in establishing that *Vertigo* is "one of the four or five most profound and beautiful films the cinema has yet given us" (108) and argues that it contains "an entirely satisfying and fully realized treatment of themes of the most fundamental human significance" (108). See also Lesley Brill, *The Hitchcock Romance: Love and Irony in Hitchcock's Films* (Princeton: Princeton University Press, 1988), 202–21. Brill similarly dehistoricizes the film by universalizing its themes. He reads Scottie and Madeleine's tragic, star-crossed love as Hitchcock's attempt to show that "lovers cannot be true. At worst, they use and abuse, lie to and deceive each other" (221).

6. Barbara Ehrenreich, *The Hearts of Men*, 14–67. For an excellent discussion of the translation of these discourses onto the screen and what they indicate about the textual politics of various films made in the 1950s, see Peter Biskind, *Seeing is Believing: How Hollywood Taught Us to Stop Worrying and Love the Fifties* (New York: Pantheon, 1983), 250–333.

7. Quoted in Ehrenreich, *The Hearts of Men*, 14.

8. Wolfe, "Angry at What," 318. Hereafter all references to this essay will be cited in the text.

9. Podhoretz, *Doings and Undoings*, 146. Hereafter all references to this essay will be cited in the text.

10. Podhoretz's attack on the Beats seems especially vicious. Only the year before, he had criticized the conformity of younger liberals in "The Young Generation," an essay originally published in *Partisan Review* but included in *Doings and Undoings*. There he complained that younger liberals had "cultivated an interest in food, clothes, furniture, manners—these being the elements of the 'richness' of life that the generation of the 30's had deprived itself of." See *Doings and Undoings*, 109. The growing popularity of the Beats and the possibility that they might influence the younger generation to resist the suburbanization of American culture seems, however, to have compelled him to pathologize the Beat rebellion in order to contain its impact.

11. Ehrenreich discusses the relation of *Playboy* to the postwar culture of consumption and the reasons why the figure of the playboy escaped pathologization in *The Hearts of Men*, 42–51. See also Andrew Ross, *No Respect: Intellec-*

tuals and Popular Culture (New York: Routledge, 1989), 173–74, and Diggins, *The Proud Decade*, 206, 216.

12. The best discussion of the growing conservatism of liberal intellectuals in the 1950s and the institutionalization of liberal cultural critique is Richard H. Pells, *The Liberal Mind in a Conservative Age: American Intellectuals in the 1940s and 1950s* (Middletown, CT: Wesleyan University Press, 1989). See also Neil Jumonville's excellent discussion of much of the same material in *Critical Crossings: The New York Intellectuals in Postwar America* (Berkeley and Los Angeles: University of California Press, 1991). Ross analyzes the hostility to popular culture of postwar liberal intellectuals in *No Respect*.

13. D'Emilio argues persuasively for the importance of the Beat rebellion. He shows that its rejection of middle-class values directly influenced the social movements of the 1960s, particularly the gay liberation movement. See D'Emilio, *Sexual Politics, Sexual Communities*, 177–95. See also Morris Dickstein, *Gates of Eden: American Culture in the Sixties* (New York: Basic Books, 1977), 3–24.

14. Leslie Fiedler, *The Collected Essays of Leslie Fiedler* (New York: Stein and Day, 1971), 1:398. Hereafter all citations refer to this edition.

15. In this respect, Fiedler's jeremiad against younger liberal intellectuals can be said to anticipate Russell Jacoby's recent obituary of the so-called "public" intellectual in his book, *The Last Intellectuals*. Jacoby argues that in the sixties progressive intellectuals failed to take over from the New York intellectuals, and he endlessly repeats the claim that "today nonacademic intellectuals are an endangered species." See Russell Jacoby, *The Last Intellectuals: American Culture in the Age of Academe* (New York: Basic Books, 1987), 9 and passim. But Jacoby's narrative of decline fails to consider the increasingly reactionary cultural politics of the New York intellectuals. It is more likely that in the sixties progressive intellectuals were put off by the mixed legacy of Cold War liberalism. For a discussion of Jacoby and other neoconservative attacks on academic leftists, see Bruce Robbins, "Introduction: The Grounding of Intellectuals," in *Intellectuals: Aesthetics, Politics, Academics,* ed. Bruce Robbins (Minneapolis: University of Minnesota Press, 1990), ix–xxvii.

16. Norman Mailer, *Advertisements for Myself* (New York: G. P. Putnam, 1959), 353. Hereafter all citations refer to this addition.

17. Interestingly enough, liberal intellectuals tended to read the Beats through the distorting lens of Mailer's analysis of them in "The White Negro" and attributed to them a fascination with violence that puzzled them and that they were quick to disown. For a discussion of the Beats' reaction to Mailer's essay, see Jumonville, *Critical Crossings*, 189–90.

18. More militant Black intellectuals, such as Eldridge Cleaver, did not share Baldwin's reservations about Mailer's essay and followed Mailer's example in trying to exploit white male anxiety about Black male sexual prowess.

250

See Dickstein, *The Gates of Eden*, 154–82. See also Ross, *No Respect*, 88–89. Dickstein also discusses the way in which more militant Black intellectuals in the sixties used Baldwin's objections to the myth of the threatening black phallus to undermine his cultural authority and to stigmatize him as an effeminate homosexual. See Dickstein, *The Gates of Eden*, 165–71.

19. James Baldwin, *Nobody Knows My Name: More Notes of a Native Son* (New York: Dial Press, 1961), 217. Hereafter all citations refer to this edition.

20. Paul Goodman, *Growing Up Absurd: Problems of Youth in the Organized System* (New York: Random House, 1960), 59. Hereafter all citations refer to this edition.

21. The best example of a reading of the film that psychoanalyzes rather than historicizes Scottie's desire for Madeleine and therefore reduces its complex determinations is Wood's. See his *Hitchcock's Films Revisited*, 108–30. See also Brill, *The Hitchcock Romance*, 202–21.

22. See in particular Tania Modleski, *The Woman Who Knew Too Much: Hitchcock and Feminist Theory* (New York: Methuen, 1988). Inadvertently ratifying the homophobic categories of the official narrative of male development in the 1950s, Modleski argues that "from the outset . . . with his failure to perform his proper role in relation to the Symbolic order and the law, Scottie is placed in the same position of enforced passivity as L. B. Jeffries [in *Rear Window*], a position that the film explicitly links to femininity and associates with unfreedom" (90). But this reading seriously misinterprets the film's representation of Scottie's sexual identity. The film does not link Scottie's problematic relation to the law to femininity, but rather the official narrative of male development does. Scottie occupies a position that has been designated by the official narrative of male development as that of "the homosexual" because he has internalized the homophobic categories of that narrative. See also Brill, *The Hitchcock Romance*, 207. According to Brill, the scene in Midge's apartment demonstrates that Scottie is emotionally and sexually immature. It seems to me, however, that Scottie appears to be emotionally and sexually immature in this scene, not because he actually is, but because he accepts the official representation of his hesitation in the line of duty, a representation that positions him as "the homosexual" of the dominant discourse of rebellion.

23. For a discussion of the homoerotics of the use of women as objects of exchange between men, see René Girard, *Deceit, Desire, and the Novel: Self and Other in Literary Structure*, trans. Yvonne Freccero (Baltimore: Johns Hopkins University Press, 1972). For an important feminist revision of Girard's mimetic theory of desire, see Eve Sedgwick, *Between Men: English Literature and Male Homosocial Desire* (New York: Columbia University Press, 1985), 21–27. See also Toril Moi, "The Missing Mother: The Oedipal Rivalries of René Girard," *Diacritics* 12 (1982): 21–31.

24. The fact that James Stewart played Jeff in Hitchcock's earlier film, *Rear Window* (1954), and that both Jeff and Scottie are handicapped at the beginning of the two films—Scottie because he is wearing a corset, Jeff because he has broken his leg and is wearing a cast—reinforces my claim that Scottie's surveillance of Madeleine is meant to represent a form of cinematic spectatorship. Certainly, Stewart's appearance in both films would have created a space of intertextuality between them that would have encouraged the spectator to make a connection between Scottie's and Jeff's behavior in these scenes. But whereas the earlier film tried to reclaim cinematic spectatorship from its contamination by the emergence of the national security state, *Vertigo* attributes its current construction to a historically specific regime of pleasure that helps to insure the reproduction of the structural inequalities between the sexes and questions whether it can in fact be recuperated for the postwar settlement.

6 Hitchcock through the Looking Glass

1. For an important exception to the critical consensus, see Raymond Bellour, "Psychosis, Neurosis, Perversion," *Camera Obscura* 3–4 (1979): 66–103. Bellour sees a logic of displacement in the film in which Norman's psychosis restages and absorbs Marion's neurosis, the feminine counterpart of psychosis, according to psychoanalytic theory. He wants to show that despite its abrupt narrative shift, the film constitutes an exemplary instance of classical Hollywood cinema. Thus he argues that in classic fashion, the end of the film replies to the beginning. Although I agree with the implication of his reading, namely that Marion and Norman function as mirror images of each other, I feel that he gives the film's narrative structure more order and coherence than it actually has. For an interesting feminist elaboration of Bellour's reading, see Barbara Klinger, "*Psycho:* The Institutionalization of Female Sexuality," in *Hitchcock Reader*, ed. Marshall Deutelbaum and Leland Poague (Ames: Iowa State University Press, 1986), 332–39.

2. See Leo Braudy, "Hitchcock, Truffaut, and the Irresponsible Audience," in *Focus on Hitchcock*, ed. Albert J. LaValley (Englewood Cliffs, NJ: Prentice-Hall, 1972), 116–27. See also Leland Poague, "Links in a Chain: *Psycho* and Film Classicism," in Deutelbaum and Poague, eds., *Hitchcock Reader*, 340–49.

3. For an excellent discussion of the rise of the expert in postwar American culture, see Elaine Tyler May, *Homeward Bound: American Families in the Cold War Era* (New York: Basic Books, 1988), 16–36. See also John Patrick Diggins, *The Proud Decades: America in War and Peace, 1941–1960* (New York: Norton, 1988), 177–219. For a good discussion of the representation of the rise of the

expert in postwar American cinema, see Peter Biskind, *Seeing is Believing: How Hollywood Taught Us to Stop Worrying and Love the Fifties* (New York: Pantheon, 1983).

4. May describes in detail the emergence of middle-class suburban culture and its impact on the structure of the family in *Homeward Bound*, 162–82.

5. For a different reading of the film's opening titles that is heavily indebted to Cavellian critical categories, see Marian Keane, "The Designs of Authorship: An Essay on *North by Northwest*," *Wide Angle* 4, no. 1 (1980): 44–52. In true Cavellian fashion, Keane seems primarily interested in establishing the canonical status of the film, which she tries to do by comparing it to Shakespearean romance.

6. The most useful discussion of the emergence of the "feminine mystique" remains Betty Friedan, *The Feminine Mystique* (New York: Dell, 1963). May discusses the outpouring of letters Friedan received in response to her book in *Homeward Bound*, 208–26. These letters suggest that for many American housewives, Friedan's book was an accurate description of gender relations in the postwar period.

7. See Michael Rogin, *Ronald Reagan, the Movie, and Other Episodes in Political Demonology* (Berkeley and Los Angeles: University of California Press, 1987), 236–71.

8. Ibid., 242.

9. Ibid., 242–43.

10. Leonard is one of a long line of villains in Hitchcock's films who are coded as homosexual or lesbian. In addition to Bruno Anthony (Robert Walker) in *Strangers on a Train* (1951), whom I discuss in chapter 2, there are also Handel Fane (Esme Percy), the female impersonator in *Murder!* (1930) who is also of racially mixed origin; Mrs. Danvers (Judith Anderson), the sadistic housekeeper in *Rebecca* (1940); and, finally, Shaw Brandon (John Dall) and Philip (Farley Granger) in *Rope* (1948). Robin Wood tries unconvincingly to show that these villains are in fact not coded as homosexual and that the assumption that they are is heterosexist. See "The Murderous Gays: Hitchcock's Homophobia," in *Hitchcock's Films Revisited* (New York: Columbia University Press, 1989), 336–57.

11. See Lesley Brill, *The Hitchcock Romance: Love and Irony in Hitchcock's Films* (Princeton: Princeton University Press, 1988), 9–10. Although Brill is quite right to call attention to the pervasive homophobia of Hitchcock's films, he tries to defend it, which indicates the extent to which his readings participate in the same network of discourses as the films he critiques. For example, in a particularly homophobic passage in which he all but states that homosexuality is a form of deviance, he cautions that "Leonard's uncertain sexuality, and that of other evil figures in Hitchcock's work, should not be dismissed as a reflection

of the director's prudery. . . . true heterosexual love between well-matched partners approaches divine grace in many of Hitchcock's films. *Deviance*, therefore, is generally demonic; and it is artistically consistent that Hitchcock's villains often show signs of *sexual perversity*" (10; emphasis added). In other words, Brill follows Hitchcock's example (not to mention that of the discourses of national security in which Hitchcock's films participated) in treating homosexuality as a form of sexual perversity.

12. It is worth pointing out that many critics of *North by Northwest* have simply assumed that Leonard is a homosexual without adequately considering the epistemological issues involved in trying to determine his sexual identity (or that of any character in classical Hollywood cinema who is not explicitly identified as homosexual). François Truffaut, for example, automatically assumed that the effeminate male characters in Hitchcock's films were homosexual. When he interviewed Hitchcock, he lauded Hitchcock's decision to make Vandamm a sophisticated, debonair character who is fastidious about his dress because it supposedly added to "the element of homosexual rivalry, with the male secretary clearly jealous of Eva Marie Saint." See François Truffaut, *Hitchcock: The Definitive Study of Alfred Hitchcock by François Truffaut*, rev. ed. (New York: Simon and Schuster, 1983), 107. Typically, Hitchcock neither confirmed nor denied that the relationship between Leonard and Vandamm was supposed to constitute a "homosexual rivalry." In this respect, I think Robin Wood is quite right to call attention to the homophobic assumptions underlying much of the Hitchcock criticism. See Wood, "The Murderous Gays."

13. Brill, for example, defines the MacGuffin as referring to "the nominal goal of a film's characters. It is only partly relevant to the real concerns of the movie, but it provides an excuse for them." He then goes on to claim that in *North by Northwest* "the MacGuffin is unspecified information, both that being smuggled out of the country by Vandamm and the knowledge of Vandamm's organization being sought by the Professor." In other words, Thornhill's espionage activities are not really relevant to the film's "real concerns." See Brill, *The Hitchcock Romance*, 7–8.

14. Truffaut, *Hitchcock*, 138–39.

15. Donald Spoto, for example, claims that "although *Notorious* seems to be a spy melodrama, in fact it is not. The espionage activities are really Hitchcock's MacGuffin, his ubiquitous pretext for more serious, abstract issues. Here, the serious issue is one of common humanity—the possibility of love and trust redeeming two lives from fear, guilt and meaninglessness." See Donald Spoto, *The Art of Alfred Hitchcock* (New York: Doubleday, 1976), 162. It seems to me that this understanding of the MacGuffin is complicit with the discourses of national security because it tries to depoliticize the film by

suggesting indirectly that politics is somehow less important than the issue of "common humanity" it supposedly addresses.

16. Tania Modleski, *The Woman Who Knew Too Much: Hitchcock and Feminist Theory* (New York: Methuen, 1988), 57–71.

17. The representation of the relationship between Sebastian and his mother as a form of "momism" can be explained by the fact that the discourses of national security constructed communism as a form of fascism and made no distinction between Hitler and Stalin. In this respect, Sebastian is no different from Vandamm and Leonard in *North by Northwest*, because they, too, are Fascists.

18. Modleski makes this point in *The Woman Who Knew Too Much*, 64. She also suggests that Alicia's name, which sounds like illicit, similarly indicates her position outside the law. This position is also indicated by Alicia's accent, which marks her as a potential enemy within. It constantly reminds the spectator that she is German and that her allegiance to America is questionable and must be demonstrated.

19. See, for example, Jean Laplanche and Jean-Bertrande Pontalis, "Fantasy and the Origins of Sexuality," in *Formations of Fantasy*, ed. Victor Burgin, James Donald, and Cora Kaplan (London: Routledge, 1986), 5–34. Laplanche and Pontalis's essay has become the classic psychoanalytic account of fantasy and its relation to desire.

20. On the role of primal fantasies in the reorganization of the pre-Oedipal sexual field, see Sigmund Freud, "The Passing of the Oedipus-Complex," in *Sexuality and the Psychology of Love* (New York: Collier Books, 1963), 176–82. For Freud's discussion of femininity and masculinity as positions in relation to desire rather than as biological categories, see his paper, "A Child is Being Beaten," in the same volume, 107–32.

21. See in particular Michael Renov, "From Identification to Ideology: The Male System of Hitchcock's *Notorious*," *Wide Angle* 4, no. 1 (1980): 3–37. For an interesting feminist critique of Renov's analysis of the shots of Devlin, an analysis deeply indebted to Bellourian categories, see Modleski, *The Woman Who Knew Too Much*, 66–67.

22. For a more detailed discussion of this aspect of fantasy and its relation to desire, see Laplanche and Pontalis, "Fantasy and the Origins of Sexuality." See also Jean Laplanche and Jean-Bertrand Pontalis, *The Language of Psychoanalysis*, trans. Donald Nicholson-Smith (New York: Norton, 1973), 314–19. For an interesting application of the psychoanalytic theory of fantasy to Hitchcock, see Victor Burgin, "Diderot, Barthes, *Vertigo*" in *Formations of Fantasy*, 85–108.

23. For a more detailed discussion of this aspect of fantasy and its role in the reorganization of the pre-Oedipal sexual field, see Burgin, "Diderot, Barthes,

Vertigo," 85–108. See also John Fletcher, "Poetry, Gender and Primal Fantasy," in *Formations of Fantasy,* 109–41.

24. Sigmund Freud, "A Special Type of Object-Choice Made by Men," in *Sexuality and the Psychology of Love,* 52.

25. See Wood, *Hitchcock's Films Revisited,* 147.

Conclusion

1. François Truffaut, *Hitchcock: The Definitive Study of Alfred Hitchcock by François Truffaut,* rev. ed. (New York: Simon and Schuster, 1983), 334.

2. Quoted in Truffaut, *Hitchcock,* 333.

3. I have borrowed the term *crisis of transformism* from Ernesto Laclau. See his *Politics and Ideology in Marxist Theory* (London: Verso, 1977), 143–98. Laclau considers a crisis of transformism one of the necessary conditions for the emergence of populist movements.

4. Quoted in Joan W. Scott, "Multiculturalism and the Politics of Identity," *October* 62 (Summer 1992): 14.

5. Quoted in Scott, "Multiculturalism and the Politics of Identity," 16.

6. Quoted in Gary Wills, "The Born-Again Republicans," *New York Review of Books,* 24 September 1992, 9. Buchanan's speech is particularly disturbing in the context of the recent proliferation of anti-gay ballot measures like the one in Oregon that seeks to classify homosexuality and lesbianism as "abnormal, wrong, unnatural and perverse." (Other measures include Amendment 2 in Colorado and an initiative in Portland, Maine, to repeal the city's recently passed gay rights ordinance.) In allowing Buchanan to address the convention on its opening night and during prime time, the Republicans helped to legitimize such measures. Such measures seek to define gays and lesbians as a special interest group rather than as an oppressed minority, which is why it is so important for gays and lesbians to continue to assert the historical existence of gay and lesbian identities, even as they interrogate the exclusionary process whereby those identities have been constructed. For an excellent discussion of the Oregon ballot measure and its legal implications, see Michelangelo Signorile, "Behind the Hate in Oregon," *New York Times,* 3 September 1992, p. A16.

7. Quoted in Wills, "The Born-Again Republicans," 9.

8. Quoted in ibid.

9. Wills, for example, sees Buchanan's declaration of war on homosexuals, lesbians, and working mothers as an attempt to find a substitute for the Cold War rather than as an attempt to prolong it, as I am claiming. Citing Bu-

Notes

256 chanan's speech, Wills concludes that "Republican campaigns, hitherto based on the cold war, must now be based on the equally important culture war." See ibid. For a discussion of the political commentators who see homosexuals and working mothers as the Willie Horton of the 1992 presidential election campaign, see Richard L. Berke, "In 1992, Willie Horton is Democrat's Weapon," *New York Times*, 24 August 1992, p. A10.

10. Laclau, *Politics and Ideology in Marxist Theory*, 143–98.

INDEX

Robert J. Corber is Assistant

Professor of English at Chatham College

in Pittsburgh, Pennsylvania.

Library of Congress Cataloging-in-Publication Data

Corber, Robert J., 1958-
In the name of national security : Hitchcock, homophobia,
and the political construction of gender in postwar America /
Robert J. Corber. ⬩
p. cm. — (New Americanists)
Includes bibliographical references (p.   ) and index.
ISBN 0-8223-1380-4 (acid-free paper). —
ISBN 0-8223-1386-3 (pbk. : acid-free paper)
1. Hitchcock, Alfred, 1899-   —Criticism and
interpretation.   2. Motion pictures—Political aspects—
United States.   3. Homosexuality in motion pictures.
I. Title.   II. Series.
PN1998.3.H58C67   1993
791.43'0233'092—dc20   93-19816   CIP